W9-CZW-505

Principles of

COMPUTER
SCIENCE

SCHAUM'S OUTLINE OF

Principles of

COMPUTER SCIENCE

CARL REYNOLDS
Department of Computer Science
Rochester Institute of Technology

PAUL TYMANN
Department of Computer Science
Rochester Institute of Technology

Schaum's Outline Series

McGRAW-HILL

New York | Chicago | San Francisco | Lisbon | London | Madrid
Mexico City | Milan | New Delhi | San Juan
Seoul | Singapore | Sydney | Toronto

CARL REYNOLDS teaches courses in database, operating systems, programming, and programming language theory in the Computer Science Department at the Rochester Institute of Technology. He has taught at the college level for 10 years, and in the computer industry for 4 years. Before coming to RIT, Dr. Reynolds spent 19 years in the computer industry working in technical and training capacities for both hardware and software suppliers, and 6 years with a Dow Jones Industrial manufacturer creating expert systems for machine control. His interests include genetic algorithms, expert systems, and image processing.

PAUL TYMANN is Professor and Chair of the Computer Science Department at the Rochester Institute of Technology. He has taught both basic and advanced programming techniques for over 15 years. More recently he has been involved with development of a new bioinformatics program at RIT. Prior to entering academia, Professor Tymann worked in industry developing control software for point-of-sale terminals. For the past 5 years he has worked in the area of bioinformatics and has completed joint software development projects at the University of Rochester and Rutgers University.

The **McGraw·Hill** Companies

Schaum's Outline of Principles of
COMPUTER SCIENCE

1 2 3 4 5 6 7 8 9 0 CUS/CUS 0 1 4 3 2 1 0 9 8

ISBN 978-0-07-146051-4
MHID 0-07-146051-9

Library of Congress Cataloging-in-Publication Data

Reynolds, Carl, date.
     Schaum's outline of principles of computer science / Carl Reynolds, Paul Tymann.
          p.   cm.—(Schaum's outline series)
     Includes index.
     ISBN 978-0-07-146051-4
     1. Computer science—Problems, exercises, etc.   I. Tymann, Paul T.   II. Title.
  QA76.28.R49   2008
  004.076—dc22   2007041732

CONTENTS

SCHAUM'S
OUTLINE OF

Principles of

COMPUTER
SCIENCE

CHAPTER 1

Introduction to Computer Science

WHAT IS COMPUTER SCIENCE?

Computer Science is defined in different ways by different authors. Wikipedia (http://en.wikipedia.org/wiki/Computer_science) defines computer science as the collection of a variety of disciplines related to computing, both theoretical and practical: theoretical foundations of information and computation, language theory, algorithm analysis and development, implementation of computing systems, computer graphics, databases, data communications, etc.

The US National Coordination Office for *Networking and Information Technology Research and Development* (NITRD) defines computer science in a similarly broad way:

> the systematic study of computing systems and computation. The body of knowledge resulting from this discipline contains theories for understanding computing systems and methods; design methodology, algorithms, and tools; methods for the testing of concepts; methods of analysis and verification; and knowledge representation and implementation. (http://www.nitrd.gov/pubs/bluebooks/1995/section.5.html)

Another broad definition comes from the *Association for Computing Machinery* (ACM) Model Curriculum. It says that computer science is the "study of computers and algorithmic processes, including their principles, their hardware and software design, their applications, and their impact on society."

A famous definition of computer science by Gibbs and Tucker (Gibbs and Tucker, "A Model Curriculum for a Liberal Arts Degree in Computer Science," *Comm. of the ACM*, vol. 29, no. 3, March 1986) emphasizes algorithm development and analysis as the central focus of computer science.

It's also a fair question to ask, "How is computer science a science?" In contrast to physics, biology, and chemistry, computer science is not based on the study of the natural world. In that sense, computer science is more like mathematics than science. Some argue that computer science is really computer art (where "art" means practice). On the other hand, computer scientists do use the scientific method to propose and test hypotheses, and some very nonobvious discoveries in computer science have important real-world implications. An example, which we will discuss later, is the discovery that some important problems simply cannot be solved by computation.

Despite many variations, essentially all definitions of computer science emphasize the study of algorithms. Algorithms, in one form or another, are central to computer science. Computer science combines the theoretical concepts of algorithm design and analysis with the practical considerations of how to implement algorithms on a computer and solve practical problems.

An algorithm defines a detailed and unambiguous sequence of actions for solving a particular problem or for performing some task. If you have ever followed a recipe when cooking, followed a set of driving directions, or filled out an income tax form, you have worked with an algorithm.

For example, at some point in time you were probably taught how to determine the *greatest common divisor* (GCD) of two numbers. In case you've forgotten, the GCD of two positive integers is the greatest integer that is an even divisor of both numbers. For example, the GCD of 42 and 30 is 6. The algorithm given below can be used to compute the GCD of two positive integers a and b:

> If b is zero, then the GCD of a and b is a. Algorithm ends.
> Set r to be the remainder obtained from the integer division of a and b.
> Repeat this process using b and r.

Consider computing the GCD of 42 and 30. Let a = 42 and b = 30. We start the process at step 1 of the algorithm. Since b is not zero, we proceed to step 2. In step 2 we compute the remainder obtained when 42 is divided by 30, which is 12. Step 3 instructs us to repeat the process, this time using 30 and 12. So on this second trip through the process a is now 30 and b is now 12. Since b is not zero, we compute the remainder of 30 and 12, which is 6, and repeat the process using 12 and 6. As before, since b is not zero, we compute the remainder of 12 and 6 and get zero. We will now repeat the process using 6 and 0. This time through, since b is now zero, we conclude that the GCD of 42 and 30 is 6.

Algorithms are essential to the way computers process information because a computer program is basically an electronic form of an algorithm that tells the computer what specific steps to perform to carry out a specified task. In order to study an electronic form of an algorithm, a computer scientist must also understand the computer that will be used to execute the steps of the algorithm. The term hardware is used to describe the physical, tangible parts of a computer. A keyboard, mouse, motherboard, graphics card, and processor are all examples of computer hardware.

Just as a racecar driver needs to understand the capabilities and limitations of the vehicle they are driving, a computer scientist must also understand the hardware platform on which computing algorithms will be implemented. It is not enough just to "know how to drive" in the case of the racecar driver, and it is not enough just to "know algorithms" to be a computer scientist. An algorithm that is optimal for a particular hardware platform may not be optimal on another.

Algorithms are typically expressed in a form that can be easily understood by a human being. For example, the algorithm given earlier to compute the GCD of two numbers was written using the English language so that it would be easy for you to understand.

Even though you may understand more than one language, the *only* language that a computer understands is *machine language*. Machine language is a system of codes that the computer is designed to interpret. Each word in machine language represents a simple action that can be performed by the computer. For example the machine language instruction "add" instructs the computer to add together two numbers. (In Chap. 3 on Computer Organization, we will explain machine language in much more detail.) The set of instructions that, when executed by a computer, executes the steps of an algorithm is called a program.

It is difficult for humans to work directly with machine language. Machine instruction words consist of rows of ones and zeros, typically 8, 16, 32, or 64 bits long, and sometimes varying in length. Since people have difficulty manipulating these strange codes directly, computer languages have been developed to ease the process of converting an algorithm into a form that the computer can act upon. We refer to these languages as *higher-level languages*, because the languages have been designed to allow humans to work at a "higher level" than at the level of ones and zeros of the computer. Machine language, on the other hand, is often referred to as a *low-level language*. Java, FORTRAN, Basic, and ADA are just a few examples of high-level languages that are used by computer scientists to express the algorithms they have developed. The act of expressing an algorithm using a low-level or high-level language is referred to as programming.

Over the years, starting in the 1950s, computer scientists have created many higher-level languages. In the early days some experts thought that it should be possible to develop one language that would be best for all uses. Since then, however, computer scientists have found that language design always trades off some features and capabilities for others. As a result, today we have many good higher-level languages, some particularly suited to symbol manipulation, some particularly good for teaching programming, some good for matrix algebra applications, some for fast one-off, one-time programs, some for mission-critical, life-dependent applications, some tuned for applications in real-time automation control, and many good ones for general-purpose use. Computer scientists study the general characteristics of computer languages and formal grammars, and usually become proficient in several or many different languages.

The term *software* is used to describe the set of instructions, or programs, that a computer uses to execute an algorithm. Software contains the instructions that direct the operation of the hardware. The software that makes the basic functions of the computer accessible is referred to as *system software*. System software is responsible for controlling and managing the hardware of a computer system, and for making the computer easy to use for program developers as well as general users. Examples of system software include *operating systems*, display managers, virus scanners, language processors (called compilers or interpreters—to be discussed in the chapter on software), and device drivers.

Programs such as word processors or spreadsheets are referred to as *application software*. Application software is used to accomplish specific tasks. Application software may consist of a single program, or a small collection of programs that work together to accomplish a task for a user of the computer.

Operating systems are particularly important and complex system software. They are important because the performance of the operating system has a dramatic influence on the quality of the computer user's experience and the efficiency of the computer system as a whole. In the days of simpler computing systems, in the 1960s and 1970s, a company might purchase a computer without an operating system, with the intention of writing or using its own operating system, but today one always buys an operating system when one buys a computer.

The operating system provides easy access to peripheral devices like printers and displays, a file system for storing information like data, documents, and programs, a user interface to make it easy to start application programs, a time-of-day clock, a connection to the Internet using the standard network protocols, a set of "calls" or "methods" that application programs can use to request services of the operating system, an efficient algorithm for allocating memory to the various programs active at the same time, and an efficient algorithm for sharing access to the computer among several people and/or programs at the same time.

Popular operating systems today include Microsoft Windows, Mac OS, Unix, Linux (a variety of Unix), and IBM's MVS, among others. In fact, the field of operating system development is still a very active one in computer science. Not only are operating systems becoming more complex (adding firewalls and other protections, for example), but operating systems are also becoming more diverse. As simpler devices like thermostats and dishwashers come under computer control, computer scientists have created specialized "embedded systems" operating systems for those requirements.

Even into the 1980s many, if not most, computers were stand-alone—not connected to one another. During the 1970s and 1980s computer scientists explored the advantages of computing networks and proposed a number of different physical connections among computers, as well as different networking protocols. At the time there was hot competition among different vendors of computers, each with a different standard, and each hoping to "lock in" customers by selling its particular networking products. IBM offered *System Networking Architecture* (SNA), Digital Equipment promoted DECnet, Hewlett Packard offered *Distributed Systems* (DS), and Xerox offered *Xerox Networking Systems* (XNS). Even General Motors got into the act, with its *Manufacturing Automation Protocol* (MAP). None was directly compatible with any other, but all offered "bridges" to other systems.

Today the problems for computer scientists in networking are different. For the most part, the world has agreed on the IEEE 801 standards and the TCP/IP protocols for the Internet. The problems now have to do with expanding the number of Internet addresses without disrupting the operation of the older "installed base," adapting to new and much faster physical connections such as optical fiber, increasing the speed of wireless connections, which are by nature slower and more susceptible to interference, managing larger data transfers such as movies, which also require strict real-time performance so the movie doesn't stop midaction, and providing low-power, low-cost protocols for the ad hoc connection of hundreds or thousands of digital sensors.

Supporting almost all applications today is database technology. The dominant database model is the relational database, first offered for commercial use in the 1980s. Computer scientists develop algorithms for storing and retrieving information quickly from absolutely enormous reservoirs of data. How is it, for example, that Google can call up almost instantly more than 400,000 images of a "red barn" from over 1.5 billion images in its database?

There is a great deal to know about creating a good database, accessing a database from a program, growing a database, and managing a database. Application programmers and database administrators need to understand databases at this level in order to use them efficiently. Even computer scientists focused on other specialties need to know about databases today. For instance, some of the newer operating systems use database technology in their file systems for the storage of all information, not just information formally devoted to a particular database. The benefits to the operating system include speed, space savings, and data security.

At a deeper level, computer scientists develop algorithms for sharing access to a database among many users simultaneously. For instance, a site like Amazon.com may serve more that 100,000 users at once, and it's important that each user's choices and purchases be kept distinct from one another. Likewise, when you reserve an airplane seat on-line, it's important that two people on-line at the same time are not promised space in the same seat!

Computer scientists also develop algorithms for making backup copies of the database to protect against the possibility of data loss due to equipment failure. For a site like Amazon, such an algorithm must allow backup without first stopping the operation of the primary database, for the site must be up at all times! Algorithms to provide such service reliably and efficiently are very challenging to perfect.

It should not be hard to convince you that computers have dramatically changed the way in which human beings live their lives. Technologies such as the Internet and the World Wide Web put a vast amount of information at our fingertips. Instant messenger systems, electronic mail, and cell phones have revolutionized the way in which human beings communicate. Computer surveillance systems are being used by police forces to make the world a safer place to live.

While all of these technologies are primarily being used for the betterment of human kind, it is also possible to use these technologies to inflict harm, obtain unauthorized access to information, or to spy on people. Coupled with the ability to develop these technologies is a need to address the social and ethical uses of the technology. It is just as important, perhaps sometimes even more important, to ask questions about the potential impact of a technology on society, as it is to build the technology. As more and more people come to depend on computing technology in their daily lives, computer science must also consider the study of social issues of the technologies that it produces.

There is a common misconception that computer science is nothing more than the study of computer hardware and programming. It should be clear to you now that computer science is much more than simply writing programs. It includes the study of computer hardware, computer languages, operating systems, networking, databases, and the social consequences of computing. In order to be effective, a computer scientist must understand and master each of these areas. Further, computer science is a young discipline that is still rapidly evolving since its beginnings in the 1940s. In the next section we will briefly explore the history of computing from both a hardware and software perspective.

COMPUTING HISTORY

Though computer science is a relatively young field that only began in earnest in the 1940s, interest in computing and computing devices started much earlier. The abacus, a simple counting device invented in Babylonia in the fourth century BC, is considered by many to be the first computing device.

In 1614 the Scottish lord John Napier, inventor of logarithms, invented a calculating device consisting of a series of rods (often called "bones") that reduced the complex process of multiplication and division into the relatively simple tasks of addition and subtraction. Some regard his inventions as the first attempt at mechanical computation.

Blaise Pascal is often credited with the invention of the first mechanical calculator, the Pascaline, in 1642 (there is evidence that Leonardo DaVinci may have beaten Pascal by 150 years). According to Pascal's memoirs, he developed the machine to help his father with his work as a tax collector. Pascal's device could only add and subtract but it was possible to perform multiplication and division operations using a series of additions or subtractions. What is noteworthy about Pascal's machine is that it was capable of calculating with eight figures, and that subtraction was performed using complement techniques. Subtracting using complementary addition is same technique that is used to implement subtraction in most modern computers.

Figure 1-1   The Pascaline, photograph by Yves Serra (http://pagesperso-orange.fr/yves.serra/).

In the early 1800s inventors were just beginning to build the power-driven machinery that would fuel the industrial revolution. One of these inventors, Joseph Marie Jacquard, invented a loom in 1801 that revolutionized the weaving industry. Although it was not the first mechanical loom, Jacquard's loom was revolutionary in that it could be used to weave complex and intricate patterns automatically.

The key idea behind the loom was that the pattern to be woven into the cloth was encoded by holes punched in a card. A group of these cards, that were literally strung together, provided the information required to

Figure 1-2   The Jacquard Loom, photograph by Frank da Cruz
(http://www.columbia.edu/acis/history/jacquard.html).

control the actions of the loom. The Jacquard loom required fewer people and little skill to operate, and versions of the loom are still in use today. The Jacquard loom also had a profound impact on computing in that it was the one of the first devices that could be programmed. The loom gave birth to the concept of punched cards, which played a fundamental role in the early days of computing.

Charles Babbage, a mathematician and inventor, grew tired of calculating astronomical tables by hand, and conceived of a way to build a mechanical device to perform the calculations automatically. In 1822 Babbage started work on a computing device, the difference engine, to automatically calculate mathematical tables. During the course of his work on the difference engine, he conceived of a more sophisticated machine he called the analytical engine. The analytical engine was meant to be programmed using punched cards, and would employ features such as sequential control, branching, and looping. Although Babbage never built a complete working model of either machine, his work became the basis on which many modern computers are built. (One of Babbage's earlier difference engines was eventually constructed from drawings by a team at London's Science Museum in the 1990s. The machine weighs 3 tons and is 10 feet wide by $6\frac{1}{2}$ feet tall.)

Figure 1-3   Jacquard Loom Cards, photograph by Doug Jones
(http://www.cs.uiowa.edu/~jones/cards/history.html).

In his work on the analytical engine, Babbage made an important intellectual leap regarding the punched cards. In the Jacquard loom, the presence or absence of each hole in the card physically allows a colored thread to pass or stops that thread. Babbage realized that the pattern of holes could be used to represent an abstract idea such as a problem statement or the raw data required for that problem's solution.

Because of the connection to the Jacquard loom, Babbage called the two main parts of his Analytic Engine the "Store" and the "Mill", as both terms are used in the weaving industry. The Store was where numbers were held, and the Mill was where they were "woven" into new results. In a modern computer these same parts are called the memory unit and the *central processing unit* (CPU).

Perhaps the key concept that separated the analytical engine from its predecessors was that it supported conditional program execution. This allows the machine to determine what to do next, based upon a condition or situation that is detected at the very moment the program is running.

Augusta Ada Byron, the countess of Lovelace, was a mathematician who worked with Charles Babbage on his analytical engine. Unlike Babbage, who was interested in building a computing device, Lovelace sought to understand and reason about methods for computing. She studied these methods, their implementations, and the properties of their implementations. Lovelace even developed a program that would have been able to compute the Bernoulli numbers. (Bernoulli numbers comprise a sequence of rational numbers that have many roles in mathematics and number theory.)

In her published analysis of the analytical engine, Lovelace outlined the fundamentals of computer programming, including looping and memory addressing. The influence of the Jacquard loom on her work was evident in her writing, "We may say most aptly that the analytical engine weaves algebraic patterns just as the Jacquard loom weaves flowers and leaves."

It is because of this work that many consider Lovelace to be the world's first programmer. The US Department of Defense named the computer language ADA in honor of Lovelace's work as a programmer.

Figure 1-4   Ada Lovelace (http://www-groups.dcs.st-and.ac.uk/~history/PictDisplay/Lovelace.html).

The 1890 census of the United States proved another milestone in the history of computing when punch cards were used with automatic sorting and tabulating equipment invented by Herman Hollerith to speed the compilation of the data. His machines reduced the time required for a full compilation of census results from 10 years to 3 months, and saved $5,000,000 in costs to the census bureau.

Building on the success of his equipment with the US Census Bureau, Hollerith founded the Tabulating Machine Company in 1896. After merging with two other companies and changing its name, the company became known as the International Business Machines (IBM) Corp. The punch card remained a staple of data storage well into the 20th century.

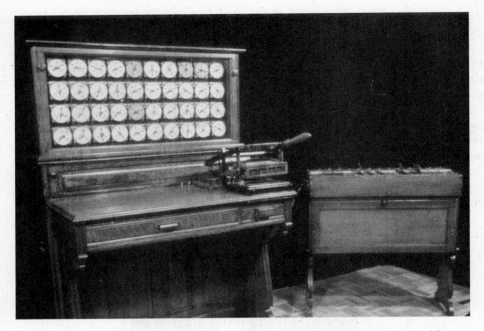

Figure 1-5   Hollerrith Tabulator & Sorter, photograph IBM Corporate Archives.

The 1940s were a decade of dramatic events for the world. World War II changed the face of the world and many lives forever. Although terrible atrocities were taking place during this period, it was also a time of innovation and invention in computing. During the 1940s the first electronic computers were built, primarily to support the war. Unfortunately the clouds of war make it difficult to determine exactly who invented the computer first.

Legally, at least in the United States, John Atanasoff is credited as being the inventor of the computer. Atanasoff was a professor of mathematics and physics at Iowa State. Atanasoff was frustrated at the difficulty his graduate students were having finding solutions to large systems of simultaneous algebraic equations for solving differential equations. Like Babbage, almost 100 years earlier, Atanasoff believed that he could build a machine to solve these equations.

Working with graduate student Clifford Berry, Atanasoff completed a prototype of his machine near the end of 1939. Atanasoff and Berry sought simplicity in their computer. The *Atanasoff–Berry*

Figure 1-6   Clifford Berry with the ABC (www.scl.ameslab.gov/ABC/Progress.html).

Computer (ABC) used only 300 vacuum tubes and was capable of performing arithmetic electronically. Perhaps what is most important about this particular machine is that is operated on base-2 numbers (binary). The ABC did not implement the stored program idea, however, so it was not a general-purpose computer.

During the same time period, Howard Aiken was working on the Mark I computer at Harvard University. As completed in 1944, the Mark I contained more than 750,000 parts, including switches, relays, rotating shafts, and clutches. The machine was huge, at 51 feet long, 8 feet high, 2 feet thick, and weighing 5 tons. It had 500 miles of wiring, and three million wire connections. The machine sounded like a "roomful of ladies knitting" when it was running. Aiken showed that it was possible to build a large-scale automatic computer capable of reliably executing a program.

Figure 1-7   The Aiden/IBM Mark 1 Computer installed at Harvard, photograph IBM Corporate Archives.

One of the people who worked with Aiken on the Mark I was Grace Murray Hopper, a freshly commissioned lieutenant in the US Naval Reserve. Hopper was involved with programming the Mark I from the very start. One of her most significant contributions to the field of computing was the concept of a compiler. Hopper was troubled by the mistake-plagued nature of code writing, and developed a piece of software that would translate an entire set of programmer's instructions, written in a high-level symbolic language, into the machine's language. The first compiler developed by Hopper was named A-0, and was written in 1952.

Grace Murray Hopper is also credited as the individual who coined the term "bug." During the summer of 1947 the Mark II computer, a successor to the Mark I, was acting strangely. At times it would produce the correct answer, and at other times the same program would produce erroneous results. Hopper traced the problem down to a faulty relay within the computer. When she physically examined the relay to correct the problem, she discovered that a moth had been trapped in the relay, causing it to malfunction. Once she removed the moth from the relay, the machine functioned normally. The "bug" was taped onto a page of the laboratory's notebook with the inscription "First actual bug found."

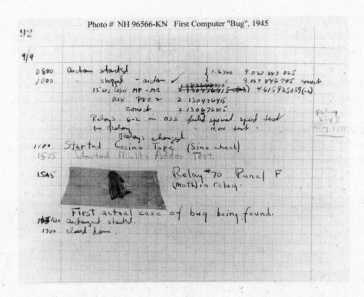

Figure 1-8 The first computer bug
(http://www.history.navy.mil/photos/images/h96000/h96566kc.htm).

After World War II ended, the allies discovered that Konard Zuse, a German engineer, had been developing computers for use by the Germans. Zuse's first computer, the Z1, was built between 1936 and 1938. The machine contained all of the parts of a modern computer; however, it was not reliable. Its mechanical construction was very complex and error-prone. Zuse's Z3 was the first fully functional program-controlled computer in the world.

The Z3 was finished in 1941 and predated Aiken's Mark I. Zuse's accomplishments are all the more incredible given the material and worker shortages in Germany during World War II. Zuse couldn't even obtain paper tape, so he had to make his own by punching holes in discarded movie film. Zuse also invented what might be the first high-level computer language, "Plankalkul", though it, too, was unknown outside Germany.

The work done by the code breakers at Bletchley Park (between London and Birmingham, UK) during World War II provided the allies with information that literally turned the tide of the war. Computers played a vital role in the work of the code breakers and made it possible for them to break the Enigma and Lorenz ciphers. Colossus, a computer developed at Bletchley Park to break ciphers, became operational in 1943. Colossus was one of the first major computers to employ vacuum tubes, and was capable of reading information stored on paper tape at a rate of 5000 characters per second. Colossus also featured limited programmability.

When the allies invaded North Africa in 1942, they discovered that the firing tables they used to aim their artillery were off. This resulted in requests for new ballistics tables that exceeded the ability to compute them. John Mauchly and J. Presper Eckert used this opportunity to propose the development of an electronic high-speed vacuum tube computer. Even though many experts predicted that, given the number of vacuum tubes in the machine, it would only run for five minutes without stopping, they were able to obtain the funding to build the machine.

Under a cloak of secrecy, they started work on the machine in the spring of 1943. They completed their work on the machine in 1946. The result was the *Electronic Numerical Integrator Analyzer and Computer* (ENIAC), a machine that weighed 30 tons and was built using 17,468 vacuum tubes and 6000 switches. The machine was more than 1000 times faster than any machine built to date. Unlike modern computers, reprogramming ENIAC required a rewiring of the basic circuits in the machine. ENIAC heralded the dawning of the computer age.

Soon after ENIAC become functional, Mauchly and Eckert formed the *Electronic Control Corporation* (ECC) and received contracts from the government to design and build a computer for the Bureau of the Census. ECC developed financial difficulties and as a result sold its patents to, and became an employee of, the Remington Rand Corporation. In 1951 Remington Rand delivered the *Universal Automatic Computer* (UNIVAC) to the census bureau.

UNIVAC was the fastest computer of the time and was the only commercially available general-purpose computer. It contained only 5000 vacuum tubes and was more compact than its predecessors. UNIVAC computers were sold to government agencies, the A.C. Neilson Company (market researchers), and Prudential Insurance. By 1957 Remington Rand had sold over 40 machines.

Probably what made UNIVAC most famous was its use by CBS to predict the results of the 1952 presidential election. Opinion polls predicted that Adalai Stevenson would beat Dwight D. Eisenhower by a landslide. UNIVAC's analysis of early returns, however, showed a clear victory for Eisenhower. Newscasters Walter Cronkite and Charles Collingwood questioned the validity of the computer's forecast, so they postponed announcing UNIVAC's prediction until very late.

For many years, Mauchly and Eckert were considered the inventors of the electronic computer. In fact they applied for, and received, a patent for their work in 1947. After purchasing ECC, Remington Rand owned the rights to their patent and was collecting royalties from firms building computers. In a legal battle, initiated by Honeywell's refusal to pay royalties, a judge ruled the original patent invalid. Part of his decision to invalidate the patent was based on the fact that Mauchly had visited John Atanasoff's laboratory in 1941, and used the knowledge he gained during the visit to build ENIAC. The results of this lawsuit legally established John Atanasoff as the inventor of the modern computer.

After the war, commercial development of computers continued, resulting in the development of many new machines that provided improved performance in terms of computing capability and speed. Computers at this time were large, cumbersome devices that were capable of performing simple operations. These machines were very expensive to build and maintain. The only organizations that could afford to purchase and run the equipment were the government and large corporations.

Not surprisingly, many individuals working in the computing field felt that the use of computers would be limited. In a 1950 article, *Business Week* noted, "Salesmen will find the market limited. The UNIVAC is not the kind of machine that every office could use." And though the story is probably apocryphal, the lore of computing attributes the following prediction to Thomas Watson, the founder of IBM, in 1943: "I think there is a world market for maybe five computers."

In the early 1950s, a group of scientists working at Bell Laboratories in New Jersey was studying the behavior of crystals as semiconductors in an attempt to replace vacuum tubes. Its work resulted in the development of the transistor, which changed the way computers and many electronic devices were built. Transistors switch and modulate electric current in much the same way as a vacuum tube. Using transistors instead of vacuum tubes in computers resulted in machines that were much smaller and cheaper, and that required considerably less electricity to operate. The transistor is one of the most important inventions in the 20th century.

While computer companies such as IBM and Honeywell focused on the development of mainframe computers, *Digital Equipment Corporation* (DEC) focused on the development of smaller computers. DEC's PDP series of computers were small and designed to serve the computing needs of laboratories. The PDP-8 was one of the first computers purchased by end users. Because of their low cost and portability, these machines could be purchased to fill a specific need. The PDP-8 is generally regarded as the first minicomputer.

The invention of the integrated circuit caused the trend toward smaller, cheaper, and faster computers to accelerate. *Popular Electronics* featured an article on a kit that home hobbyists could purchase that would enable them to build a computer at home. This machine, offered first in 1974, was the Altair 8800, manufactured by a company named MITS. It ushered in the personal computer era. These initial machines were designed to be built at home, which was fine for the home hobbyist but limited the availability of the machine. The first programming language for the Altair was Altair BASIC, the first product of a little company called Microsoft.

In 1981 IBM introduced its personal computer, or PC, which changed the face of computing forever. It was now possible for individuals to simply purchase these machines and use them at home.

A ROADMAP

After reading this chapter, you should realize that there is much more to computer science than simply writing programs. Like any professional, a computer scientist must have an understanding of all of the subdisciplines of the field. Some of the major disciplines of computer science are algorithms, programming, programming languages, computer hardware, networking, operating systems, database systems, distributed computing, and the ethical issues surrounding the use of computer technology.

There are two major schools of thought when it comes to the education of computer scientists. The depth-first approach is to study one particular topic in depth. For example, many computer science degree programs start out with a course in programming. After taking such a course, students will be proficient programmers, but clearly they will not have enough knowledge of the other subdisciplines of the field to be considered computer scientists.

A second approach is to cover many of the subdisciplines of computer science, but only to the depth required to teach a basic understanding of the principles of each discipline. After obtaining an overall view of the field, students will then study certain subdisciplines in depth. This is referred to as the breadth-first approach, and is the approach we chose to use in this book.

The organization of this text follows the description of computing given in the first section of this chapter. It begins with a discussion of algorithms, how they are developed, and how they may be compared. We also introduce a formal model of computation. After reading this chapter you will have a basic understanding of algorithm development and will be able to develop algorithms to solve simple problems.

After studying algorithms, the text will focus on the basics of computer hardware. In this chapter you will learn what the major components of the computer are and how they work together. You will also learn about the binary number system and see how it can be used to encode information at the hardware level.

The next two chapters will focus on programming. We will first study software in general and discuss how high-level languages can be constructed to provide models in which algorithms can be expressed, and ultimately expressed in a way that the hardware can work with. In the next chapter we will focus on programming using the programming language Java. The goal of this chapter is not to make you an expert programmer, but instead to introduce you to the basics of programming using a language that is readily available and in wide use.

After learning the fundamentals of programming we will focus on operating systems, networking, and databases. The topics covered in these chapters will address common techniques used to manage computer hardware, provide access to network resources, and manage and store data. Almost every modern computer application uses the technologies discussed in these chapters.

The last chapter in the book will discuss some of the social issues of computing. In this chapter we will discuss intellectual property rights and conflicts, privacy of data, "hacking," and viruses. We will also discuss our professional responsibilities when lives depend on the systems on which we work.

REVIEW QUESTIONS

1.1 Write an algorithm for your morning routine, from the time the alarm clock rings until you leave the house for work or school.

1.2 Find or invent an algorithm to calculate the square root of any number. Apply the algorithm to the number 2046, finding its square root to 2 decimal places. Do not use a computer or calculator!

1.3 Perl is a computer language that is often used for quick, one-off programming jobs, like converting text in a document from one format to another. ADA is a language used for Department of Defense applications where human life may be at stake. What differences would you imagine to find when you compare Perl with ADA?

1.4 Why might a computer scientist with a primary interest in databases also need to know about networking?

1.5 The acronym API stands for Application Programming Interface. What do you suppose API means with respect to an operating system?

1.6 If you were offered a job with Microsoft and permitted to choose between working on operating systems, database products, or applications products like Word or Excel, which would you choose, and why?

1.7 Whom do you believe should be credited as "the inventor of the modern computer?"

1.8 What applications of computing seem to you to be unethical? What are some principles you can declare with respect to the ethical and unethical use of computers and software?

1.9 List some important ways in which computing has contributed to the welfare of humanity. Which people, if any, have suffered from the advance of computing technology?

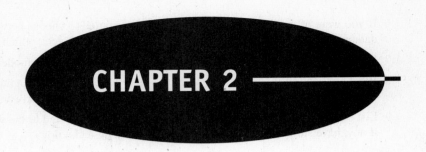

Algorithms

DEFINITION OF AN ALGORITHM

An algorithm is a method for solving a class of problems. While computer scientists think a lot about algorithms, the term applies to any method of solving a particular type of problem. The repair manual for your car will describe a procedure, which could also be called an algorithm, for replacing the brake pads. The turn-by-turn travel instructions from MapQuest could be called an algorithm for getting from one place to another.

EXAMPLE—DESIGNING A STAIRCASE

You may be surprised, as we were, to know that every staircase must be custom-designed to fit the circumstances of total elevation (total "rise") and total horizontal extent (total "run"). Figure 2-1 shows these dimensions. If you search the web, you can find algorithms—methods—for designing staircases.

To make stairs fit a person's natural gait, the relationship of each step's rise (lift height) to its run (horizontal distance) should be consistent with a formula. Some say the following formula should be satisfied:

```
(rise * 2) + run = 25 to 27 inches
```

Others say the following simpler formula works well:

```
rise + run = 17 to 18 inches
```

Many say the ideal rise for each step is 7 in, but some say outdoor steps should be 6 in high because people are more likely to be carrying heavy burdens outside. In either case, for any particular situation, the total rise of the staircase will probably not be an even multiple of 6 or 7 in. Therefore, the rise of each step must be altered to create a whole number of steps.

These rules lead to a procedure for designing a staircase. Our algorithm for designing a set of stairs will be to:

1 Divide the total rise by 7 in and round the result to the nearest whole number to get the number of steps.
2 We will then divide the total run by (the number of steps − 1) (see Fig. 2-1) to compute the run for each step.
3 We will apply one of the formulas to see how close this pair of rise and run parameters is to the ideal.
4 Then we will complete the same computations with one more step and one less step, and also compute the values of the formula for those combinations of rise and run.
5 We will accept the combination of rise and run that best fits the formula for the ideal.

An algorithm is a way of solving a type of problem, and an algorithm is applicable to many particular instances of the problem. A good algorithm is a tool that can be used over and over again, as is the case for our staircase design algorithm.

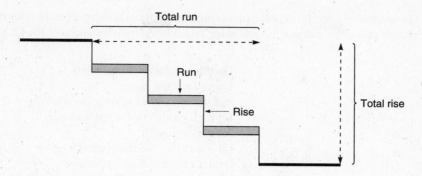

Figure 2-1   Staircase dimensions.

EXAMPLE—FINDING THE GREATEST COMMON DENOMINATOR

In mathematics, a famously successful and useful algorithm is Euclid's algorithm for finding the *greatest common divisor* (GCD) of two numbers. The GCD is the largest integer that will evenly divide the two numbers in question. Euclid described his algorithm about 300 BCE.

Without having Euclid's algorithm, how would one find the GCD of 372 and 84? One would have to factor the two numbers, and find the largest common factor. As the numbers in question become larger and larger, the factoring task becomes more and more difficult and time-consuming. Euclid discovered an algorithm that systematically and quickly reduces the size of the problem by replacing the original pair of numbers by smaller pairs until one of the pair becomes zero, at which point the GCD is the other number of the pair (the GCD of any number and 0 is that number).

Here is Euclid's algorithm for finding the GCD of any two numbers A and B.

    Repeat:
        If B is zero, the GCD is A.
        Otherwise:
            find the remainder R when dividing A by B
        replace the value of A with the value of B
        replace the value of B with the value of R

For example, to find the GCD of 372 and 84, which we will show as:

GCD(372, 84)

Find GCD(84, 36) because 372/84 —> remainder 36
Find GCD(36, 12) because 84/36 —> remainder 12
Find GCD(12, 0) because 36/12 —> remainder 0; Solved! GCD = 12

More formally, an algorithm is a sequence of computations that operates on some set of inputs and produces a result in a finite period of time. In the example of the algorithm for designing stairs, the inputs are the total rise and total run. The result is the best specification for the number of steps, and for the rise and run of each step. In the example of finding the GCD of two numbers, the inputs are the two numbers, and the result is the GCD.

Often there are several ways to solve a class of problems, several algorithms that will get the job done. The question then is which algorithm is best? In the case of algorithms for computing, computer scientists have developed techniques for analyzing the performance and judging the relative quality of different algorithms.

REPRESENTING ALGORITHMS WITH PSEUDOCODE

In computer science, algorithms are usually represented as pseudocode. Pseudocode is close enough to a real programming language that it can represent the tasks the computer must perform in executing the algorithm. Pseudocode is also independent of any particular language, and uncluttered by details of syntax, which characteristics make it attractive for conveying to humans the essential operations of an algorithm.

There is no standard pseudocode form, and many computer scientists develop a personal style of pseudocode that suits them and their tasks. We will use the following pseudocode style to represent the GCD algorithm:

```
GCD ( a, b )                        Function name and arguments
    While b ! = 0 {                 ! = means "not equal"
                                    indentation shows what to do while b ! = 0

        r <-- a modulo b            set r = a modulo b ( = remainder a/b)
        a <-- b                     set a = original b
        b <-- r                     set b = r (i.e., the remainder)
    }                               border of the "while" repetition
return a                            when b = 0, return value of a as the GCD
```

CHARACTERIZING ALGORITHMS

To illustrate how different algorithms can have different performance characteristics, we will discuss a variety of algorithms that computer scientists have developed to solve common problems in computing.

Sequential search

Suppose one is provided with a list of people in the class, and one is asked to look up the name Debbie Drawe. A sequential search is a "brute force" algorithm that one can use. With a sequential search, the algorithm simply compares each name in the list to the name for which we are searching. The search ends when the algorithm finds a matching name, or when the algorithm has inspected all names in the list.

Here is pseudocode for the sequential search. The double forward slash "//" indicates a comment. Note, too, the way we use the variable index to refer to a particular element in list_of_names. For instance, list_of_names[3] is the third name in the list.

```
Sequential_Search(list_of_names, name)
    length <-- length of list_of_names
    match_found <-- false
    index <-- 1

    // While we have not found a match AND
    // we have not looked at every person in the list,
    // (The symbol <= means "less than or equal to.")
    // continue ...
    // Once we find a match or get to the end of the list,
    // we are finished
    while match_found = false AND index <= length {

        // The index keeps track of which name in the list
        // we are comparing with the test name.
        // If we find a match, set match_found to true
        if list_of_names[index] = name then
            match_found <-- true
        index <-- index + 1
    }
    // match_found will be true if we found a match, and
    // false if we looked at every name and found no match
    return match_found
end
```

ANALYZING ALGORITHMS

If we know how long each statement takes to execute, and we know how many names are in the list, we can calculate the time required for the algorithm to execute. However, the important thing to know about an algorithm is usually not how long it will take to solve any particular problem. The important thing to know is how the time taken to solve the problem will vary as the size of the problem changes.

The sequential search algorithm will take longer as the number of comparisons becomes greater. The real work of the algorithm is in comparing each name to the search name. Most other statements in the algorithm get executed only once, but as long as the while condition remains true, the comparisons occur again and again.

If the name we are searching for is in the list, on average the algorithm will have to look at half the names on the list before finding a match. If the name we are searching for is not on the list, the algorithm will have to look at all the names on the list.

If the list is twice as long, approximately twice as many comparisons will be necessary. If the list is a million times as long, approximately a million times as many comparisons will be necessary. In that case, the time devoted to the statements executed only once will become insignificant with respect to the execution time overall. The running time of the sequential search algorithm grows in proportion to the size of the list being searched.

We say that the "order of growth" of the sequential search algorithm is n. The notation for this is T(n). We also say that an algorithm whose order of growth is within some constant factor of T(n) has a theta of NL say. "The sequential search has a theta of n." The size of the problem is n, the length of the list being searched. Since for large problems the one-time-only or a-few-times-only statements make little difference, we ignore those constant or nearly constant times and simply focus on the fact that the running time will grow in proportion to the length of the list being searched.

Of course, for any particular search, the time required will depend on where in the list the match occurs. If the first name is a match, then it doesn't matter how long the list is. If the name does not occur in the list, the search will always require comparing the search name with all the names in the list.

We say the sequential search algorithm is $\Theta(n)$ because in the average case, and the worst case, its performance slows in proportion to n, the length of the list. Sometimes algorithms are characterized for best-case performance, but usually average performance, and particularly worst-case performance are reported. The average case is usually better for setting expectations, and the worst case provides a boundary upon which one can rely.

Insertion sort—An example of order of growth n^2—$\Theta(n^2)$

Programmers have designed many algorithms for sorting numbers, because one needs this functionality frequently. One sorting algorithm is called the insertion sort, and it works in a manner similar to a card player organizing his hand. Each time the algorithm reads a number (card), it places the number in its sorted position among the numbers (cards) it has already sorted.

On the next page we show the pseudocode for the insertion sort. In this case, we use two variables, number_index and sorted_index, to keep track of two positions in the list of numbers.

We consider the list as two sets of numbers. We start with only one set of numbers—the numbers we want to sort. However, immediately the algorithm considers the list to be comprised of two sets of numbers; the first "set" consists of the first number in the original list, and the second set consists of all the rest of the numbers.

The first set is the set of "sorted" numbers (like the cards already sorted in your hand), and the second set is the remaining set of unsorted numbers. The sorted set of numbers starts out containing only a single number, but as the algorithm proceeds, more and more of the unsorted numbers will be moved to their proper position in the sorted set.

The variable number_index keeps track of where we are in the list of unsorted numbers; it starts at 2, the first number which is "unsorted." The variable sorted_index keeps track of where we are among the sorted numbers; it starts at 1, since the first element of the original list starts the set of "sorted" numbers.

The algorithm compares the next number to be inserted into the sorted set against the largest of the sorted numbers. If the new number is smaller, then the algorithm shifts all the numbers up one position in the list. This repeats, until eventually the algorithm will find that the new number is greater than the next sorted number, and the algorithm will put the new number in the proper position next to the smaller number.

It's also possible that the new number is smaller than all of the numbers in the sorted set. The algorithm will know that has happened when sorted_index becomes 0. In that case, the algorithm inserts the new number as the first element in the sorted set.

```
Insertion_Sort(num_list)

length <-- length of num_list

// At the start, the second element of the original list
// is the first number in the set of "unsorted" numbers.
number_index <-- 2

// We're done when we have looked at all positions in the list.
while(number_index <= length) {

    // newNum is the no. being considered for sorting
    newNum        <-- num_list[number_index]

    // sorted_index marks the end of previously sorted numbers.
    sorted_index <-- number_index - 1

    // From high to low, look for the place for the new number.
    // If newNum is smaller than the previously sorted numbers,
    // move the previously sorted numbers up in the num_list.
    while newNum < num_list[sorted_index] AND sorted_index > 0 {
        num_list[sorted_index + 1]   <-- num_list[sorted_index]
        sorted_index                 <-- sorted_index - 1
    }

    // newNum is not smaller than the number at sorted_index.
    // We found the place for the new number, so insert it.
    num_list[sorted_index + 1] = newNum

}
end
```

To repeat, the variable `number_index` keeps track of where the algorithm is in the unsorted set of numbers. The algorithm starts with the second number (`number_index = 2`). Then the algorithm compares the number to the largest number that has been sorted so far, `num_list[sorted_index]`. If the number is smaller than the previously sorted number, the algorithm moves the previously sorted number up one position in `num_list`, and checks the new number against the next largest number in the previously sorted elements of `num_list`. Finally, the algorithm will encounter a previously sorted number which is smaller than the number being inserted, or it will find itself past the starting position of `num_list`. At that point, the number can be inserted into the `num_list`. The algorithm completes when all of the positions in the `num_list` have been sorted.

To analyze the running time of the insertion sort, we note first that the performance will be proportional to n, the number of elements to be sorted. We also note that each element to be sorted must be compared one or many times with the elements already sorted. In the best case, the elements will be sorted already, and each element will require only a single comparison, so the best-case performance of the insertion sort is $\Theta(n)$.

In the worst case, the elements to be sorted will be in reverse order, so that every element will require comparison with every element already sorted. The second number will be compared with the first, the third with the second and first, the fourth with the third, second, and first, etc. If there were four numbers in reverse order, the number of comparisons would be six. In general, the number of comparisons in the worst case for the insertion sort will be:

$$n^2/2 - n/2$$

The number of comparisons will grow as the square of the number of elements to be sorted. The negative term of $-n/2$, and the division of n^2 by the constant 2, mean that the rate of growth in number of comparisons will not be the full rate that n^2 would imply. However, for very large values of n, those terms other than

n^2 become relatively insignificant. Imagine the worst case of sorting a million numbers. The n^2 term will overwhelm the other terms of the equation.

Since one usually reports the order of growth for an algorithm as the worst-case order of growth, the insertion sort has a theta of n^2, or $\Theta(n^2)$. If one computes the average case order of growth for the insertion sort, one also finds a quadratic equation; it's just somewhat smaller, since on average each new element will be compared with only half of the elements already sorted. So we say the performance of the insertion sort is $\Theta(n^2)$.

Merge sort—An example of order of growth of n(lg n)— Θ(n lg n)

Another algorithm for sorting numbers uses recursion, a technique we will discuss in more detail shortly, to divide the problem into many smaller problems before recombining the elements of the full solution. First, this solution requires a routine to combine two sets of sorted numbers into a single set.

Imagine two piles of playing cards, each sorted from smallest to largest, with the cards face up in two piles, and the two smallest cards showing. The merge routine compares the two cards that are showing, and places the smaller card face down in what will be the merged pile. Then the routine compares the two cards showing after the first has been put face down on the merged pile. Again, the routine picks up the smaller card, and puts it face down on the merged pile. The merge routine continues in this manner until all the cards have been moved into the sorted merged pile.

Here is pseudocode for the merge routine. It expects to work on two previously sorted lists of numbers, and it merges the two lists into one sorted list, which it returns. The variable index keeps track of where it is working in sorted_list.

The routine compares the first (top) numbers in the two original lists, and puts the smaller of the two into sorted_list. Then it discards the number from the original list, which means that the number that used to be the second one in the original list becomes the first number in that list. Again the routine compares the first numbers in the two lists, and again it moves the smaller to sorted_list.

The routine continues this way until one of the original lists becomes empty. At that point, it adds the remaining numbers (which were in sorted order originally, remember) to sorted_list, and returns sorted_list.

```
merge(list_A, list_B)
  // index keeps track of where we are in the
  // sorted list
  index <-- 1

  // Repeat as long as there are numbers in both
  // original lists.
  while list_A is not empty AND list_B is not empty
    // Compare the 1st elements of the 2 lists.
    // Move the smaller to the sorted list.
    // "<" means "smaller than."
    if list_A[1] < list_B[1]
        sorted_list[index] <-- list_A[1]
        discard list_A[1]
    else
        sorted_list[index] <-- list_B[1]
        discard list_B[1]
    index <-- index + 1

  // If numbers remain only in list_A, move those
  // to the sorted list
  while list_A is not empty
        sorted_list[index] <-- list_A[1]
        discard list_A[1]
  index <-- index + 1
```

```
// If numbers remain only in list_B, move those
// to the sorted list
while list_B is not empty
        sorted_list[index] <-- list_B[1]
        discard list_B[1]
        index <-- index + 1

// Return the sorted list
return sorted_list
```

The performance of merge is related to the lengths of the lists on which it operates, the total number of items being merged. The real work of the routine is in moving the appropriate elements of the original lists into the sorted list. Since the total number of such moves is equal to the sum of the numbers in the two lists, merge has a theta of $n_A + n_B$, or $\Theta(n_A + n_B)$, where $n_A + n_B$ is equal to the sum of the numbers in the two lists.

The merge_sort will use the merge routine, but first the merge_sort will divide the problem up into smaller and smaller sorting tasks. Then merge_sort will reassemble the small sorted lists into one fully sorted list.

In fact, merge_sort divides the list of numbers until each sublist consists of a single number, which can be considered a sorted list of length 1. Then the merge_sort uses the merge procedure to join the sorted sublists.

The technique used by merge_sort to divide the problem into subproblems is called recursion. The merge_sort repeatedly calls *itself* until the recursion "bottoms out" with lists whose lengths are one. Then the recursion "returns," reassembling the numbers in sorted order as it does. Here is pseudocode for the merge sort. It takes the list of numbers to be sorted, and it returns a sorted list of those numbers.

```
merge_sort(num_list)
length <-- length of num_list

// if there is more than 1 number in the list,
if length > 1

  // divide the list into two lists half as long
  shorter_list_A <-- first half of num_list
  shorter_list_B <-- second half of num_list

  // Perform a merge sort on each shorter list
  result_A <-- merge_sort(shorter_list_A)
  result_B <-- merge_sort(shorter_list_B)

  // Merge the results of the two sorted sublists
  sorted_list <-- merge(result_A, result_B)

  // Return the sorted list
  return sorted_list
else
  // If there's only 1 number in the list,
  // just return it
  return num_list
end
```

Let's follow the execution of merge_sort when one calls it with this list of numbers:

    NUMS = { 1, 6, 4, 2 }

1 First, we call merge_sort passing the list NUMS. This is what we call the "top-level" of recursion, level 0.

2 merge_sort calls merge_sort again, passing a list of the first two numbers in NUMS. This will sort the front half of the list. This is level 1 of recursion.

3 Now merge_sort calls merge_sort again, passing only the first number in NUMS. This is level 2.

4 Now merge_sort simply returns; it's down to one element in the list, merge_sort returns to level 1.

5 Now merge_sort calls merge_sort again, passing only the second of the first two numbers in NUMS. This is level 2.

6 Again, merge_sort simply returns; it's down to one element in the list, merge_sort returns to level 1.

7 At level 1 of recursion, merge_sort now has result_A and result_B. merge_sort calls merge to put those two numbers in order, and then it returns the sorted pair of numbers back to level 0. The first half of the list is sorted.

8 From level 0, merge_sort calls merge_sort again, passing a list of the last two numbers in NUMS. This will sort the back half of NUMS. It's back to level 1 of recursion.

9 merge_sort calls merge_sort again, passing only the first of the last two numbers of NUMS. This is level 2 of recursion again.

10 Since the list contains only one number, merge_sort simply returns back to level 1.

11 merge_sort calls merge_sort again, passing only the last of the numbers of NUMS. This is level 2 of recursion again.

12 Since the list contains only one number, merge_sort simply returns back to level 1.

13 At level 1 of recursion, merge_sort now has result_A and result_B. merge_sort calls merge to put the two lists in order, and then it returns the sorted set of two numbers back to level 0.

14 At level 0 of recursion, merge_sort now has result_A and result_B. merge_sort calls merge to put the two lists of numbers in order, and then it returns the entire set of four numbers in sorted order.

Aside from being an interesting exercise in recursion, the merge_sort provides attractive performance. The merge sort has a theta of n(lg n), which for large problems is much better than the theta of n^2 for the insertion sort.

The recursion in merge_sort divides the problem into many subproblems by repeatedly halving the size of the list to be sorted. The number of times the list must be divided by two in order to create lists of length one is equal to the logarithm to the base 2 of the number of elements in the list.

In the case of our 4-element example, the logarithm to the base 2 of 4 is 2, because $2^2 = 4$. This can be written as $\log_2 n$, but in computer science, because of the ubiquity of binary math, this is usually written as lg n, meaning logarithm to the base 2 of n.

The total running time T of the merge sort consists of the time to recursively solve two problems of half the size, and then to combine the results. One way of expressing the time required is this:

```
T = 2T(n/2) + merge
```

Since merge runs in $\Theta(n_A + n_B)$, and since $n_A + n_B = n$, we will restate this:

```
T = 2T(n/2) + Θ(n)
```

A recursion tree is a way to visualize the time required. At the top level, we have the time required for merge $\Theta(n)$, plus the time required for the two subproblems:

```
Θ(n)
T(n/2) T(n/2)
```

At the next level, we have the time required for the two merges of the two subproblems, and for the further subdivision of the two subproblems:

```
Θ(n)
Θ(n/2)        Θ(n/2)
T(n/4) T(n/4) T(n/4) T(n/4)
```

We can continue this sort of expansion until the tree is deep enough for the size of the overall problem:

$$\Theta(n)$$
$$\Theta(n/2) \qquad \Theta(n/2)$$
$$\Theta(n/4) \quad \Theta(n/4) \quad \Theta(n/4) \quad \Theta(n/4)$$

. . .

. . .

Adding across each row, we find:

	Sum	
$\Theta(n)$	$\Theta(n)$	
$\Theta(n/2)$	$\Theta(n/2)$	$\Theta(n)$
$\Theta(n/4) \quad \Theta(n/4) \quad \Theta(n/4) \quad \Theta(n/4)$	$\Theta(n)$	

. . .

. . .

For any particular problem, because we repetitively divide the problem in two, we will have as many levels as (lg n). For instance, our example with four numbers had only two levels of recursion. A problem with eight numbers will have three levels, and a problem with 16 numbers will have four.

Summing over the whole problem, then, we find the merge sort has a theta of n(lg n). There are (lg n) levels, each with a theta of n. So the merge sort has an order of growth of $\Theta(n(\lg n))$.

This is a very big deal, because for large sets of numbers, n(lg n) is very much smaller than n^2. Suppose that one million numbers must be sorted. The insertion sort will require on the order of $(10^6)^2$, or 1,000,000,000,000 units of time, while the merge sort will require on the order of 10^6 (lg 10^6), or 10^6 (20), or 20,000,000 units of time. The merge sort will be almost five orders of magnitude faster. If a unit of time is one millionth of a second, the merge sort will complete in 20 seconds, and the insertion sort will require a week and a half!

Binary search—An example of order of growth of (lg n)—Θ(lg n)

Earlier we discussed the sequential search algorithm and found its performance to be $\Theta(n)$. One can search much more efficiently if one knows the list is in order to start with. The improvement in efficiency is akin to the improved usefulness of a telephone book when the entries are sorted by alphabetical order. In fact, for most communities, a telephone book where the entries were not sorted alphabetically would be unthinkably inefficient!

If the list to be searched is already ordered from smallest to largest, the binary search algorithm can find any entry in (lg n) time. If the list contains 1,000,000 entries, that means the binary search will locate the item after reading fewer than 20 entries. The sequential search, on average, will have to read 500,000 entries. What a difference!

The binary search works by repetitively dividing the list in half. It starts by comparing the element in the middle of the list with the item sought. If the search item is smaller than the element in the middle of the list, the binary search reads the element at the middle of the first half of the list. Then, if the search item is larger than that element, the binary search next reads the element at the middle of the second half of the front half of the list. Eventually, the search finds the element sought, or concludes that the element is not present in the list.

Here is pseudocode for a binary search:

```
BinarySearch(list, search_item)
begin        <-- 1
end          <-- length of list
match_found <-- false

// Repeat search as long as no match has been found
// and we have not searched the entire list.
while match_found = false AND begin <= end

   // Find the item at the midpoint of the list
   midpoint <-- (begin + end) / 2
```

```
    // If it's the one we're looking for, we're done
    if list[midpoint] = search_item
       match_found = true
    // If the search item is smaller, the next
    // list item to check is in the first half
    else if search_item < list[midpoint]
        end <-- midpoint - 1

    // Otherwise, the next list item to check
    // is in the back half of the list
    else
        begin <-- midpoint + 1

// Return true or false, depending on whether we
// found the search_item
return match_found
```

With each iteration, the binary search reduces the size of the list to be searched by a factor of 2. So, the binary search generally will find the search item, or conclude that the search item is not in the list, when the algorithm has executed (lg n) iterations or fewer. If there are seven items in the list, the algorithm will complete in three iterations or fewer. If there are 1,000,000 items in the list, the algorithm will complete in 20 iterations or fewer.

If the original list happens to be a perfect power of 2, the maximum number of iterations of the binary search can be 1 larger than (lg n). When the size of the list is a perfect power of 2, there are two items at the (lg n) level, so one more iteration may be necessary in that circumstance. For instance, if there are eight items in the list, the algorithm will complete in (3 + 1) iterations or fewer.

In any case, the running time of the binary search is $\Theta(\lg n)$. This efficiency recommends it as a search algorithm, and also, therefore, often justifies the work of keeping frequently searched lists in order.

Intractable problems

The algorithms discussed so far all have an order of growth that can be described by some polynomial equation in n. A "polynomial in n" means the sum of some number of terms, where each term consists of n raised to some power and multiplied by a coefficient. For instance, the insertion sort order of growth is $(n^2/2 - n/2)$.

When an algorithm has an order of growth that is greater than can be expressed by some polynomial equation in n, then computer scientists refer to the algorithm as intractable. If no better algorithm can be discovered to solve the problem, computer scientists refer to the problem as an intractable problem.

As an example of an intractable problem, consider a bioinformatics problem. The Department of Genetics at Yale School of Medicine maintains a database of genetic information obtained from different human populations. ALFRED (ALlele FREquency Database) is a repository of genetic data on 494 anthropologically defined human populations, for over 1600 polymorphisms (differences in DNA sequences between individuals). However, researchers have collected data for only about 6 percent of the possible population–polymorphism combinations, so most of the possible entries in the database are absent.

When population geneticists seek to find the largest possible subset of populations and polymorphisms for which complete data exist (that is, measures exist for all polymorphisms for all populations), the researchers are confronted by a computationally intractable problem. This problem requires that every subset of the elements in the matrix be examined, and the number of subsets is very large!

The number of subsets among n elements is 2^n, since each element can either be in a particular subset or not. For our problem, the number of elements of our set is the number of possible entries in the database. That is, the ALFRED database presents us with $2^{(494 * 1600)}$ subsets to investigate! To exhaustively test for the largest subset with complete data, we would have to enumerate all the subsets, and test each one to see if all entries in the subset contained measurements!

Clearly, the order of growth of such an algorithm is 2^n; $\Theta(2^n)$. This is an exponential function of n, not a polynomial, and it makes a very important difference. An exponential algorithm becomes intractable quickly.

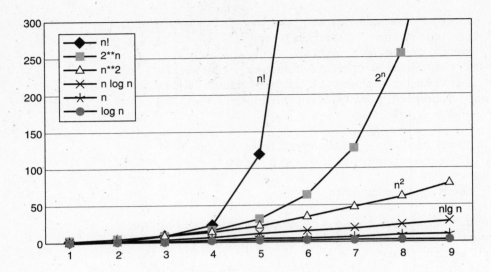

Figure 2-2   Comparison of orders of growth.

For instance, solving the problem for a matrix of 20 entries will require about a million units of time, but solving the problem for a matrix of 50 entries will require about a million billion units of time. If a unit of time is a millionth of a second, the problem of size 20 will require a second to compute, but the problem of size 50 will require more than 25 years. The ALFRED database is of size $494 * 1600 = 790,400$. Students hoping to graduate need a better algorithm or a different problem!

Another example of an intractable problem is the famous ***traveling salesman problem***. This problem is so famous it has its own acronym, TSP. The salesman needs to visit each of several cities, and wants to do so without visiting any city more than once. In the interest of efficiency, the salesman wants to minimize the length of the trip.

The salesman must visit each city, but he can visit the cities in any order. Finding the shortest route requires computing the total distance for each permutation of the cities the salesman must visit, and selecting the shortest one. Actually, since a route in one direction is the same distance as the reverse route, only half of the permutations of cities need to be calculated. Since the number of permutations of n objects is equal to n-factorial (n! or $n * (n-1) * (n-2) \ldots * 2 * 1$), the number of routes to test grows as the factorial of the number of cities, divided by 2. So the order of growth for the TSP problem is n-factorial; $\Theta(n!)$.

Table 2-1

Θ	Classification
k	Constant: run time is fixed, and does not depend upon n. Most instructions are executed once, or only a few times, regardless of the amount of information being processed.
lg n	Logarithmic: when n increases, so does run time, but much more slowly than n does. When n doubles, lg n increases by a constant, but does not double until n increases to n^2. Common in programs which solve large problems by transforming them into smaller problems.
n	Linear: run time varies directly with n. Typically, a small amount of processing is done on each element.
n lg n	When n doubles, run time slightly more than doubles. Common in programs which break a problem down into smaller subproblems, solve them independently, and then combine solutions.
n^2	Quadratic: when n doubles, runtime increases fourfold. Practical only for small problems; typically the program processes all pairs of input (e.g., in a double nested loop).
2^n	Exponential: when n doubles, run time squares. This is often the result of a natural, "brute force" solution. Such problems are not computable in a reasonable time when the problem becomes at all large.

A factorial order of growth is even more extreme than an exponential order of growth. For example, there are about 3.6 million permutations of 10 cities, but more than 2 trillion billion permutations of 20. If the computer can compute the distance for a million permutations a second, the TSP problem will take 1.8 seconds for 10 cities, but tens of thousands of years for 20 cities.

Figure 2-2 shows the rates of growth for lg n, n, n(lg n), n^2, 2^n, and n!

Table 2.1 summarizes some different orders of growth, and the characteristics of associated algorithms.

ALGORITHMS AS TECHNOLOGY

It's pretty exciting to buy a new computer with twice, four times, or even ten times the clock rate of the old computer. Many people think of computer hardware speed as the measure of technological advance. Having discussed algorithms and their performance, consider whether a better algorithm on a slower computer might be better than a slower algorithm on a faster computer.

As an example, consider a sorting task. Suppose you need to sort a million numbers (social security numbers, for example). You have the choice of using your current computer with a merge sort program, or of buying a new computer, which is 10 times faster, but which uses an insertion sort.

The insertion sort on the new computer will require on the order of $(10^6)^2$, or a million million cycles, while the merge sort will require on the order of $10^6(\lg 10^6)$, or $10^6(20)$, or 20 million cycles. Even when it runs on your old computer, the merge sort will still run four orders of magnitude faster than the insertion sort on the new machine. If it takes 20 seconds to run the merge sort on your old machine, it will take over 27 hours to run the insertion sort on the new machine!

Algorithm design should be considered important technology. A better algorithm can make the difference between being able to solve the problem or not, and a better algorithm can make a much greater difference than any near-term improvement in hardware speed.

FORMAL MODELS OF COMPUTATION

The theory of computing has advanced by adopting formal models of computation whose properties can be explored mathematically. The most influential model was proposed by the mathematician Alan Turing in 1936.

Turing used the human as the model computing agent. He imagined a human, in a certain state of mind, looking at a symbol on paper. The human reacts to the symbol on paper by

1 erasing the symbol, or erasing the symbol and writing a new symbol, or neither,
2 perhaps changing his or her state of mind as a result of contemplating the symbol, and then
3 contemplating another symbol on the paper, next to the first.

This model of computation captures the ability to accept input (from the paper), store information in memory (also on the paper), take different actions depending on the input and the computing agent's "state of mind," and produce output (also on the paper). Turing recast this drastically simple model of computation into mathematical form, and derived some very fundamental discoveries about the nature of computation. In particular, Turing proved that some important problems cannot be solved with any algorithm. He proved not that these problems have no known solution; he proved that these problems cannot ever have a solution. For instance, he proved that one will never be able to write one program that will be able to determine whether any other arbitrary program will execute to a proper completion, or crash.

Hmmm... that's too bad... it would be nice to have a program to check our work and tell us whether or not our new program will ever crash.

The mathematical conception of Turing's model of computation is called a *Turing machine* or TM. A TM is usually described as a machine reading a tape.

- The tape contains symbols or blanks, and the tape can be infinitely long.
- The machine can read one symbol at a time, the symbol positioned under the "read/write head" of the TM.
- The machine can also erase the symbol, or write a new symbol, and it can then position the tape one cell to the left or right.
- The machine itself can be in one of a finite number of states, and reading a symbol can cause the state of the TM to change.
- A special state is the halting state, which is the state of the machine when it terminates normally.

- When the machine starts, it is in state 1, it is positioned at the extreme left end of the tape, and the tape extends indefinitely to the right.

A particular TM will have a set of instructions it understands. Each instruction consists of a 5-tuple (rhymes with couple), which is a mathematical way of saying that one instruction consists of five values. These values are

1 the current state
2 the current symbol being read
3 the symbol with which to replace the current symbol
4 the next state to enter
5 the direction to move the tape (Right, Left, or Stationary)

As a first example, suppose a TM includes these three instructions (Δ means blank):

```
1 (1,  0,  1,  1,     Right      )
2 (1,  1,  0,  1,     Right      )
3 (1,  Δ,  Δ,  halt,  Stationary)
```

The first says that if the symbol being read is a 0, replace it with a 1 and move right. The second says that if the symbol being read is a 1, replace it with a 0 and move right. The third says that if the symbol being read is a blank, halt the machine without moving the tape.

Assume the tape presented to this TM contains the symbols:

```
1 1 0 1 0 1 0 0 Δ Δ Δ...
```

Starting in state 1, and positioned at the extreme left of the tape, the machine reads the symbol 1. Instruction 2 applies to this situation, so the instruction causes the 1 to be replaced by a 0, the machine state to remain 1, and the machine to move 1 cell to the right on the tape.

Next the TM reads another 1. Instruction 2 applies again, so the TM changes the second 1 to a 0, and moves right again, remaining in state 1.

When the TM reads the symbol 0, instruction 1 applies, so instruction 1 causes the 0 to be replaced by a 1, the machine to stay in state 1, and the machine to move right once again.

As the machine advances down the tape, every 1 will be changed to a 0, and every 0 will be changed to a 1. Finally, the machine will read a blank. In that case, instruction 3 will apply, and the machine will halt.

This simple TM is a machine for complementing (inverting) the bits of a binary number. The result of the computation will be a tape that contains these symbols:

```
0 0 1 0 1 0 1 1 Δ Δ Δ...
```

Complementing the bits of a binary number is a frequently required task, so this is a useful TM.

A slightly more complex task is that of complementing and incrementing a binary number. That operation is often used by computers to perform binary subtraction. In fact, in the "old days" when the only calculating machines available were mechanical adding machines, people performed subtraction the same way in base 10, using the 10's complement method. To subtract 14 from 17 in base 10, they found the 9's complement of 14, which is 85 (subtract 1 from 9 to get the 8, and subtract 4 from 9 to get the 5). They incremented 85 by 1, to get 86, or what's called the 10's complement. Adding 17 and 86 gave 103. Ignoring the carry digit gave the answer of 3!

To perform binary subtraction by the 2's complement method, the subtrahend is complemented and incremented, and then added to the minuend. For instance, to subtract 2 from 5, we can complement and increment 2, and add that to 5 to get 3:

```
  010      2 (in base 2: 0 fours, 1 two, 0 units)
  101      2 complemented (1s --> 0s; 0s --> 1s)

  110      2 complemented & incremented
           (adding 001 to 101 --> 110 in base 2)
 +101      5 (1 four, 0 twos, 1 unit)
 1011      3 (in base 2: 0 fours, 1 two, 1 unit --
           ignore the carry bit to the left)
```

Since subtraction is often required, a TM for complementing and incrementing a binary number is interesting. Here are the instructions for such a machine:

```
1 (1, 0, 1, 1, Right )
2 (1, 1, 0, 1, Right )
3 (1, Δ, Δ, 2, Left  )
4 (2, 0, 1, 3, Right )
5 (2, 1, 0, 2, Left  )
6 (3, 1, 1, 3, Right )
7 (3, 0, 0, 3, Right )
8 (3, Δ, Δ, halt, Stationary)
```

Instructions 1 and 2 are the same as for the simpler TM which complemented the bits on the tape. Instruction 3 will apply when the TM has complemented all the bits and encountered the blank on the right end of the tape. When that happens, the machine will go into state 2 and move left.

If the machine is in state 2 and encounters a 0, instruction 4 will cause the 0 to be replaced by a 1, the machine to enter state 3, and move right. Once the machine is in state 3, instructions 6 and 7 will cause the machine to move right without further changing the contents of the tape. When the machine finally encounters the blank on the right again, instruction 8 will cause the machine to halt.

If the machine is in state 2 and encounters a 1, instruction 5 will cause the 1 to be replaced by a 0, the machine to stay in state 2, and move left again. This will continue in such manner until the TM encounters a 0, in which case instruction 4 will apply, as described in the previous paragraph.

Using the binary number 2 as the example again, the TM will create the following contents on the tape as it executes:

```
0 1 0 Δ Δ       original tape
1 0 1 Δ Δ       complementing complete
1 0 0 Δ Δ       after executing instruction 5
1 1 0 Δ Δ       after executing instruction 4
1 1 0 Δ Δ       halted after executing instruction 8
```

This TM works for many inputs, but not all. Suppose the original input tape were all zeros:

```
0 0 0 Δ Δ       original tape
```

After the complementing is complete, and all the 0s become 1s, the TM will back up over the tape repeatedly executing instruction 5. That is, it will back up changing each 1 to 0. In this case, however, the TM will never encounter a 0, where instruction 4 would put the TM into state 3 and start the TM moving toward the end of the tape and a proper halt.

Instead, the TM will ultimately encounter the first symbol on the tape, and instruction 5 will command it to move again left. Since the machine can go no further in that direction, the machine "crashes."

Likewise, the TM will crash if one of the symbols on the tape is something other than 1 or 0. There are no instructions in this TM for handling any other symbol, so an input tape such as this will also cause the TM to crash:

```
0 3 0 Δ Δ       original tape
```

Another way a TM can fail is by getting into an infinite loop. If instruction 7 above specified a move to the left instead of the right, certain input tapes containing only 1s and 0s would cause the TM to enter an endless loop, moving back and forth endlessly between two adjacent cells on the tape.

Algorithms can be specified as TMs and, like all algorithms, TMs must be tested for correctness, given expected inputs.

CHURCH–TURING THESIS

The Turing machine is thought to be a very general model of computation. In 1936, logician Alonzo Church advanced the thesis that any algorithmic procedure to manipulate symbols, conducted by humans or any machine, can be conducted by some TM.

It is not possible to prove this proposition rigorously, for the notion of an algorithm is not specified mathematically. However, the Church–Turing thesis has been widely tested, and is now accepted as true. One would not want to write a TM for a complex task like designing a set of stairs for a staircase, but it could be done.

The significance of having such a model of computation is that the model has been used to show that some tasks cannot be accomplished with a TM. If the Church–Turing thesis is true, then tasks for which a TM cannot be successful are tasks which simply have no algorithmic solution.

UNSOLVABLE PROBLEMS

It would be very useful to have a way of quickly knowing whether any particular program, when provided with any particular set of inputs, will execute to completion and halt, or instead continue endlessly. In computer science, this is known as the "halting problem." Given a program, and a set of inputs, will the program execute to completion or not? Is there some algorithm one can apply that will, for any program and any set of inputs, determine whether the program will run to completion or not?

One might suggest simply running the program, providing the particular inputs, and seeing whether the program halts or not. If the program were to run to completion and halt, you would know that it halts. However, if the program were to continue to run, you would never know whether the program would continue forever, or halt eventually. What is needed is an algorithm for inspecting the program, an algorithm which will tell us whether the program will eventually halt, given a particular set of inputs.

If there is such an algorithm for inspecting a program, there is a TM to implement it. Unfortunately however, the halting problem has been shown to be an unsolvable problem, and the proof that there is no solution is a proof by contradiction. We begin by assuming there is, indeed, a TM that implements a solution to the halting problem. We will call this TM 'H', for it solves the big halting problem.

The input to H must include both the program under test p, and the input to the program i. In pseudocode, we call H like this:

```
H(p, i)
```

We assume that H must itself halt, and that the output from H must be true or false—the program under test must be found either to halt, or not to halt. Whatever H does, it does not rely on simply running the program under test, because H itself must always halt in a reasonable time.

Now suppose that we create another TM called NotH that takes a symbolic argument that will include the encoding of a program, p. NotH will call H, passing the code for p as both the program p and the input data i to be tested. (TMs can be linked this way, but the details are not important to this discussion.) NotH will return true if H fails to halt under these conditions, and will loop forever if H does halt. In pseudocode NotH looks like this:

```
NotH(p)
  if(H(p, p) is false) return true
  else
      while(true) {} //loop forever
endNotH
```

Now suppose we test NotH itself with this approach. That is, suppose we pass the code for NotH itself to NotH. We will refer to the code for NotH as 'nh', and we can ask, "Does the program NotH halt when it is run with its own code as input?" Saying this another way, does NotH(nh) halt?

If NotH(nh) halts, this can only be because H(nh,nh) reports that NotH does not halt. On the other hand, if NotH(nh) does not halt, this can only be because H(nh,nh) reports that NotH does halt. These are obviously contradictions.

The original assumption, that a TM does exist that can determine whether any particular program will run to completion when presented with any arbitrary input data, must be incorrect. That assumption led to the contradictory state illustrated by NotH. Therefore, computer scientists conclude that there can be no one algorithm that can determine whether any particular program will run to completion, or fail to run to completion, for every possible set of inputs.

It would be very nice to have a program to which we could submit new code for a quick determination as to whether it would run to completion given any particular set of inputs. Alas, Turing proved that this cannot be. One can and should write test programs, but one will never succeed in writing one program which can test every program.

The "halting problem" is one of the provably unsolvable problems in computing (Turing, Alan, "On computable Numbers with an Application to the Entscheidungsproblem", *Proceedings of the London Mathematical Society*, 2:230–265, 1936). No one algorithm will ever be written to prove the correct or incorrect execution of every possible program when presented with any particular set of inputs. While no such algorithm can be successful, knowing that allows computer scientists to focus on problems for which there are solutions.

SUMMARY

An algorithm is a specific procedure for accomplishing some job. Much of computer science has to do with finding or creating better algorithms for solving computational problems.

We usually describe computational algorithms using pseudocode, and we characterize the performance of algorithms using the term "order of growth" or "theta." The order of growth of an algorithm tells us, in a simplified way, how the running time of the algorithm will vary with problems of different sizes. We provided examples of algorithms whose orders of growth were $(\lg n)$, n, $n(\lg n)$, n^2, 2^n and $n!$.

Algorithm development should be considered an important part of computing technology. In fact, a better algorithm for an important task may be much more impactful than any foreseeable near-term improvement in computing hardware speed.

The Turing machine is a formal mathematical model of computation, and the Church–Turing thesis maintains that any algorithmic procedure to manipulate symbols can be conducted by some Turing machine. We gave example Turing machines to perform the simple binary operations of complementing and incrementing a binary number.

Some problems in computing are provably unsolvable. For instance, Turing proved that it is impossible to write one computer program that can inspect any other program and verify that the program in question will, or will not, run to completion, given any specific set of inputs. While the "Holy Grail" of an algorithm to prove the correctness of programs has been proven to be only a phantom in the dreams of computer scientists, computer scientists at least know that is so, and can work instead on practical test plans for real programs.

REVIEW QUESTIONS

2.1 Write pseudocode for an algorithm for finding the square root of a number.

2.2 Write pseudocode for finding the mean of a set of numbers.

2.3 Count the primitive operations in your algorithm to find the mean. What is the order of growth of your mean algorithm?

2.4 Write pseudocode for finding the median of a set of numbers.

2.5 What is the order of growth of your algorithm to find the median?

2.6 Suppose that your algorithm to find the mean is $\Theta(n)$, and that your algorithm to find the median is $\Theta(n \lg n)$, what will be the execution speed ratio between your algorithm for the mean and your algorithm for the median when the number of values is 1,000,000?

2.7 A sort routine which is easy to program is the bubble sort. The program simply scans all of the elements to be sorted repeatedly. On each pass, the program compares each element with the one next to it, and reorders the two, if they are in inverse order. For instance, to sort the following list:

    6 7 3 1 4

Bubble sort starts by comparing 6 and 7. They are in the correct order, so it then compares 7 and 3. They are in inverse order, so bubble sort exchanges 7 and 3, and then compares 7 and 1. The numbers 7 and 1 are in reverse order, so bubble sort swaps them, and then compares 7 and 4. Once again, the order is incorrect, so it swaps 7 and 4. End of scan 1:

   6 3 1 4 7

Scanning left to right again results in:

   3 1 4 6 7

Scanning left to right again results in a correct ordering:

   1 3 4 6 7

Write pseudocode for the bubble sort.

2.8 What is the bubble sort T?

2.9 How will the bubble sort compare for speed with the merge sort when the task is to sort 1,000,000 social security numbers which initially are in random order?

CHAPTER 3

Computer Organization

VON NEUMANN ARCHITECTURE

Most computers today operate according to the "von Neumann architecture." The main idea of the von Neumann architecture is that the program to be executed resides in the computer's memory, along with the program's data. John von Neumann published this idea in 1945.

Today this concept is so familiar it seems self-evident, but earlier computers were usually wired for a certain function. In effect, the program was built into the construction of the computer. Think of an early calculator; for example, imagine an old hand-cranked mechanical calculator. The machine was built to do one well-defined thing. In the case of an old hand-cranked calculator, it was built only to add. Put a number in; crank it; get the new sum.

To subtract, the operator needed to know how to do complementary subtraction, which uses addition to accomplish subtraction. Instead of offering a subtract function, the old calculator required the operator to add the "ten's complement" of the number to be subtracted. You can search for "ten's complement" on Google to learn more, but the point for now is that early computing devices were built for certain functions only. One could never, for instance, use an old adding machine to maintain a list of neighbors' phone numbers!

The von Neumann architecture is also called the "stored program computer." The program steps are stored in the computer's memory, and the computation cycle of the machine retrieves the next step (instruction to be executed) from memory, completes that computation, and then retrieves the next step. This cycle simply repeats until the computer retrieves an instruction to "halt."

There are three primary units in the von Neumann computer. Memory is where both programs and data are stored. The *central processing unit* (CPU) accesses the program and data in memory and performs the calculations. The I/O unit provides access to devices for data input and output.

DATA REPRESENTATION

We're used to representing numbers in "base 10." Presumably this number base makes sense to us because we have 10 fingers. If our species had evolved with 12 fingers, we would probably have 2 more digits among the set of symbols we use, and we would find it quite natural to compute sums in base 12. However, we have only 10 fingers, so let's start with base 10.

Remember what the columns mean when we write a number like 427. The seven means we have 7 units, the two means we have 2 tens, and the four means we have 4 hundreds. The total quantity is 4 hundreds, plus

2 tens, plus 7. The column on the far right is for units (which you can also write as 10^0), the next column to the left is for 10s (which you can also write as 10^1), and the next column is for 100s (which you can write as 10^2). We say that we use "base 10" because the columns correspond to powers of 10—10^0, 10^1, 10^2, etc.

Suppose that we had evolved with 12 fingers and were more comfortable working in base 12, instead. What would the meaning of 427 be? The seven would still mean 7 units (12^0 is also equal to 1), but now the two would mean 2 dozen (12^1 equals 12), and the four would mean 4 gross (12^2 equals 144). The value of the number 427 in base 12 would be 4 gross, plus 2 dozen, plus 7, or 607 in our more familiar base-10 representation.

Some people say we would be better off using base 12, also known as the duodecimal or dozenal system. For example, you can readily find a sixth, a third, a quarter, or a half in base 12, whereas you can only find a half easily in base 10. Twelve is also a good match for our calendar, our clock, and even our compass. Ah well, the decision to use base 10 in daily life was made long ago!

The point of this discussion is to show that base 10 is simply one number system of many. One can compute in base 10, or base 12, or base-any-other-number. Our choice of number system can be thought of as arbitrary—we've got 10 fingers, so let's use base 10. We could compute just as competently in base 7, or base 12, or base 2.

Computers use base 2, because it's easy to build hardware that computes based on only two states—on and off, one and zero. Base 2 is also called the "binary number system," and the columns in a base-2 number work the same way as in any other base. The rightmost column is for units (2^0), the next column to the left is for twos (2^1), the next is for fours ($2^2 = 4$), the next is for eights ($2^3 = 8$), the next is for sixteens ($2^4 = 16$), etc.

What is the base-10 value of the binary number 10011010? The column quantities from right to left are 128 (2^7), 64 (2^6), 32 (2^5), 16 (2^4), 8 (2^3), 4 (2^2), 2 (2^1), 1 (2^0). So, this number represents 128, plus 16, plus 8, plus 2—154 in base 10.

We can calculate in base 2 after learning the "math facts" for binary math. You learned the math facts for base 10 when you studied your addition, subtraction, and multiplication tables in elementary school. The base-2 math facts are even simpler:

```
0 + 0 = 0
0 + 1 = 1
1 + 1 = 10  (remember, this means 2; and also 0 carry 1 to the next column)
```

Let's add the binary value of 1100 to 0110:

```
  1100   (12 in base 10)
  0110   (6 in base 10)
 10010   (18 in base 10)
```

rightmost digit:	0 + 0 = 0
next rightmost:	0 + 1 = 1
next rightmost:	1 + 1 = 10 (or 0 carry 1)
next rightmost:	carried 1 + 1 + 0 = 10 (or 0 carry 1)
last digit:	1 (from the carry)

So, any kind of addition can be carried out using the binary number system, and the result will mean the same quantity as the result from using base 10. The numbers look different, but the quantities mean the same value.

COMPUTER WORD SIZE

Each computer deals with a certain number of bits at a time. The early hobbyist computers manipulated 8 bits at a time, and so were called "8-bit computers." Another way to say this was that the computer "word size" was 8 bits. The computer might be programmed to operate on more than 8 bits, but its basic operations dealt with 8 bits at a time.

If our program must count, how large a count can an 8-bit computer maintain? Going back to our discussion of the binary number system, this is the largest number we can represent with 8 bits:

    11111111

This number is 128, plus 64, plus 32, plus 16, plus 8, plus 4, plus 2, plus 1—255. That's it for an 8-bit computer, unless we resort to some "workaround."

The first IBM PC used the Intel 8088 processor. It had an 8-bit data bus (meaning it read and wrote 8 bits at a time from/to peripheral devices), but internally it was a 16-bit computer. How large a count can a 16-bit computer maintain? Here's the number, broken into two 8-bit chunks (bytes) for legibility:

    1111111 11111111

This number is 32,768 (2^{15}), plus 16,384, plus 8192, plus 4096, plus 2048, plus 1024, plus 256, plus 255 (the lower 8 bits we already computed above)—65,535. That's a much bigger number than the maximum number an 8-bit computer can work with, but it's still pretty small for some jobs. You'd never be able to use a 16-bit computer for census work, for instance, without some "workaround."

Today, most computers we're familiar with use a 32-bit word size. The maximum count possible with 32 bits is over 4 billion. The next generation computers will likely use a 64-bit word size, and the maximum count possible with 64 bits is something like a trillion billions!

The ability to represent a large number directly is nice, but it comes at a cost of "bit efficiency." Here's what the number 6 looks like in a 32-bit word:

    00000000000000000000000000000110

There are a lot of wasted bits (leading zeros) there! When memory was more expensive, engineers used to see bit-efficiency as a consideration, but memory is now so inexpensive that it usually is no longer a concern.

INTEGER DATA FORMATS

So far our discussion has been of whole numbers only, and even of positive whole numbers. Computers need to keep track of the sign of a number, and must also be able to represent fractional values (real numbers).

As you might expect, if we need to keep track of the sign of a number, we can devote a bit of the computer word to maintaining the sign of the number. The leftmost bit, also known as the most significant bit ("msb"—in contrast to the least significant bit, "lsb," at the right end of the word), will be zero if the number is positive, and 1 if the number is negative. Here is a positive 6 for an 8-bit computer:

    00000110

The msb is 0, so this is a positive number, and we can inspect the remaining 7 bits and see that the value is 6. Now here's a counter-intuitive observation. How do we represent −6? You might think it would be like this:

    10000110

That would be incorrect, however. What happens if we add 1 to that representation? We get 10000111, which would be −7, not −5! This representation does not work correctly, even in simple arithmetic computations.

Let's take another tack. What number would represent −1? We can test our idea by adding 1 to −1. We should get 0 as a result. How about this for negative 1:

    11111111

That actually works. If we add 1 to that number, we get all zeros in the sum (and we discard the final carry).

In fact, the correct representation of a negative number is called the "two's complement" of the positive value. To compute the two's complement of a number, simply change all the zeros to ones and all the ones to zeros, and then add one. Here is the two's complement of 6:

```
  11111001       All the bits of +6 are "complemented" (reversed)
 +00000001       Add one
  11111010       The two's complement of 6 = −6
```

You can check to see that this is correct by adding 1 to this representation 6 times. You will find that the number becomes 0, as it should (ignoring the extra carry off the msb). You can also verify that taking the two's complement of −6 correctly represents +6.

Larger word sizes work the same way; there are simply more bits with which to represent the magnitude of the number. These representations are called "integer" or "integral" number representations. They provide a means of representing whole numbers for computation.

REAL NUMBER FORMATS

Numbers containing fractions are more difficult to represent. Real numbers consist of a mantissa and an exponent. Computer designers decide how to allocate the bits of the computer word so that some can be used for the mantissa and some for the exponent. In addition, the mantissa can be positive or negative, and the exponent can be positive or negative.

You might imagine that different designers could create different definitions for real number formats. A larger mantissa will provide greater precision; a larger exponent will provide for larger and smaller magnitudes (scale). As recently as the 1980s, different computer manufacturers used different representations, and those differences made it difficult to move data between computers, and difficult to move ("port") programs from one make of computer to another.

Since then, the IEEE has created a standard for binary floating-point number representation using 32 and 64 bits. The 32-bit format looks like this:

```
SEEEEEEEEmmmmmmmmmmmmmmmmmmmmmmm
```

The msb is the sign of the number, the 8-bit field is the exponent of 2, and the 23-bit field is the mantissa. The sign of the exponent is incorporated into the exponent field, but the IEEE standard does not use simple two's complement for representing a negative exponent. For technical reasons, which we touch on below, it uses a different approach.

How would we represent 8.5? First we convert 8.5 to binary, and for the first time we will show a binary fractional value:

```
1000.1
```

To the left of the binary point (analogous to the decimal point we're familiar with) we have 8. To the right of the binary point, we have ½. Just as the first place to the right of the decimal point in base 10 is a tenth, the first place to the right of the binary point in base 2 is a half.

In a manner akin to using "scientific notation" in base 10, we normalize binary 1000.1 by moving the binary point left until we have only the 1 at the left, and then adding a factor of 2 with an exponent:

```
1.0001 * 2³
```

From this form we can recognize the exponent in base 2, which in this case is 3, and the mantissa, which is 0001.

The IEEE 32-bit specification uses a "bias" of 127 on the exponent (this is a way of doing without a separate sign bit for the exponent, and making comparisons of exponents easier than would be the case with two's complements—trust us, or read about it on-line), which means that the exponent field will have the binary value of 127 + 3, or 130. After all this, the binary representation of 8.5 is:

```
01000001000010000000000000000000
```

The sign bit is 0 (positive), the exponent field has the value 130 (10000010), and the mantissa field has the value 0001 (and lots of following zeros).

As you can imagine, computing with real numbers requires the computer to do more work than computing with integers. The mantissa and exponent fields must be considered appropriately in all mathematical operations. In fact, some computers have special floating-point processor hardware to speed such calculations.

CHARACTER FORMATS

We think of computing as work with numbers, but in fact most computing operates on character data rather than numeric data—names, addresses, order numbers, gender, birthdates, etc. are usually, or often, represented by strings of characters rather than numeric values.

Characters are mapped to integer numbers. There have been many character–to-integer mappings over the years. IBM invented a mapping called *binary coded decimal* (BCD), and later *extended BCD interchange coded* (EBCDIC), which became a de facto standard with IBM's early success in the computer market.

The American standard *American Standard Code for Information Interchange* (ASCII) was defined in the 1960s and became the choice of most computer vendors, aside from IBM. Today Unicode is becoming popular because it is backwards compatible with ASCII and allows the encoding of more complex alphabets, such as those used for Russian, Chinese, and other languages. We will use ASCII to illustrate the idea of character encoding, since it is still widely used, and it is simpler to describe than Unicode.

In ASCII each character is assigned a 7-bit integer value. For instance, 'A' = 65 (1000001), 'B' = 66 (1000010), 'C' = 67 (1000011), etc. The 8th bit in a character byte is intended to be used as a parity bit, which allows for a simple error detection scheme.

If parity is used, the 8th or parity bit is used to force the sum of the bits in the character to be an even number (even parity) or an odd number (odd parity). Thus, the 8 bits for the character 'B' could take these forms:

```
01000010  even parity
11000010  odd parity
01000010  no parity
```

If parity is being used, and a noisy signal causes one of the bits of the character to be misinterpreted, the communication device will see that the parity of the character no longer checks. The data transfer can then be retried, or an error announced. This topic is more properly discussed under the heading of data communications, but since we had to mention the 8th bit of the ASCII code, we didn't want you to be left completely in the dark about what parity bits and parity checking are.

The lowercase characters are assigned a different set of numbers: 'a' = 97 (1100001), 'b' = 98 (1100010), 'c' = 99 (1100011), etc. In addition, many special characters are defined: '$' = 36 (0100100), '+' = 43 (0101011), '>' = 62 (01111110), etc.

A number of "control characters" are also defined in ASCII. Control characters do not print, but can be used in streams of characters to control devices. For example, 'line feed' = 10 (0001010), 'tab' = 11 (0001011), 'backspace' = 8 (0001000), etc.

For output, to send the string "Dog" followed by a linefeed, the following sequence of bytes would be sent (the msb is the parity bit, and in this example parity is being ignored, and the parity bit set to 0):

```
01000100      01101111     01100111     00001010
D             o            g            lf (line feed)
```

Likewise for input, if a program is reading from a keyboard, the keyboard will send a sequence of integer values that correspond to the letters being typed.

How does a program know whether to interpret a series of bits as an integer, a character, or a floating-point number? Bits are bits, and there is no label on a memory location saying this location holds an integer/character/real. The answer is that the program will interpret the bits based on its expectation.

If the program expects to find a character, it will try to interpret the bits as a character. If the bit pattern doesn't make sense as a character encoding, either the program will fail or an error message will result. Likewise, if the program expects an integer, it will interpret the bit pattern as an integer, even if the bit pattern originally encoded a character. It is incumbent on the programmer to be sure that the program's handling of data is appropriate.

CPU/ALU

The CPU is the part of the computer one thinks of first when describing the components of a computer. The repetitive cycle of the von Neumann computer is to a) load an instruction from memory into the CPU, and b) decode and execute the instruction. Executing the instruction may include performing arithmetic or logical operations, and also loading or storing data in memory. When the instruction execution is complete, the computer fetches the next instruction from memory, and executes that instruction. The cycle continues indefinitely, unless the instruction fetched turns out to be a HALT instruction.

The CPU is usually described as consisting of a *control unit* and an *arithmetic and logic unit* (ALU). The control unit is responsible for maintaining the steady cycle of fetch-and-execute, and the ALU provides the hardware for arithmetic operations, value comparisons (greater than, less than, equal to), and logical functions (AND, OR, NOT, etc.).

Both the control unit and the ALU include special, very high-performance memory cells called *registers*. Registers are intimately connected to the wiring of the control unit and the ALU; some have a special purpose, and some are general purpose. One special-purpose register is the *program counter* (PC).

The PC keeps track of the address of the instruction to execute next. When the control unit begins a fetch–execute cycle, the control unit moves the instruction stored at the address saved in the PC to another special register called the *instruction register* (IR). When such a fetch of the next instruction occurs, the control unit automatically increments the PC, so that the PC now "points" to the next instruction in sequence.

The control unit then decodes the instruction in the IR, and executes the instruction. When execution is complete, the control unit fetches the instruction to which the PC now points, and the cycle continues.

Other registers of the ALU are general purpose. General-purpose registers are used to store data close to the processor, where the processor can access the information even more quickly than when the value is in memory. Different computers have different numbers of registers, and the size of the registers will be congruent with the word size of the computer (16-bit, 32-bit, etc.).

The number of registers, and the nature of the special-purpose registers, comprise an important part of the computer architecture. In the case of the Intel x86 architecture, there are four 32-bit general-purpose registers (EAX, EBX, ECX, and EDX), and four 32-bit registers devoted to address calculations and storage (ESP, EBP, ESI, and EDI). One could say much more about registers in the Intel x86 architecture, but they are now too complex to describe completely, as the architecture has been cleverly expanded while maintaining complete compatibility with earlier designs.

INSTRUCTION SET

The quintessential definition of a computer's architecture is its "instruction set." The actual list of things the computer hardware can accomplish is the machine's instruction set. Given the wide variety of computer applications, and the sophistication of many applications, it can be surprising to learn how limited and primitive the instruction set of a computer is.

Machine instructions include loading a CPU register from memory, storing the contents of a CPU register in memory, jumping to a different part of the program, shifting the bits of a computer word left or right, comparing two values, adding the values in two registers, performing a logical operation (e.g., ANDing two conditions), etc. For the most part, machine instructions provide only very basic computing facilities.

A computer's assembly language corresponds directly to its instruction set; there is one assembly language mnemonic for each machine instruction. Unless you program in assembly language, you will have very little visibility of the machine instruction set. However, differences in instruction sets explain why some programs run on some machines but not others. Unless two computers share the same instruction set, they will not be able to execute the same set of machine instructions.

The IBM 360 family of computers was the first example of a set of computers which differed in implementation, cost, and capacity, but which shared a common machine instruction set. This allowed programs written for one IBM 360 model to run on other models of the family, and it allowed customers to start with a smaller model, and later move up to a larger model without having to reinvest in programming. At the time, this capability was a breakthrough.

Today, most programming is done in higher-level languages, rather than assembly language. When you program in a higher-level language, you write statements in the syntax of your programming language (e.g., Java, C, Python), and the language processor translates your code into the correct set of machine instructions to execute your intent. If you want to run the same program on a different computer with a different instruction set, you can often simply supply your code to the appropriate language processor on the new computer. Your source code may not change, but the translation of your code into machine instructions will be different because the computer instruction sets are different. The language processor has the responsibility to translate standard higher-level programming syntax into the correct machine instruction bit patterns.

Machine instructions are represented as patterns of ones and zeros in a computer word, just as numbers and characters are. Some of the bits in the word are set aside to provide the "op-code," or operation to perform. Examples of op-codes are ADD, Jump, Compare, and AND. Other bits in the instruction word specify the values to operate on, the "operands." An operand might be a register, a memory location, or a value already in the instruction word operand field.

An example machine instruction is the following ADD instruction for the Intel x86 computers. The Intel x86 instruction set is an unusually complex one to describe, because Intel has expanded the instruction set as it has evolved the computer family. It would have been easier to create new instruction sets when computing evolved from 16-bit processing in 1978, to 32-bit processing in 1986, to 64-bit processing in 2007. Instead, the Intel engineers very cleverly maintained compatibility with earlier instruction sets, while they added advanced capabilities. This allowed old programs to continue to run on new computers, and that greatly eased upgrades among PC users. The result, however effective technically and commercially, is an instruction set that is somewhat complex to describe. Here is the bit pattern, broken into bytes for readability, which says, "Add 40 to the contents of the DX register:"

```
00000001 11000010 00000000 00101000
```

The first byte is the op-code for ADD immediate (meaning the number to add resides in the instruction word itself). The second byte says that the destination operand is a register, and in particular, the DX register. The third and fourth bytes together comprise the number to add; if you evaluate the binary value of those bits, you will see that the value is 40.

To look at the content of a computer word, you cannot tell whether the word contains an instruction or a piece of data. Fetched as an instruction, the bit pattern above means add 40 to the DX register. Retrieved as an integer, the bit pattern means 29,491,240. In the Intel architecture, instructions ("code") are stored in a separate section of memory from data. When the computer fetches the next instruction, it does so from the code section of memory. This mechanism prevents a type of error that was common with earlier, simpler computer architectures, the accidental execution of data, as if the data were instructions.

Here is an example JMP instruction. This says, "Set the program counter (transfer control) to address 20,476 in the code:"

```
11101001 11111100 01001111
```

The first byte is the op-code for JMP direct (meaning the address provided is where we want to go, not a memory location holding the address to which we want to go). The second byte is the *low-order* byte for the address to which to jump. The third byte is the *high-order* byte for the address! How odd is that, you may think? To get the proper address, we have to take the two bytes and reorder them, like this:

```
01001111 11111100
```

This "peculiarity" is due to the fact that the Intel processor line is historically "little endian." That is, it stores the least significant byte of a multiple byte value at the lower (first) address. So, the first byte of a 2-byte address contains the low-order 8 bits, and the second byte contains the high-order 8 bits.

An advantage of the little endian design is evident with the JMP instruction because the "short" version of the JMP instruction takes only an 8-bit (1-byte) operand, which is naturally the low-order byte (the only byte). So the JMP direct with a 2-byte operand simply adds the high-order byte to the low-order byte. To say this another way, the value of the jump destination, whether 8 bits or 16 bits, can be read starting at the same address.

Other computers, such as the Sun SPARC, the PowerPC, the IBM 370 and the MIPS, are "big endian," meaning that the most significant byte is stored first. Some argue that big endian form is better because it reads more easily when humans look at the bit pattern, because human speech is big endian (we say, "four hundred, forty," not "forty and four hundred"), and because the order of bits from least significant to most significant is the same within a byte as the ordering of the bytes themselves. There is, in fact, no performance reason to prefer big endian or little endian formats. The formats are a product of history. Today, big endian order is the standard for network data transfers, but only because the original TCP/IP protocols were developed on big endian machines.

Here is a representative sampling of machine instructions from the Intel x86 machine instruction set. Most x86 instructions specify a "source" and a "destination," where each can in general be a memory location or a register. This list does not include every instruction; for instance, there are numerous variations of the jump instruction, but they all transfer control from one point to another. This list does provide a comprehensive look at all the types of instructions:

MOV	move "source" to "destination," leaving source unchanged
ADD	add source to destination, and put sum in destination
SUB	subtract source from destination, storing result in destination
DIV	divide accumulator by source; quotient and remainder stored separately
IMUL	signed multiply
DEC	decrement; subtract 1 from destination
INC	increment; add 1 to destination
AND	logical AND of source and destination, putting result in destination
OR	inclusive OR of source and destination, with result in destination
XOR	exclusive OR of source and destination, with result in destination
NOT	logical NOT, inverting the bits of destination
IN	input data to the accumulator from an I/O port
OUT	output data to port
JMP	unconditional jump to destination
JG	jump if greater; jump based on compare flag settings
JZ	jump if zero; jump if the zero flag is set
BSF	find the first bit set to 1, and put index to that bit in destination
BSWAP	byte swap; reverses the order of bytes in a 32-bit word
BT	bit test; checks to see if the bit indexed by source is set
CALL	procedure call; performs housekeeping and transfers to a procedure
RET	performs housekeeping for return from procedure
CLC	clear the carry flag
CMP	compare source and destination, setting flags for conditions
HLT	halt the CPU
INT	interrupt; create a software interrupt
LMSW	load machine status word
LOOP	loop until counter register becomes zero
NEG	negate as two's complement
POP	transfer data from the stack to destination
PUSH	transfer data from source to stack
ROL	rotate bits left
ROR	rotate bits right
SAL	shift bits left, filling right bits with 0
SAR	shift bits right, filling left bits with the value of the sign bit
SHR	shift bits right, filling left bits with 0
XCHG	exchange contents of source and destination

Other computer families will have machine instructions that differ in detail, due to the differences in the designs of the computers (number of registers, word size, etc.), but they all do the same, simple, basic things. The instructions manipulate the bits of the words mathematically and logically. In general, instructions fall into these categories: data transfer, input/output, arithmetic operations, logical operations, control transfer, and comparison. Upon such simple functions all else is built.

MEMORY

Computer memory is organized into addressable units, each of which stores multiple bits. In the early days of computing (meaning up until the 1970s), there was no agreement on the size of a memory unit. Different computers used different size memory "cells." The memory cell size was also referred to as the computer's "word size." The computer word was the basic unit of memory storage. The word size of the IBM 704 was 36 bits; the word size of the Digital Equipment PDP-1 was 18 bits; the word size of the Apollo Guidance Computer was 15 bits; the word size of the Saturn Launch Vehicle Computer was 26 bits; the word size of the CDC 6400 was 60 bits. These machines existed during the 1950s, 1960s, and 1970s.

The IBM 360 family, starting in the mid-1960s, introduced the idea of a standard memory cell of 8 bits called the "byte." Since then, computer manufacturers have come to advertise memory size as a count of standard bytes.

The idea of the computer word size is still with us, as it represents the number of bits the computer usually processes at one time. The idea of word size has become less crystalline, however, because newer computer designs operate on units of data of different sizes. The Intel Pentium processes 32 or 64 bits at a time, but it is also backwards compatible to the Intel 8086 processor of 1980 vintage, which had a word size of 16 bits. To this day, the Intel family of processors calls 16 bits a word, and in any case each byte has its own address in memory.

Today the byte is the measure of computer memory, and most computers, regardless of word size, offer "byte addressability." Byte addressability means that each byte has a unique memory address. Even though the computer may be a 32-bit machine, each byte in the 4-byte computer word (32 bits) can be addressed uniquely, and its value can be read or updated.

As you probably know, the industry uses prefixes to set the scale of a measure of memory. A kilobyte is 1024 bytes, or 2^{10} bytes—roughly a thousand bytes. A megabyte is 1,048,576 bytes, or 2^{20} bytes—roughly a million bytes. A gigabyte is 1,037,741,824 bytes, or 2^{30} bytes—roughly a billion bytes.

We hear larger prefixes occasionally, too. A terabyte is 1,099,511,627,776 bytes, or 2^{40} bytes—roughly a trillion bytes. A petabyte is 1,125,899,906,842,624, or 2^{50} bytes—roughly a quadrillion bytes. Such numbers are so large that their discussion usually accompanies speculation about the future of computing. However, we are starting to hear about active databases in the terabyte, and even the petabyte range (http://www.informationweek.com/ story/IWK20020208S0009).

Memory is used to store program instructions and data. The basic operations on memory are store and retrieve. Storing is also referred to as "writing." Retrieval is also referred to as "fetching," "loading," or "reading." Fetch is an obvious synonym for retrieve, but what about load? By loading one means loading a register in the CPU from memory, which from the point of view of the memory system is retrieval.

There are at least two registers associated with the memory control circuitry to facilitate storage and retrieval. These are the *memory address register* (MAR) and the *memory data register* (MDR). When writing to memory, the CPU first transfers the value to be written to the MDR, and the address of the location to be used to the MAR. At the next memory access cycle, the value in MDR will be copied into the location identified by the contents of the MAR.

When retrieving from memory, the CPU first stores the address to read in the MAR. When the read occurs on the next memory access cycle, the value in that location is copied into the MDR. From the MDR in the memory controller, the data value can be transferred to one of the CPU registers or elsewhere.

Main computer memory, such as we have in our PCs, is referred to as *random access memory* (RAM). That means we can access any element of memory at will, and with roughly the same speed, regardless of address.

By contrast, consider information and data stored on a magnetic tape. Magnetic tape is a kind of memory (we can store data on a magnetic tape), but magnetic tape is definitely not random access. Magnetic tape is serial access. We can read the contents of memory location 4000 only after having read and passed over all those locations that come before.

In addition to main memory, which has been the focus of our discussion so far, computer designers also usually provide small, high-performance memories, called *cache memories*, that are located close to the CPU. Cache memory may even be located on the same electronic chip as the CPU.

Cache is the French word for "hiding place." Cache memory is used to hold a copy of the contents of a small number of main memory locations. This turns out to be very useful, because program execution demonstrates a property called "locality of reference."

By locality of reference, we mean that for relatively long periods of time, the execution of a program will reference and affect a small number of memory locations. Accesses to memory are not random. Rather, for one period of time the program will read and write one part of memory, for example, an array of numbers, and for another period of time the program will store and retrieve from a different part of memory, for example, a record from a database.

When the computer copies the contents of main memory currently being accessed to cache memory, the CPU can avoid waiting for access to slower main memory, and access the cache instead. Since access times for cache memory are typically 5 to 10 times faster than access times for main memory, this tactic has proven very generally effective. Almost all computers built since 1980 have incorporated one or more cache memories in their design.

The management of cache memory is challenging, because the system must keep the contents of the cache memory synchronized with the contents of main memory. Engineers call this cache "coherency." As long as the program is reading from memory, but not writing, there is no problem. When the program writes to memory, however, both main memory and cache must be updated.

Also, when the program begins to access a new area of memory, one for which the contents are not already reflected in the cache, the cache management algorithm will typically bring to the cache the needed word as well as a number of following words from memory. At the same time, the cache management algorithm must decide which contents of the current cache to discard. As complex as this management is, use of cache memory usually makes a very noticeable difference in performance, with speedup of average memory access often in the neighborhood of 50 percent.

INPUT AND OUTPUT (I/O)

Obviously, most data on which we compute resides outside of the computer itself; perhaps it's originally on paper receipts, or in lists on paper. And when computation is complete, we want to see the results outside of the computer's own memory; on a display, or on paper, for example.

While there is variation in the way CPUs, memory, and caches are implemented, there is even more variation in the ways in which I/O is implemented. First of all, there are many different I/O devices. Some are for interacting with humans, such as keyboards, mice, touch screens, and displays. Others are for use by the computer directly, such as disk drives, tape drives, and network interfaces.

I/O devices also vary enormously in speed, and they're all much slower than the CPU and main memory. A typist working at 40 words per minute is going pretty fast, and striking about 200 keys a minute, or one key every .3 seconds. Let's compute how many instructions a 1 GHz personal computer might execute during that .3 seconds.

Some instructions execute on one clock cycle, but many require more than one. Let's assume that an average instruction requires 3 cycles. If that's the case, then the 1 GHz computer executes 330 million instructions per second, or 99 million instructions in the time it takes to type one letter.

To get a feel for the difference in speed between the keyboard and the CPU, imagine that the typist walks one foot in the time it takes to type one letter, and imagine also that the computer travels one foot in the time it takes to execute an instruction. If that were the case, then in the time the typist walks a foot, the computer travels 18,750 miles, or about three quarters of the way around the earth!

In the early days of computing, the CPU would wait for each character to be typed. A machine instruction would ready the keyboard interface to accept a character from the keyboard, and the next instruction would test to see if the character had been received. If the character had not yet been received, the program would simply loop, testing ("polling") to see if the character had been received. This is called "programmed I/O with polling," or "busy waiting." It's a simple but prohibitively costly approach.

Today computers use an "interrupt system" to avoid busy waiting, and the operating system supervises all I/O. Each I/O device is connected to the computer via an "I/O controller." An I/O controller is a small, special-purpose computer within the computer. It has a few well-defined functions, and a small amount of memory of its own with which to "buffer" (store temporarily) the information being sent or received.

When a program requires output, for example, the operating system moves the data to the buffer memory of the I/O controller for the device, and commands the I/O controller to start the operation. From that point on, the main computer is free to do other work, while the I/O controller handles the details and timing of moving the data to its destination. When the data transfer is complete, the I/O controller creates an "interrupt" which notifies the main computer that the transfer is now finished. The operating system responds to the interrupt in an appropriate way, perhaps by starting another output operation to the same device (think of multiple lines going to a printer).

When a program requires input, the operating system will suspend the execution of the requesting program and command the I/O controller of the device to start reading the necessary data. The operating system will then transfer control of the CPU to a different program, which will execute while the first program is waiting for its input. When the requested data become available, the I/O controller for the device will generate an interrupt. The operating system will respond by suspending the execution of the second program, moving the data from the buffer on the I/O controller to the program that requested the data initially, and restarting the first program.

The interrupt system is used for all data transfers today. While that is so, there are also some useful categorizations of device types. Devices may be categorized as *character* devices or *block* devices. A keyboard is a character device, and a disk is a block device. A character device transfers a character (8 bits) at a time, and a block device transfers a buffer, or set of data, at a time.

Other examples of character devices include telephone modems and simple terminals. Other examples of block devices include CD-ROM drives, magnetic tape drives, network interfaces, sound interfaces, and blocks of memory supporting devices like displays. Character devices interrupt on each character (8 bits) transferred, and block devices interrupt only when the entire block has been transferred.

Modern computer designs usually include a facility called *direct memory access* (DMA) for use with block devices. The DMA controller is its own special computer with access to memory, and it shares access to main memory with the CPU. DMA moves data directly between the buffer in the I/O controller and main memory, and it does so without requiring any service from the CPU.

Block devices can be used without DMA and, when they are used that way, the practice is called "programmed I/O with interrupts." With programmed I/O, the block device interrupts when the buffer is ready, but the operating system must still use the CPU to move the data between the buffer on the I/O controller and the destination in main memory.

When DMA is used with a block device, the data are transferred directly between the device and main memory, without requiring assistance from the operating system and the CPU. The operating system starts the transfer by specifying an address at which to start and the count of bytes to transfer. The CPU is then free to continue computing while the data are moved in or out. This is a further improvement in system efficiency, and today DMA is almost universally used for disk and other block transfers.

SUMMARY

Modern computers implement the von Neumann architecture, or stored program computer design. Program instructions and data are both stored in main memory. The components of the computer design are the CPU (including the control unit and the ALU), memory, and input/output.

Computers operate in base-2 arithmetic. Any number base can be used for computation and, just as humans find 10 fingers a convenient basis for computation, machine builders find 2-state (on–off) devices easy to build and convenient for computation. We discussed the simple math facts for binary math, and showed how subtraction is accomplished using 2's-complement addition. We also discussed the concept of the computer word, and the implications of computer word sizes of different numbers of bits.

Data are encoded in different ways, depending on the type of data. We described integer, floating-point and character encodings. The program interprets the bit pattern in a computer word depending on what it expects to find in that memory location. The same bit pattern can be interpreted in different ways when the program expects one data type or another. The programmer is responsible for insuring that the program correctly accesses its data.

The CPU consists of two parts. The control unit is responsible for implementing the steady cycle of retrieving the next instruction, decoding the bit pattern in the instruction word, and executing the instruction.

The arithmetic and logic unit (ALU) is responsible for performing mathematical, logical, and comparison functions.

The instruction set of a computer is the list of primitive operations that the computer hardware is wired to perform. Modern computers have between 50 and 200 machine instructions, and instructions fall into the categories of data movement, arithmetic operations, logical operations, control transfer, I/O, and comparisons. Most programmers today write in higher-level languages, and so are isolated from direct experience of the machine instruction set, but at the hardware level, the machine instruction set defines the capability of the computer.

Main memory provides random access to data and instructions. Today all manufacturers measure memory with a count of 8-bit bytes. Most machines, regardless of 16-bit, 32-bit, or 64-bit word size, also offer byte addressability.

Since access to memory takes longer than access to registers on the CPU itself, modern designs incorporate cache memory near the CPU to provide a copy of the contents of a section of main memory in order to obviate the need to read from main memory so frequently. Cache memory entails complexity to manage cache coherency, but it typically results in speedup of average memory access time by 50 percent.

Input and output functions today are based on I/O controllers, which are small special-purpose computers built to control the details of the I/O device, and provide a local memory buffer for the information being transferred in or out. Computers today use an interrupt system to allow the CPU to process other work while I/O occurs under the supervision of the I/O controller. When the transfer is complete, the I/O controller notifies the CPU by generating an interrupt.

A further improvement in I/O efficiency is direct memory access (DMA). A DMA controller is another special-purpose computer within the computer, and it shares access to main memory with the CPU. With DMA, the CPU does not even get involved in moving the data into or out of main memory. Once the CPU tells the DMA controller where the data reside and how much data to transfer, the DMA controller takes care of the entire task, and interrupts only when the entire task is complete.

REVIEW QUESTIONS

3.1 Write the number 229 in base 2.

3.2 What is the base-10 value of 11100101?

3.3 What are the units (values) of the first 3 columns in a base-8 (octal) number?

3.4 What is the base-2 value of the base-8 (octal) number 377?

3.5 Convert the following base-10 numbers to base 2:
   37
   470
   1220
   17
   99

3.6 Convert the following base-2 numbers to base 10:
   00000111
   10101010
   00111001
   01010101
   00110011

3.7 Assume a 16-bit signed integer data representation where the sign bit is the msb.
   a What is the largest positive number that can be represented?
   b Write the number 17,440.
   c Write the number −20.
   d What is the largest negative number that can be represented?

3.8 Using ASCII encoding, write the bytes to encode your initials in capital letters. Follow each letter with a period.

3.9 Referring to the list of Intel x86 instructions in this chapter, arrange a set of instructions to add the values stored in memory locations 50 and 51, and then to store the result in memory location 101. You need not show the bit pattern for each instruction; just use the mnemonics listed, followed in each case by the appropriate operand(s).

3.10 What Intel x86 instructions would you use to accomplish subtraction using 2's complement addition? This instruction set has a SUB instruction, but don't use that; write your own 2's complement routine instead.

3.11 What are the advantages of a larger computer word size? Are there disadvantages? If so, what are the disadvantages?

3.12 Assume that cache memory has an access time of 10 nanoseconds, while main memory has an access time of 100 nanoseconds. If the "hit rate" of the cache is .70 (i.e., 70 percent of the time, the value needed is already in the cache), what is the average access time to memory?

3.13 Assume our 1 GHz computer, which averages 3 cycles per instruction, is connected to the Internet via a 10 Mbit connection (i.e., the line speed allows 10 million bits to pass every second). From the time the computer receives the first bit, how many instructions can the computer execute while waiting for a single 8-bit character to arrive?

3.14 What complexity does DMA present to the management of cache memory?

3.15 Discuss the concept of a "memory hierarchy" whereby memory closer to the CPU is faster, more expensive, and smaller than memory at the next level. Arrange the different types of memory we have discussed in such a hierarchy.

CHAPTER 4

Software

This chapter will introduce a wide variety of topics related to computer software and programming languages. We will discuss some of the history of computer languages, and describe some of the varieties of languages. Then we will discuss the operation of language processing programs that build executable code from source code written by programmers. All these discussions will be incomplete—they are intended only to introduce the topics. However, we hope to impart a sense of the variety of approaches to computer programming, the historical variety of languages, and the basic mechanisms of compilers and interpreters.

GENERATIONS OF LANGUAGES

To understand the amazing variety of languages, programs, and products which computer scientists collectively refer to as software, it helps to recall the history of this young discipline.

Each computer is wired to perform certain operations in response to instructions. An instruction is a pattern of ones and zeros stored in a word of computer memory. By the way, a "word" of memory is the basic unit of storage for a computer. A 16-bit computer has a word size of 16 bits, or two bytes. A 32-bit computer has a word size of 32 bits, or four bytes. A 64-bit computer has a word size of 64 bits, or eight bytes. When a computer accesses memory, it usually stores or retrieves a word of information at a time.

If one looked at a particular memory location, one could not tell whether the pattern of ones and zeros in that location was an instruction or a piece of data (number). When the computer reads a memory location expecting to find an instruction there, it interprets whatever bit pattern it finds in that location as an instruction. If the bit pattern is a correctly formed machine instruction, the computer performs the appropriate operation; otherwise, the machine halts with an illegal instruction fault.

Each computer is wired to interpret a finite set of instructions. Most machines today have 75 to 150 instructions in the machine "instruction set." Much of the "architecture" of a computer design is reflected in the instruction set, and the instruction sets for different architectures are different. For example, the instruction set for the Intel Pentium computer is different from the instruction set for the Sun SPARC. Even if the different architectures have instructions that do the same thing, such as shift all the bits in a computer word left one place, the pattern of ones and zeros in the instruction word will be different in different architectures. Of course, different architectures will usually also have some instructions that are unique to that computer design.

The earliest computers, and the first hobby computers, were programmed directly in the machine instruction set. The programmer worked with ones and zeros to code each instruction. As an example, here is code (and an explanation of each instruction), for a particular 16-bit computer. These three instructions will add the value stored in memory location 64 to that in location 65, and store the result in location 66.

```
0110000001000000   (Load the A-register from 64)
0100000001000001   (Add the contents of 65)
0111000001000010   (Store the A-register in 66)
```

Once the programmer created all the machine instructions, probably by writing the bit patterns on paper, the programmer would store the instructions into memory using switches on the front panel of the computer. Then the programmer would set the P register (program counter register) contents to the location of the first instruction in the program, and then press "Run." The basic operational loop of the computer is to read the instruction stored in the memory location pointed to by the P register, increment the P register, execute the instruction found in memory, and repeat.

An early improvement in programming productivity was the assembler. An assembler can read mnemonics (letters and numbers) for the machine instructions, and for each mnemonic generate the machine language in ones and zeros.

Assembly languages are called *second-generation languages*. With assembly language programming, the programmer can work in the world of letters and words rather than ones and zeros. Programmers write their code using the mnemonic codes that translate directly into machine instructions. These are typical of such mnemonics:

```
LDA  m       Load the A-register from memory location m.
ADA  m       Add the contents of memory location m to the contents of the A-register, and leave
             the sum in the A-register.
ALS          A Left Shift; shift the bits in the A-register left 1 bit, and make the least significant bit zero.
SSA          Skip on Sign of A; if the most significant bit in the A-register is 1, skip the next
             instruction, otherwise execute the next instruction.
JMP  m       Jump to address m for the next instruction.
```

The work of an assembler is direct; translate the mnemonic "op-codes" into the corresponding machine instructions.

Here is assembly language code for the program above that adds two numbers and stores the result in a third location:

```
LDA 100   //Load the A-register from 100 octal = 64
ADA 101   //Add to the A-reg the contents of 101 (65)
STA 102   //Store the A-register contents in 102 (66)
```

Almost no one codes directly in the ones and zeros of machine language anymore. However, programmers often use assembly language for programs that are very intimate with the details of the computer hardware, or for programs that must be optimized for speed and small memory requirements. As an educational tool, assembly language programming is very important, too. It is probably the best way to gain an intuitive feel for what computers really do and how they do it.

In 1954 the world saw the first *third-generation language*. The language was FORTRAN, devised by John Backus of IBM. FORTRAN stands for FORmula TRANslation. The goal was to provide programmers with a way to work at a higher level of abstraction. Instead of being confined to the instruction set of a particular machine, the programmer worked with statements that looked something like English and mathematical statements. The language also included constructs for conditional branching, looping, and I/O (input and output).

Here is the FORTRAN statement that will add two numbers and store the result in a third location. The variable names X, Y, and Z become labels for memory locations, and this statement says to add the contents of location Y to the contents of location Z, and store the sum in location X:

```
X = Y + Z
```

Compared to assembly language, that's quite a gain in writeability and readability!

FORTRAN is a "procedural language". Procedural languages seem quite natural to people with a background in automation and engineering. The computer is a flexible tool, and the programmer's job is to lay out the sequence of steps necessary to accomplish the task. The program is like a recipe that the computer will follow mechanically.

Procedural languages make up one category of "imperative languages," because the statements of the language are imperatives to the computer—the steps of the program specify every action of the computer. The other category of imperative languages is "object-oriented" languages, which we will discuss in more detail later. Most programs today are written in imperative languages, but not all ...

In 1958, John McCarthy at MIT developed a very different type of language. This language was LISP (for LISt Processing), and it was modeled on mathematical functions. It is a particularly good language for working with lists of numbers, words, and objects, and it has been widely used in *artificial intelligence* (AI) work.

In mathematics, a function takes arguments and returns a value. LISP works the same way, and LISP is called a "functional language" as a result. Here is the LISP code that will add two numbers and return the sum:

```
(+ 2 5)
```

This code says the function is addition, and the two numbers to add are 2 and 5. The LISP language processor will return the number 7 as a result. Functional languages are also called "declarative languages" because the functions are declared, and the execution of the program is simply the evaluation of the functions. We will return to functional languages later.

In 1959 a consortium of six computer manufacturers and three US government agencies released Cobol as the computing language for business applications (COmmercial and Business-Oriented Language). Cobol, like FORTRAN, is an imperative, procedural language. To make the code more self-documenting, Cobol was designed to be a remarkably "wordy" language. The following line adds two numbers and stores the result in a third variable:

```
ADD Y, Z GIVING X.
```

Many students in computer science today regard Cobol as old technology, but even today there are more lines of production code in daily use written in Cobol than in any other language (http://archive.adaic.com/docs/reports/lawlis/content.htm).

Both PL/1 and BASIC were introduced in 1964. These, too, are procedural, imperative languages. IBM designed PL/1 with the plan of "unifying" scientific and commercial programming. PL/1 was part of the IBM 360 project, and PL/1 was intended to supplant both FORTRAN and Cobol, and become the one language programmers would henceforth use for all projects (Pugh, E., Johnson, L., & Palmer, J. *IBM's 360 and Early 370 Systems*. Cambridge, MA: MIT Press, 1991). Needless to say, IBM's strategy failed to persuade all those FORTRAN and Cobol programmers.

BASIC was designed at Dartmouth by professors Kemeny and Kurtz as a simple language for beginners. BASIC stands for Beginner's All-purpose Symbolic Instruction Code. Originally BASIC really was simple, too simple, in fact, for production use; it had few data types and drastic restrictions on the length of variable names, for example. Over time, however, an almost countless number of variations of BASIC have been created, and some are very rich in programming power. Microsoft's Visual Basic, for example, is a powerful language rich in modern features.

Dennis Ritchie created the very influential third-generation language C in 1971. C was developed as a language with which to write the operating system Unix, and the popularity of C and Unix rose together. C is also an imperative programming language. An important part of C's appeal is its ability to perform low-level manipulations, such as manipulations of individual bits, from a high-level language. C code is also unusually amenable to performance optimization. Even after 34 years, C is neck-and-neck with the much newer Java as the most popular language for new work (http://www.tiobe.com/tpci.htm).

During the 1970s, the language Smalltalk popularized the ideas of object-oriented programming. Object-oriented languages are another subcategory of imperative languages. Both procedural and object-oriented languages are imperative languages. The difference is that object-oriented languages support object-oriented programming practices such as inheritance, encapsulation, and polymorphism. We will describe these ideas in more detail later. The goal of such practices is to create more robust and reusable modules of code, and hence improve programming productivity.

In the mid-1980s, Bjarne Stroustrup, at Cambridge University in Britain, invented an object-oriented language called C++. C++ is a superset of C; any C program is also a C++ program. C++ provides a full set of object-oriented features, and at one time was called "C with classes." Until Java emerged in the late 1990s, C++ was the most popular object-oriented development language.

The most popular object-oriented language today is Java, which was created by James Gosling and his colleagues at Sun Microsystems. Java was released by Sun in 1994, and became an immediate hit due to its appropriateness for web applications, its rich language library, and its hardware independence. Java's growth in use among programmers has been unprecedented for a new language. Today Java and C are the languages most frequently chosen for new work (http://www.tiobe.com/tpci.htm).

The variety of third-generation languages today is very great. Some are more successful than others because they offer unusual expressive power (C, Java), efficiency of execution (C, FORTRAN), a large installed base of code (Cobol), familiarity (BASIC), portability between computers (Java), object orientation (Java, C++), or the backing of important sponsors (such as the US Department of Defense sponsorship of ADA).

COMPILERS AND INTERPRETERS

With the development of FORTRAN came a new and more complex program for creating machine language from a higher-level expression of a programmer's intent. The new program was called a compiler, and the job of a compiler is to translate a high-level programming language into machine code.

The input to a compiler is the source code written by the programmer in the high-level language. We will show a simple example program from a seminal book in statistics entitled *Multivariate Data Analysis*, written by William Cooley and Paul Lohnes in 1971. The book was remarkable in its time for its inclusion of many FORTRAN programs in source code form.

In 1971 the input would have been from punched cards, and the output would have been to a printer. In the read statements below we have replaced the card reader device ID of 7 with the asterisk character to allow the program to read from the keyboard of the PC. Likewise, in the write statements, we have replaced the printer device ID of 6 with an asterisk. This permits the output to go to the computer display.

FORTRAN of that time was a column-oriented language (newer FORTRAN standards have allowed "free format" statements). Statement numbers appeared in columns 1–5, and statements were written in columns 7–72. Putting a number in column 6 meant that the line was a continuation of the previous line. Putting a C in column 1 meant that the line was a comment, not a program statement.

Variables beginning with letters I, J, K, L, M, or N were integers, and all others were floating point (characters could be read into integer-type variables).

If you are interested in trying out this program, a free FORTRAN compiler, called GNU FORTRAN G77, is available from the Free Software Foundation. You can find the download link at http://kkourakis.tripod.com/.

The following program from Cooley and Lohnes was used to compute average scores on each of several tests for each student in a study.

```
     PROGRAM CLAVG
C
C     COMPUTE AVERAGE OF M SCORES FOR EACH OF N SUBJECTS
C     INPUT:
C      FIRST CARD CONTAINS N IN COLS 1-5, AND M IN COLS 6-10
C      FOLLOWING CARDS ARE SCORE CARDS, ONE SET PER SUBJECT.
C       FIRST CARD PER SET CONTAINS ID IN COLS 1-5 AND UP TO
C        25 SCORES IN 3-COLUMN FIELDS. ID FIELD MAY BE
C        BLANK IN ADDITIONAL CARDS IN A SET
C     COOLEY, W & LOHNES, P, MULTIVARIATE DATA ANALYSIS, 1971
C
     DIMENSION X(1000)
     READ( *, 1 ) N, M
   1 FORMAT( 2I5 )
     WRITE( *, 2 ) M, N
   2 FORMAT( 'AVERAGES ON ', I6, ' TESTS FOR EACH OF ', I6,
    1' SUBJECTS' )
     EM=M
```

```
      DO 5 J=1, N
      READ( *, 3 ) ID, ( X(K), K=1, M )
    3 FORMAT( I5, 25F3.0/ (5X, 25F3.0) )
      SUM = 0.0
      DO 4 K=1, M
    4 SUM = SUM + X(K)
      AV = SUM / EM
    5 WRITE( *, 6 ) J, ID, AV
    6 FORMAT( I6, 3X, 'SUBJECT ', I6, 3X, 'AV= ', F9.2 )
      STOP
      END


Example input cards:
  5   5
821 3 7 9 4 7
812 1 4 3 3 2
813 3 2 3 1 1
824 7 9 9 9 9
825 6 9 8 8 5
```

This program starts by reserving an array of 1000 elements for real numbers. Then it reads the first line of input to get values for N and M, the number of students and the number of scores for each student. Then it writes a message summarizing the task ahead.

The main loop starts next at the keyword DO. The loop starts there and ends at the statement numbered 5. The work of the loop begins with reading another line of input, which the program expects to consist of a student identifier and five test scores. Inside the main loop, there is a smaller loop that starts at the next DO and continues just to the following line, numbered 4. The inner loop sums all the scores for that line of input. The last work of the main loop is to divide the sum of test scores for the student by the number of tests in order to compute an average score for that student. After writing the result for that student, the loop resumes with the next student, until the scores for all the students have been averaged.

Obviously, translating such English-like or mathematical statements into machine code is much more challenging than the work done by an assembler. Compilers process source code in a series of steps.

The first step is called "scanning" or "lexical analysis," and the output is a stream of *tokens*. Tokens are the words of the language, and "READ", "FORMAT", "AV", "4", and "3X" are all tokens in the example program.

Next, the compiler "parses" the token stream. This step is also called "syntax analysis." Referring to the "grammar" or rules of the language, the compiler uses a "parse tree" to verify that the statements in the source code comprise legal statements in the language. It is at this step that the compiler will return error messages if a comma is missing, for example, or a key word is misspelled. Later in this chapter we will return to the topics of parsing and parse trees.

If all of the statements are legal statements, the compiler proceeds with "semantic analysis." In this phase, the *meaning* of the statements is created. By meaning, we mean implementing the programmer's intent in executable code. Modern compilers often create a program in an intermediate language that is later converted into machine code, but early compilers either created assembly language code that was then assembled by the trusty assembler, or created machine language directly. The advantage of the modern approach is that compilers for different languages can create intermediate code in the common form, which intermediate code can be fed to a common machine language generator.

The result of compiling a program is a file of *object code*, which is the binary file of machine instructions that will be executed when the program is run. Compilers create a special type of object code called *relocatable code*, which is object code that can be loaded into any part of memory. When the program is loaded into memory to run, addresses and references in relocatable files are adjusted to reflect the actual location of the program in memory.

With compilers, the translation of source code to executable code is accomplished once. Once the program is compiled, executing the program requires no translation, and the program in machine code form executes swiftly.

Interpreters operate differently. Interpreters translate the source code to machine code one source code line at a time, and they do this every time the program executes. The interpreter is always the program in control; it is the interpreter that is actually executing when a program in an interpreted language is run. BASIC is a language that is usually implemented with an interpreter.

In general, a program executed by an interpreter will run more slowly than a program that is first compiled into object code. The reason, of course, is that the interpreter must analyze each line and convert each line to machine code each time the program runs.

On the other hand, interpreters have other compensating advantages in some situations. For instance, when students are learning to program, the interactivity of an interpreter, and the savings of recompilation time on long programs, can be more important than final execution speed. Interpreters often can provide better diagnostic messages, too, since they work directly from the source code, line by line. In addition, with the continuing increases in hardware computation speeds, speed of execution sometimes becomes less important to users than other features of a language.

The distinctions are sometimes "fuzzy." First of all, some languages are implemented both as interpreted and compiled languages (e.g., BASIC, PERL, LISP). The modern Java language also blurs compiler/interpreter boundaries, as we will now discuss.

VIRTUAL MACHINES

Java is both compiled and interpreted. The Java *compiler* (javac) translates Java source code into Java "bytecode," which is a platform-independent intermediate code. When the Java program (java) runs, the *Java Virtual Machine* (JVM) *interprets* the Java bytecode.

A virtual machine such as the Java JVM is a computer defined by software rather than hardware. A virtual machine runs programs like a real computer, but the virtual machine is really another program, a construction in software, that fetches, decodes, and executes the program's instructions. The instructions are referred to as bytecode.

In the case of Java, the JVM implements a machine described by the official JVM specification by Lindholm and Yellin, which you can view on the Sun Microsystems website: http://java.sun.com/docs/books/vmspec/.

> The Java Virtual Machine is the cornerstone of the Java and Java 2 platforms. It is the component of the technology responsible for its hardware and operating system independence, the small size of its compiled code, and its ability to protect users from malicious programs.

> The Java Virtual Machine is an abstract computing machine. Like a real computing machine, it has an instruction set and manipulates various memory areas at run time.

Java is both compiled and interpreted; the source code is compiled into bytecode, and the bytecode is interpreted by the JVM. Further, many current implementations of the JVM offer *just-in-time compilation* (JITC), which means that when the program first executes, the JVM actually compiles the bytecode into machine instructions. Henceforth, executing the program runs a compiled program in object code form. The goal of this design is to provide the advantages of both compilers and interpreters.

By the way, the term *virtual machine* in general describes an additional layer of abstraction between the user and the hardware, and so computer scientists also use the term to describe software that makes one type of computer appear to be another. For instance, the Digital Equipment Corporation VAX product line, running the VMS operating system, was very popular in the 1980s and 1990s, and many programs were written for that environment. Since those computers are no longer available, some people install virtual machines (software) to make Linux (http://www.wherry.com/gadgets/retrocomputing/vax-simh.html) or Windows computers (http://www.dynawell.com/charon-vax/) execute VAX programs and appear to be VAX/VMS computers.

Another use of the term virtual machine is that by IBM, whose VM operating system provides each user the illusion of having a complete IBM 370 machine for their personal use.

PROCEDURAL PROGRAMMING

For many new programmers, procedural programming is the natural paradigm. A program can often be conceived simply as a list of instructions to be executed in order; that is, a procedure to be followed by the computer. Procedural programming languages are also called *imperative* languages.

In procedural programming, the code for a specific job is contained in a named procedure. Another name for a procedure is often *subroutine*. For instance, one might create a procedure to find the standard deviation of an array of numbers.

The standard deviation of a measure is defined as the square root of the average squared deviation from the mean. Here σ is the population standard deviation, and μ is the population mean:

$$\sigma = \sqrt{\sum_{i=1}^{n}(x_i - \mu)^2 / n} \qquad (4.1)$$

If one is working from a sample and intending to infer the standard deviation of the larger population, the best estimate will be obtained by dividing the sum of deviations by $(n-1)$ instead of n. Here s is the sample standard deviation, and $\bar{x}$ is the sample mean:

$$s = \sqrt{\sum_{i=1}^{n}(x_i - \bar{x})^2 / (n-1)} \qquad (4.2)$$

An equivalent formula often useful for computation is the following:

$$s = \sqrt{(\sum_{i=1}^{n} x_i^2 - n\bar{x}^2) / (n-1)} \qquad (4.3)$$

To write a procedure to perform this calculation, one might write a program to do the following:

    Set SUM and SUMSQUARES equal to 0.0
    Set n = size of the array of scores
    Start with the first score, and continue until all the scores have been processed
        Set SUM = SUM + score
        Set SUMSQUARES = SUMSQUARES + score^2
    End of loop
    Set MEAN = SUM/n
    Return the SquareRoot of (SUMSQUARES – n * MEAN^2) / (n – 1)

This is the recipe, the procedure, the pseudocode, for calculating the standard deviation of an array of numbers. Here is a Java class called `Sd` that implements such a procedure in a routine called `stdDev`:

```
import java.lang.Math;
class Sd {
public static void main( String args[] ){
   float[] numbers = { 3, 5, 7, 9 };
   System.out.println( "Std. dev. = " + stdDev( numbers) );
}
public static float stdDev( float scores[] ) {
   float sum         = 0;
   float sumSquares  = 0;
   int   n           = scores.length;
   for( int i = 0; i < n; i++ ) {
      sum            = sum + scores[i];
      sumSquares     = sumSquares + scores[i]*scores[i];
   }
   float mean        = sum / n;
   float variance = (sumSquares - n*mean*mean) / (n - 1);
   return (float)Math.sqrt( variance );
}
}
```

Execution starts at `main`. The main program creates an array of four floating-point numbers, and then it prints the character string `"Std. dev. = "`, followed by the number returned from the `stdDev` routine when `stdDev` is passed the array of four numbers. The code in `stdDev` follows our pseudocode above, using a `for` loop to iterate through all the numbers in the array that the main passed to `stdDev`.

Java was designed to be an object-oriented language, and object orientation provides even more sophisticated ways to create modules of code than a strictly procedural language like FORTRAN offers. Nevertheless, one can program procedurally in Java, as we have done above.

Procedural programming captures standard solutions to computational problems in blocks of code that can be accessed by name, that are reusable by means of a standard set of inputs (arguments—the variables passed into the routine), and that return a standard set of outputs. Notice, too, that variables have procedure "scope;" variables that are declared within the procedure, like `sum` and `sumSquares`, and are visible only within the procedure. This helps avoid confusion regarding the variables being used, and thus adds to program reliability.

Once you have a routine that calculates the standard deviation of an array of numbers, that routine can be used again and again. Such reuse can be accomplished by including the routine in whatever new program one writes, or by adding the routine to a library where other programs can access the procedure by name.

This structuring of code is a giant step beyond *unstructured programming* where the entire program, whatever it is, consists of a single monolithic block of code. With unstructured code, branching and repetitive use of code are accomplished using conditional statements and `GOTO` or `JUMP` statements. The result can be programs that are difficult to read, prone to errors, and difficult to debug—"spaghetti code."

Structured programming divides the programming task into modular procedures. This important advance in program design greatly improves program readability, reliability, and reusability. The larger task is broken down into a series of subprocedures. The subprocedures are then defined (written), and the structured programming task then becomes one of calling the well-tested subprocedures in the appropriate order.

OBJECT-ORIENTED PROGRAMMING

Object-oriented (OO) programming is a more recent development that provides approaches that further advance software reliability and reuse, and that often allow the software to "fit" better with our understanding of the real world that our programs may be reacting to, or trying to control.

Instead of procedures, OO programming relies on software objects as the units of modularity. An individual object is an instance of a type, or "class." One creates an instance by using the specifications of the class. As an analogy, my car is an instance of the class automobile—it has four wheels, a motor, seats, etc., like all cars do, but my car is one specific car among the many automobiles in the world.

An instance of a class has its own "state," or values of its characteristics. My car is red; your car is blue; both are automobiles. My car has 170 hp; yours has 200 hp. My car is not moving at this moment; your car is traveling at 34 mph. The class automobile specifies that all automobiles have color, horsepower, and speed (among other things) as *attributes* or *instance variables*.

Objects also have behavior. Behavior is determined by procedures of the class, and such procedures are called *methods*. An automobile class will have methods such as `changeSpeed` (to accelerate or decelerate), `park`, `refuel`, and `turn`. Given an instance of the automobile class, a program could invoke the `changeSpeed` method, for example, to cause that particular car to go faster. The `changeSpeed` method is called an *instance method*, because it affects an instance of the class automobile (one particular automobile).

Making the software object the unit of modularity has some important advantages. First, OO programming "encapsulates" the state and behavior of objects. Programs wishing to use the code of an object can access that code only through public instance variables and public instance methods. When a program invokes the `changeSpeed` method of an automobile, the invoking program has no visibility of how the change is effected. This prevents programmers from taking advantage of details of implementation.

It may sound like a disadvantage to prevent programmers from taking advantage of knowledge of implementation details. However, over many years programmers have learned that "things change." When one takes advantage of some particular implementation detail, one risks having one's program fail when the class is upgraded. So, in OO programming, the "contract" between the class and the user is entirely in the specification of the interface, i.e., the method parameters and the return values. Even if the creator of the class decides to make a change internally, the interface will remain effective. This *encapsulation* means reliable operation, even as "things change."

Another very big idea supported by OO programming languages is *inheritance*. Many times a new programming effort is, "the same as the last effort, but different ..." When that is the case, it's helpful to take advantage of the earlier code by creating a new class that inherits from the old, and simply adds the new features.

For instance, if a program requires a limousine object, the limousine class might be designed as a subclass of automobile. A limousine might have additional instance variables, or attributes, related to cost, beverages on board, schedule, etc. Otherwise, the limousine class could take advantage of the color, horsepower, and speed attributes already defined for automobiles. A limousine could also share the behavior of automobiles via the `changeSpeed`, `park`, and other methods already defined.

In describing inheritance, computer scientists say that the relationship between a subclass and a superior class constitutes an "is-a" relationship. The subclass is also an instance of the superior class. The limousine is also an automobile.

Inheritance allows one class to take advantage of the attributes and behavior of another. Often the design of an OO programming project is focused in large part on the class hierarchy (the set of classes to be written), and the relationships via inheritance of the classes to one another. A well-defined class hierarchy can substantially increase code reuse (decrease the code required), and improve reliability through reduced redundancy or duplication.

Related to inheritance is the concept of *polymorphism*. Polymorphism means, "taking many forms." In OO programming, polymorphism means that the execution of a method of a given name may be different depending on the class of the object for which the method is invoked.

For instance, suppose that instances of both the automobile class and the limousine class must be parked from time to time. However, parking a limousine may require a different behavior; in particular, a limousine will require a much bigger parking space. Therefore, the `park()` method of the limousine class will seek a space of a different size than the `park()` method of the automobile class.

Suppose that the object `vehicle` can sometimes be an automobile, and sometimes be a limousine. When `vehicle` must be parked, the program will invoke the `park()` method on the particular car or limousine (e.g., `vehicle.park()`). The programmer doesn't have to worry about whether `vehicle` is an automobile or a limousine. If the instance is an automobile, the automobile method will be invoked; if the instance is a limousine, the limousine method will be invoked. The method *appears* to be the same for both types of object, but the execution differs depending on the class to which the object belongs. The `park()` method takes different forms.

Polymorphism allows programmers to think about their programs in natural ways. For instance, lawnmowers, cars, boats, and diesel trucks all must be "started," but the means of starting the different machines can be very different. Suppose that each type is a subclass of vehicle. Rather than write a differently named procedure for each activity, the class designer simply implements different `start()` methods in the different classes, as appropriate. Then the user of the classes can naturally invoke the `start()` method of the lawnmower object and the `start()` method of the automobile object, without confusion and without complexity of naming. If the object being started is a lawnmower, starting may involve pulling a rope; if it is an automobile, starting will involve turning a key.

Variables such as color, horsepower, and speed, which comprise elements of the state of an individual object, are called *instance variables*. Likewise, methods such as `changeSpeed()` and `park()`, which affect the state of an individual object, are called *instance methods*. If the designer declares such instance variables and methods to be public, other programs and objects can access them. On the other hand, the designer can also give a class private instance variables and methods, and such private "members" enable the encapsulation virtue of OO programming. Private variables and methods are not even visible outside the object.

In addition to instance variables and methods, classes can have *static variables* and *static methods*. Whereas instance members (variables and methods) are associated with individual objects, static members are associated with a class as a whole. Suppose, for example, that the class automobile includes a static variable called `countOfCars`. Each time an automobile is created, the static variable `countOfCars` gets incremented. The count, because it is a static variable, is associated with the class, not with any individual automobile. Assuming the static variable `countOfCars` is public, any object can discover the number of automobiles created so far by reading the value of `Automobile.countOfCars`. The dot notation says to return the value of `countOfCars` from the Automobile class.

The most common use of static variables is for *class constants*. If you read the Javadoc for the class `StreamTokenizer`, for example, you will see a set of four class constants that are declared static. These constants are `TT_EOF`, `TT_EOL`, `TT_NUMBER`, and `TT_WORD`. These constants represent the possible values (the token types) that a `StreamTokenizer` will return when it extracts a token (a String, a number, or an EndOfFile/EndOfLine flag) from an InputStream. Another example from Java is the class `Color`, which defines a long list of static constants used to represent commonly used colors.

Aside from using static variables for class constants, it is generally wise to avoid static variables unless you have a special reason to use them (as, for example, a need to keep a count of all the objects created). The reason is that, typically, many objects can modify a static variable, and over time the probability of some new class taking such liberties will grow. Discovering the cause of unexpected behavior related to static variables can be difficult.

Static methods likewise are associated with a class as a whole, and are accessible from any object simply by referencing the class name that provides the static method. For instance, the Java class `Integer` has a set of static methods related to integer numbers. One is the static method `Integer.valueOf(String)`, which returns a Java `Integer` object when passed a `String` that properly represents an integer number.

The Java `Math` class provides many more examples of static methods. Any object can take advantage of the static methods in the `Math` class to compute a transcendental function, square root, log, etc. The object using the routine must simply reference the class name, followed by the dot notation, and the name of the static method; for example, `Math.sqrt(X)` will return the square root of X.

Unless there is a special reason to do so, such as providing a library of functions as the `Math` class does, it is better practice to avoid static methods. The reason is the same as for static variables; the shared code provides more opportunity for unexpected "side effects" to occur. The exception to this rule is the Java program's `main()` method. The JVM must find a public static method called `main` in the class being executed.

Visual Basic .NET uses the term "shared" instead of "static," and the word shared is a better description of the concept. The term static has been used in several ways in different programming languages. For instance, a static variable in a C procedure (C is a procedural language, not an OO language) is one whose address does not change between executions of the procedure. While other variables in the procedure get pushed onto and popped off the stack dynamically, a static variable in C gets allocated to a fixed memory location, and so the address associated with the variable name remains static. Static variables in C are used for things like counters, when one must keep track of the number of times a procedure has been executed. A static variable will allow the count to persist between calls to the procedure.

For OO programming, and specifically for Java, think of static members as shared members. Static members are accessible to all. Understand how they differ from instance members, and use static members only when they satisfy a need that a corresponding instance member cannot.

SCRIPTING LANGUAGES

Today there is a large set of programming languages collectively referred to as scripting languages. The original idea of a "script" was a set of operating system commands placed in a file. When a user "executes" the script file, the set of commands in the file is executed in order. This notion of a script is still heavily used. Scripts are very useful for automating routine tasks which otherwise would require a person to sit at a keyboard and type the same commands again and again.

Here is an example from the author's experience. This script is for a Unix computer. The script runs a grading program against an output file for a student's project, then runs the student's original program against a smaller "extract" file as a second test, and finally prints a set of documents for the student. The script automates the execution of a set of commands by accepting a set of parameters in the command line, and then using the values of those variables to construct the appropriate commands and execute them. When using the script, the user types "gradeP" followed by six character strings giving the name of the student's output file, the comments file to be created, etc., and at last the student's name:

```
#! /bin/sh
#  Script gradeP for grading the access_log projects
#  Variables:
#                   $1 student's output file
#                   $2 comments/grading file to be created by
#                   program gradeProj.pl
#                   $3 student's source code
#                   $4 access_log_extract-report
#                   $5 path to student's directory
#                   $6 Name

# Run the grading program against the student's output file
gradeProj.pl $6 $5$1 $5$2

# Test the student's program against the extract file
$5$3 /home/fac/chr/public_html/plc/access_log_extract $5$4

# Print the results
nenscript -2 -r $5$2 $5$1 $5$3 $5$4
```

This script is a script in the Bourne shell (command interpreter) for Unix, and it flexibly executes a set of commands that otherwise would require much more typing and be much more prone to errors of execution.

The first line, the one beginning with #! (called a shebang), tells Unix to execute the commands in the file using the program sh, also known as the Bourne shell. The lines beginning with # are comment lines. The remaining lines are commands whose parameters are constructed from the variables defined by the original command line arguments.

The Bourne shell scripting language is one of many scripting languages one can categorize as *job control language* (JCL) scripting languages. Others include the C shell (csh), the Korn shell (ksh), Bash (Bourne Again SHell), JCL and JES2 (IBM's languages for mainframes), and MS-DOS Batch. They are all similar in that they can accept a file of commands as input, incorporate values of parameters available at execution time, and execute the sequence of commands. Except for JCL and JES2, they all have limited programming controls as well, and include conditional expressions and the ability to loop and branch during execution of the command file.

Here's an example MS-DOS Batch file that will copy a list of files to a directory called DUPLICAT. Lines beginning with twin colons are comment lines. Lines beginning with a single colon are "labels" referred to by other statements. Note the conditional statement that creates the directory only if it does not already exist. Also note the looping structure using the GOTO statement with the COPY-FILES label.

```
:: myCopy.bat
:: Copies a set of files to a (possibly new) directory
::  called DUPLICAT
:: Wildcards (* and ?) may be Used in File Names
::
@ECHO OFF

::Stops the Batch File if no file is specified
IF "%1" == "" GOTO END

::Makes the new directory only if it does not exist already
IF NOT EXIST DUPLICAT MKDIR DUPLICAT

::Loop to copy all the files.
::Uses the DOS "SHIFT" command to move
:: each file name specified at the
:: command line to the "1" parameter,
:: until none is left to copy.

:COPY-FILES
XCOPY %1 DUPLICAT
SHIFT
IF "%1" == "" GOTO END
GOTO COPY-FILES

:END
```

These JCL scripting languages have very limited programming tools and primitive error-handling abilities. They are very useful nonetheless, especially to system administrators who need quick "one-off" applications to automate repetitive tasks.

The usefulness of scripting languages inspired many authors and inventors to develop new languages with various features and conveniences. For text processing, for example, the languages awk, sed, and Perl are popular. Perl has also become popular for general-purpose programming, and the languages PHP, Ruby, and Python are other languages useful for larger applications.

In general, these scripting languages are interpreted, so execution speed is not their main attraction. Instead, scripting languages offer a compact, simplified syntax that speeds program development. In many cases, this write-time advantage outweighs any run-time disadvantage. This is especially true for one-time systems tasks like reformatting a text file or interpreting a system activity log.

Suppose one wanted to print a copy of a file, with line numbers added to the front of each line. Here's a Perl program called `lineNumberFile.pl` to do that; run it by typing

>lineNumberFile.pl < fileToPrint.

```
#!/usr/local/bin/perl        # Location of Perl interpreter
#
# Program to open the source file, read it in,
# print it with line numbers, and close it again.

$file = $0;                  # $0, the 1st cmd line arg
print "$0\n";                # Prints name of file & newLine

open(INFO, $file);           # Open the file
while($line = <INFO>)        # Read lines of file
  {                          # Add line number
    print " $. ". "$line"; # $. has the input line no
  }
close(INFO);                 # Close the file
>
```

That's only seven lines of code, and the job is done.

FUNCTIONAL LANGUAGES

Functional languages were invented early in the history of computing. In 1958 John McCarthy at MIT invented LISP. Functional languages represent computing as solving mathematical functions. A function takes one or more arguments, and returns a value. For example, an equation for a parabola is:

$$f = 2x^2 + 5 \tag{4.4}$$

When one supplies a particular value for x, the function returns a particular result:

$$f(3) = 2(3)^2 + 5 = 23 \tag{4.5}$$

With a functional language, computing proceeds by passing input parameters to a function, which then returns the result of the function. The return value(s) typically provides the input parameter(s) for another function(s), and so any level of computational complexity can be programmed.

In any functional language, some basic functions are built in, and they're called primitives. In LISP these include the mathematical functions of addition, subtraction, multiplication and division, for example, as well as the function car, which returns the first element in a list, and cdr, which returns all but the first element in a list. (By the way, the function names car and cdr come from acronyms for two registers used by LISP on the old IBM 704 computer.)

As our example functional language, we will use Scheme, a newer (1975) descendent of LISP, which has particularly consistent syntax. An expression in Scheme is an *atom* or a *list*. An atom is a single number, character string, name, or function. A list is a collection of expressions contained within parentheses. Note that the elements of a list may be atoms or other lists.

Computing in Scheme means evaluating the Scheme expressions. In particular, to evaluate a list, Scheme expects the first element of the list to be a function, and the following elements of the list to be arguments to the function. Since the elements of the list may themselves be lists, evaluation proceeds recursively, by first evaluating the lists at the lowest level, and then proceeding to final evaluation of the function at the top level.

To add two numbers in Scheme, one creates a list. The first element within parentheses is the function '+', and the following elements are the arguments to the function. When an expression is complete, the Scheme interpreter evaluates the function and returns the result. This cycle is called the REPL—the Read, Evaluate, Print, Loop. Here is the code to add 3 and 5 together:

```
(+  3  5  )
8
```

If we wish to add more than two numbers, we simply include more parameters to the function. For example, to add five numbers, we simply increase the number of arguments:

```
(+  3  5  7  4  2  )
21
```

Expressions can be evaluated as arguments, too, so this Scheme expression divides the sum of 3 and 5 by the difference between 7 and 5:

```
( /  (+  3  5  )  ( -  7  5)  )
4
```

Another primitive function in LISP and Scheme is the function list, which takes a series of arguments and makes a list:

```
( list 1 5 6 )
( 1 5 6 )
```

If we need the first element in a list, the function car will return that:

```
( car (list 1 5 6) )
1
```

The function cdr will return all but the first element of the list:

```
( cdr (list 1 5 6) )
( 5 6 )
```

A list can include many elements, only one element, or no elements:

```
( list 8 )
( 8 )
( list )
()
```

One can define a new function at any time using the "lambda notation." This code creates a new function called 'sum' which adds two numbers together, just like the built-in primitive '+' does, but for only two arguments:

```
(define sum
  (lambda (n m)
    ( + n m)))
```

The name sum is associated with a function that expects two arguments. The function completes after adding the arguments n and m together, and the result of evaluating the function is the sum of the two arguments. Our function sum produces the same result as the built-in function '+' when presented with two arguments, but sum will not accept an arbitrary number of input parameters:

```
> (sum 4 3)
7
> (+ 4 3)
7
> (sum 4 3 2)

[Repl(25)] Error: incorrect number of arguments to
#<procedure>.
Type (debug) to enter the debugger.
```

Looping in a functional language is accomplished by recursion, that is, by having the function call itself repetitively. Indeed, one of the reasons to study functional programming is to become comfortable using recursion. Even programmers using the popular imperative programming languages can take advantage of recursion, which can make some programming tasks more compact, self-documenting, and reliable.

For instance, suppose we need a function to compute the factorial of an integer. One way to write such code in C or Java is this:

```
int factorial( int n ){
    int fact = 1;
    while( n > 1 ) {
        fact = fact * n;
        n--;
    }
    return fact;
}
```

This version of the factorial function starts with the number passed in, and then iteratively multiplies that number by each smaller number until the function works its way down to 1.

A different way to write this function in C or Java, using recursion, is this way:

```
int factorial( int n ){
    if( n <= 1 ) return 1;
    return( n * factorial( n-1 ));
}
```

If the number passed in is greater than 1, the recursive function simply multiplies the number passed in by the factorial of that number minus 1. The factorial function calls itself repeatedly until the number passed in is 1, at which point it returns the value 1 to the last caller, which can then return to its caller, etc.

Some would say that the recursive function is more self-descriptive. It's certainly shorter, and simpler to write.

To write a recursive function, one first defines the "grounding condition," or "base case," at which the recursion terminates. In the example of factorial, both 1! and 0! return 1 by definition, and no further computation is necessary. When the grounding condition occurs, the function should stop calling itself and simply return the value 1.

The factorial for a larger number can be defined as the larger number times the factorial of the next smaller integer. So the factorial function can be thought of as a process: multiply the number times the factorial of the next smaller number. The process continues until the number being evaluated is 1. At that point, the function returns 1, which provides the factor for computing 2!, which answer provides the factor for computing 3!, which answer provides the factor for computing 4!, etc. The recursion "unwinds" providing the answer for the factorial of the larger number.

In a functional language, all computation proceeds by means of evaluating functions. Assignment of values to variables in order to maintain state is not permitted, so we cannot use a variable like 'n' to keep track of our progress in a loop. Looping must be accomplished by recursion. Here is a Scheme function to compute the factorial:

```
(define factorial
  (lambda (n)
    (if (<= n 1) 1 (* n (factorial (- n 1)))
    )))
```

Here we also see the conditional execution function if. The if function in Scheme is followed by three expressions. The first is evaluated for its truth. If the first expression following if is true, the second expression is evaluated and returned (in this case, if n <= 1, return 1). If the first expression is false, the third expression is evaluated and returned (in this case, if n > 1, return the product of n and the factorial of n−1).

We can elaborate on our simple summation function and illustrate some more ideas. Here is a version of sum that takes a list as an argument. This way, our sum function can compute the sum of any number of integers:

```
(define listSum
  (lambda (n)
    (cond ((null? n) 0)
          ( (null? (cdr n)) (car n) )
          (else (+ (car n) (listSum (cdr n)))))
    )))
```

The cond (condition) operator is like multiple if and else-if statements in C or Java. Following the function cond is a list of condition/action pairs. Cond tests the first condition and, if it's true, cond executes the associated action. If the first condition is false, cond checks the second condition. If the second condition is true, cond executes the action associated with the second condition. There can be any number of conditions, and cond will execute only the action associated with the first true condition. At the end can be an else condition that cond will execute if no other condition is true. The else condition is not required, however.

The listSum function tests to see whether the list it was passed is null. If so, the function returns 0. If not, then it tests to see if the cdr of the list is null. That will be true if the list consists of a single element, and in that case the function will simply return the value of the first and only element. Otherwise, the function recursively adds the first element of the list to the sum of the elements in the back (cdr) of the list.

When we evaluate listSum, we get the correct result:

```
> (listSum (list 2 4 5))
11
```

We can go one step further and make a function that behaves like the '+' function, which accepts any number of addends. Notice that next to lambda, n appears without parentheses. Scheme will accept any number of parameters; in this case, create a list of the parameters, and pass the list to the function giving the list the name n.

```
(define sum
  (lambda n
    (cond ((null? n) 0)
          ( (null? (cdr n)) (car n) )
          ( else (+ (car n) (listSum (cdr n)))))
      )))
```

The code for sum is similar to listSum in its checking for the length of n (the set of parameters in the case of sum), but if the number of parameters is two or greater, sum uses the listSum function to compute the sum of elements 2 through n. That is because listSum expects a list as an argument, whereas sum expects one or more separate arguments that get concatenated into a new list. If sum were to recursively call itself passing (cdr n), the next call to sum would create ((cdr n)), a list of one element (the element is another list, the cdr of the list of parameters), and the second line of cond would return a list instead of a number.

Our version of sum now behaves like '+' and will accept any number of parameters and return the sum.

```
> (sum 2 4 5 6)
17
```

A more elegant solution accepts the list, builds a new expression by putting the '+' in front of the list, and passes the new list to the Scheme eval function directly. The eval function is the function that Scheme itself uses to evaluate expressions.

```
(define sum
  (lambda n
    (cond ((null? n) 0)
          ( else (eval (cons '+ n)))
      )))
```

This solution introduces two new elements of Scheme syntax. To understand this version, you need to know that the single quote before the '+' stops Scheme from evaluating the function '+', and instead forces Scheme to treat '+' as a simple character atom. In addition, the function cons creates a new list by adding an element to the front of a list, in this case adding the '+' to the front of the list of numbers to be summed.

Functional programming has the desirable properties of simple syntax and semantics, and compact code. Also, since a function may not change any of the parameters passed to it, and since assignment is not used to change program state, "side effects" (any changes in variables that endure after execution of the code) are eliminated, with resulting improvements in reliability.

Historically, functional programming has found advocates in the fields of artificial intelligence and expert systems. The popular editor Emacs is written in LISP, too, as is the on-line fare search program employed by Orbitz (http://www.paulgraham.com/icad.html).

LANGUAGE DESIGN

Computer programming languages are developed to make it easier for humans to direct computation. At some times in the past it was thought that a single language could be best for all programming tasks. For instance, IBM planned to "unify" scientific and business programming in the 1960s with PL1, replacing both FORTRAN and Cobol. In the 1980s there was talk of Pascal replacing all other languages because of its superior type checking and block structure.

As time has passed, however, more languages, not fewer, have come into use, and new ones still appear. We think this is due to the maturing of the programming discipline. Just as any able mechanic will carry several different tools for working with a 10 mm nut (open-end wrench, box wrench, crows-foot wrench, shallow socket, deep socket, etc.), any able programmer will carry knowledge of several different languages so that they can select the best one for a particular circumstance.

Some languages provide better run-time performance, some provide unusually compact syntax for quick "one-off" programs, some offer particularly strong features for manipulating text, some for working with matrices of numbers, etc. In evaluating a language, computer scientists consider many properties.

From the earliest days, efficiency of execution has been a desirable property. In fact, FORTRAN was widely adopted in large part because it created code that was very nearly as fast as assembly language code. Without its characteristic efficiency, FORTRAN would have been adopted much more slowly by the programmers of the 1950s and 1960s who worked in an environment where the cost of running a program was an expensive multiple of the CPU seconds the program consumed.

Human readability is another desirable trait in a language. Cobol syntax is as "wordy" as it is because the designers of Cobol wanted the code to be self-documenting. The designers hoped to guarantee that Cobol would be easy for a human to read, regardless of the commenting style of the author.

A language that is easy to implement has an advantage. The language ADA can serve as a contrary example. While ADA is an excellent and carefully designed language, ADA has been adopted more slowly than some others, in part because its size and complexity initially made it more difficult to implement, especially on smaller computers.

Computer scientists also praise a language for *expressiveness*. This is a somewhat subjective judgment, but an example of unusual expressiveness will illustrate the property. Perl offers the "if" conditional familiar to us in most languages, and Perl also offers the "unless" conditional, which is the converse of "if." Having both forms can be called "syntactical sugar," since there is no functional requirement for a language to have both, but having both allows more natural expression of some conditions.

Expressiveness is also relative to particular types of applications. C's built-in facilities for manipulating bits mark it as unusually expressive in that way, and make it an especially good language for writing operating systems and drivers. Matlab's matrix manipulation syntax is wonderfully expressive for matrix algebra applications like statistics and image processing.

Another very desirable trait in a language is *regularity*. Regularity means consistency of behavior, consistency of appearance, and avoidance of special cases. In C, an example of an irregularity is the use of the == Boolean operator. Any two values can be compared using ==, but two arrays cannot be compared using ==; arrays must be compared element by element. The == operator cannot be applied in a general way to all data structures. There are almost always good reasons for irregularities, but, other things being equal, a more regular language is more desirable.

Computer scientists praise languages that are extensible. Many languages today allow the writer to define new data types, for instance. That was not an option in early versions of FORTRAN, which came on the scene supporting only integers and floating-point data types. Languages can also be extended by adding to libraries of shared routines. A language like LISP even allows the writer to extend the keywords of the language by writing new functions.

Standardization is another advantage; a language with a formal standard encourages wider adoption. Ada, C, Cobol, Java, and many others now boast international standards for the languages. Perl, on the other hand, does not—Perl is whatever Larry Wall and the Perl Porters decide they want "everyone's favorite Swiss Army Chainsaw" to be (http://www.perl.com/pub/a/2000/04/whatsnew.html).

Another desirable property of a language is machine independence. Java is the best example of a machine-independent language. Given that a Java Virtual Machine is available for the host hardware, the same Java source code should run the same way on any machine. (This promise of "write once, run anywhere" has largely been fulfilled today, but in the beginning days of Java, the popular quip was, "Java: write once, run away.")

On the other hand, programmers using C must keep in mind the hardware platform on which the code will run since, for example, the sizes of data types vary on different machines. An int variable may be 16 bits long on one computer, and 32 bits long on another. The programmer seeking to write a C program to run on multiple platforms must accommodate these differences somehow.

Finally, some languages are more secure than others. Strict type checking is one feature designed to enhance security. This was one of the lauded virtues of Pascal, when Pascal was being promoted in the 1980s as the answer to all programming problems. Boundary checking on arrays is another feature designed to promote security, and descriptions of the Java security model boast Java's array boundary checking as an advance over languages such as C.

While all these properties may be desirable, they are not all possible to achieve in the same language. For instance, the security of strict type checking probably will reduce some forms of programmer expressiveness (e.g., treating characters as integers, which can be used to improve execution speed in some applications), increase program size, and perhaps reduce ultimate efficiency. Tradeoffs make language design a challenging occupation, and different tradeoffs make different languages more suitable for different types of tasks.

LANGUAGE SYNTAX AND SEMANTICS

To prepare a user-written program for execution, the language processor must perform several tasks. In order, computer scientists refer to these tasks as scanning (lexical analysis), parsing (syntax analysis), and code generation (semantic analysis).

Scanning, the first step, reads the character sequence that is a source code file and creates a sequence of *tokens* of the language. Tokens are the words of a language, and tokens fall into several categories. A token may be a key word like `return` or a reserved word like `String`, a special symbol like '+', a variable name or identifier like `myCount`, or a literal constant like the number `3.14` or the character string `Please enter your name:`.

After the scanner "tokenizes" the source code, the parser accepts the list of tokens as input and builds a "parse tree" according to the syntax rules of the language. The parser tests the token stream against the syntax, or grammar rules, of the language, and in the process finds many of the errors we programmers make.

The syntax of a language describes the allowable statements in the language. Following correct syntax does not guarantee correct programming, but correct programming requires correct syntax. For instance, in English, the sentence, "The octopus combed his hair" is syntactically correct, but foolish. On the other hand, the sentence, "The mab ran after the bus" is not syntactically correct because the dictionary does not recognize the token 'mab'. In programming languages, as in English, many syntax errors occur because of misspellings and typographical errors.

Today, language syntax rules are usually expressed in *Backus-Naur form* (BNF), or *extended Backus-Naur form* (EBNF), after John Backus (inventor of FORTRAN) and Peter Naur. BNF uses a set of rules or "productions" to describe the grammar, or syntax.

On the left-hand side of a production, BNF shows a linguistic concept known as a "non-terminal." Examples of non-terminals from English include "verb-phrase" and "sentence." In a programming language, examples of non-terminals might be "term" or "expression."

Non-terminals are so-called because they can be broken down into combinations of smaller concepts. For instance, a verb-phrase can consist of a verb and a direct-object-phrase. Ultimately, the grammar defines the units of the language that cannot be further reduced, the words of the language, and these are called "terminals."

On the right-hand side of a production, BNF shows the possible combinations of non-terminals and/or terminals that can be substituted for the higher-level non-terminal on the left-hand side. Here is a grammar for mathematical expressions:

```
1 expression -> term | expression add_op term
2 term       -> factor | term mult_op factor
3 factor     -> identifier | number | - factor | (expression)
4 add_op     -> + | -
5 mult_op    -> * | /
```

The vertical lines mean "or." To simplify the discussion so that we need not also supply rules for creating "identifiers" and "numbers," assume that identifiers are valid variable names and numbers are valid numbers. We will treat them as terminals.

Production 1 says that an expression can consist either of a term, or of an expression plus an add_op (addition operator) plus a term. Production 2 says that a term can be a factor, or it can be another term plus a mult_op (multiplication operator) plus a factor.

For example, we can parse the following expression according to the grammar:

```
X * 3 + 4
```

We can, by rule 1, replace the original expression with another expression (X * 3), an add_op (+), and a term (4). By rule 2 the single-token term (4) can be replaced by a factor, which can, by rule 3 be replaced by a number (4), which is a terminal for us.

It remains for us to parse the expression (X * 3). At this point, by rule 1 the only legal substitution for (X * 3) is a term. By rule 2 the term (X * 3) can be replaced by another term (X), a mult_op (*), and a factor (3). Again, rule 3 says the factor (3) can be replaced by a number (3), which is a terminal.

By rule 2 the term (X) can be replaced by a factor (X), which by rule 3 can be replaced by an identifier (X), which we said was a terminal for us.

Such decomposition of a more complex expression into its terminals according to the rules of the grammar is called a derivation. The result of a successful derivation is a parse tree or syntax tree. Here is the parse tree for the derivation we just completed:

```
        ( X * 3 + 4 ) expression
         /       |   \
        /        |    \
     (X * 3)     +      4 expression add_op term
      / | \             4 factor
     /  |  \            4 number
    /   |   \
   /    |    \
  X     *       3 term mult_op factor
  X factor      3 number
  X identifier
```

To compute the meaning of the expression, the parse tree can be traversed from the bottom up, computing the multiplication first and then performing the addition.

If an expression can be parsed according to the grammar of the language, the expression conforms to the syntax of the language. Once the parser creates the parse tree, the compiler can work from the bottom of the tree to the top, creating the machine instructions to implement the expression. This last phase is called code generation.

Today most descriptions of language syntax use a version (there are several) of EBNF. Some notational changes simplify the representations of productions. In particular, EBNF uses curly brackets to denote "zero or more occurrences of," and it uses square brackets to denote optional parts of a production. EBNF uses parentheses and vertical "or" separators to denote multiple-choice options for a single element. We can rewrite the grammar above using this EBNF notation:

```
expression -> term   { (+ | -) term }
term       -> factor { (* | /) factor }
factor     -> identifier | number | - factor | ( expression )
```

If it is not obvious that these rules agree with our earlier grammar, consider our earlier first rule for expressions:

```
expression -> term | expression add_op term
```

From this rule, we can generate:

```
expression -> term
expression -> expression + term
expression -> expression + term + term
expression -> expression + term + term + term
...
expression -> term + term + term + term ...+ term
```

So, the EBNF notation says more simply:

```
expression -> term   { (+ | -) term }
```

An expression is a term followed by zero, one, or many additive terms.

Here is an example of EBNF used to represent an optional element in a production:

```
if-statement -> if( expression ) statement [else statement]
```

This production says that an if-statement consists of the key word if, followed by an open parenthesis, followed by an expression, followed by a closed parenthesis, followed by a program statement, optionally followed by the key word else and another program statement.

A very important requirement for a programming language grammar is that it be unambiguous. Given an expression in the language, there must be one and only one valid derivation in the language. To illustrate an ambiguous grammar, consider this simplification of the grammar for mathematical expressions:

```
1 expression -> expression operator expression | identifier |
  number | - expression | ( expression )
2 operator    -> + | - | * | /
```

We can again parse the expression (X * 3 + 4) proceeding from the left to the right, and the result will be the same parse tree we derived from the more complex grammar. However, this simpler grammar would also allow a rightmost approach, with the following result:

```
( X * 3 + 4 ) expression
  /  |    \
 /   |     \
X    *    (3 + 4) expression operator expression
|          \
X Identifier \
           (3 + 4) expression operator expression
             /    \
            /  |   \
           /   |    \
          /    |     \
       3 number +     4 number
```

The meaning of the second parsing is very different from the first, because in the rightmost parsing the addition occurs before the multiplication. That is not the customary hierarchy of operations, and the second parse tree will, in general, produce a different value for the expression than the first.

Because the simpler grammar can produce two different and valid parse trees for the same expression, the grammar is ambiguous. Programming language grammars must be unambiguous.

Look again at the first grammar, the more complex example, and notice how the grammar enforces a hierarchy of operations; multiplication and division occur before addition or subtraction. Correct grammars place higher "precedence" operations lower in the cascade of productions.

Another key to a correctly specified grammar is the "associativity" of language elements. Does a mathematical operator associate left to right, or right to left? This makes a difference with expressions like (9 - 4 - 2). Left associativity of operators yields 3, while right associativity yields 7. How do the grammar rules express associativity?

A production like this is left-associative:

```
expression -> term | expression add_op term
```

A production like this is right-associative:

```
expression -> term | term add_op expression
```

The significant difference is that the recursion (where an expression is part of an expression) is on the left in the first case, and on the right in the second case.

Using the left-associative production to parse (9 - 4 - 2) results in this parse tree:

```
    ( 9 - 4 - 2 ) expression
       /    |  \
      /     |   \
  (9 - 4)   -    2 expression add_op term
```

Using the right-associative production to parse the same expression results in this tree:

```
( 9 - 4 - 2 ) expression
  / |     \
 /  |      \
9   -   (4 - 2) term add_op expression
```

The result is 3 in the left-associative grammar, and 7 in the right-associative grammar.

SUMMARY

The machine instruction sets themselves constituted the first generation programming languages. Programs were conceived as sequences of machine operations, and programmers worked directly with the hardware, often entering code in ones and zeros directly through the front panel switches. Assembly languages, using mnemonic character strings to represent machine instructions, made up the second generation of programming languages. Beginning with FORTRAN in 1954, third-generation languages allowed programmers to work at a higher level, with languages that were much more independent of the computer hardware.

Programs can be compiled or interpreted. Compilers generate machine instructions that can run directly on the computer, independent of further availability of the compiler program. Interpreters, on the other hand, are programs that read and execute source code a line at a time. Java is an environment that uses both. Java source code is compiled into machine-independent bytecode, and the Java Virtual Machine interprets the bytecode at execution. Many JVM implementations today also compile bytecode to machine instructions.

Some languages are described as imperative, and of these we discussed procedural, object-oriented, and scripting languages. Other languages are described as declarative, and of these we discussed functional languages.

When designing a new language, computer scientists value execution efficiency, human readability, ease of implementation, expressiveness, regularity, extensibility, standardization, hardware and operating system independence, and security. It is not possible to achieve all virtues simultaneously, so language design means making wise tradeoffs for the intended use.

Language processing programs like compilers and interpreters go through the phases of scanning, parsing, and code generation. Scanning is also known as lexical analysis, and the output of the scanner is a stream of tokens in the language (key words, variable names, etc.). Parsing is also known as syntactical analysis, and the parser must verify that the stream of tokens conforms to the rules of the language grammar. The output of the parser is a parse tree. Finally, code generation, also known as semantic analysis, consists of traversing the parse tree from the bottom up, creating the necessary machine instructions.

Half a century into the computer age, the world of software encompasses a wide variety of general-purpose and special-purpose languages based on formal definitions and grammars. Interpreters, compilers, virtual machines, or all three, support the myriad programs written in these languages. The future will probably bring further differentiation and specialization of languages and programs as computer scientists further refine their thinking about how best to translate human intention into machine instructions.

REVIEW QUESTIONS

4.1 Why was it important to the history of programming languages that, even at its introduction, FORTRAN generated efficient programs?

4.2 Given what you know of computer languages, what language would be a good choice for:
   a Processing a file of text, such as a system error log, looking for particular types of events?
   b Developing an artificial intelligence application to diagnose disease, given a list of symptoms?
   c Writing driver software for a new computer printer?

4.3 Here is a C function that computes the sum of a range of integers. You can assume that `begin` will always be less than or equal to `end` (`begin <= end`):

```
int summation( int begin, int end ) {
  int result = begin;
  begin = begin + 1;

  while( begin <= end ) {
    result = result + begin;
    begin = begin + 1;
  }
  return result;
}
```

Rewrite this function so that it uses recursion instead of iteration.

4.4 Assume that a language describes a *statement-sequence* as a sequence of one or more *statements* separated by *semicolons* (assume statements are defined elsewhere), but with no punctuation at the end of the statement-sequence. Write the EBNF production.

4.5 Given the following grammar:

```
expr       → term + expr | term
term       → factor * term | factor
factor     → (expr) | number
number     → number digit | digit
digit      → 0|1|2|3|4|5|6|7|8|9
```

Draw the full parse tree for the expression:

```
2 * (3 + 5) + (6 + 8)
```

4.6 Describe the form in which a program is passed from:
       a The scanner to the parser.
       b The parser to the semantic analyzer.

4.7 Here is a context-free grammar in BNF form:

```
expr       --> expr + term    | expr - term   | term
term       --> term * factor  | term / factor | factor
factor     --> ex ** factor   | ex
ex         --> (expr) | id
```

Rewrite this grammar in EBNF form.

4.8 What does this Scheme function do?

```
(define whatsThis
  (lambda (n)
    (cond((null? n) 0)
      ((null? (cdr n)) (car n))
      ((> (car n) (whatsThis (cdr n))) (car n))
      ( else (whatsThis (cdr n)))
    )))
```

4.9 Give an example of an irregularity in a language with which you are familiar.

4.10 Would it ever make sense to write a program in one language, planning from the beginning to rewrite the program later in a different language? Give an example of a situation in which such a plan might make sense, and not simply result in wasted time and effort.

CHAPTER 5

Programming in Java

INTRODUCTION

Java is one of a great many computer programming languages in use today. Since it is a fairly new language, having been first released in 1994 by Sun Microsystems, its design takes advantage of modern ideas about what makes a good programming language. Historically, new programming languages have usually taken years to become popular, but Java enjoyed unprecedented growth in popularity from the very day of its release. In fact, today Java is by some measures the most popular language for new work (http://www.tiobe.com/tpci.htm).

Many long books have been written teaching Java programming, and it is not our purpose in this chapter to provide a complete tutorial on Java programming. Instead, we will introduce basic programming structures and techniques with Java. We hope this exposure to one very good language will help readers to understand ideas presented in other chapters on topics of software, algorithms, operating systems, etc.

In this chapter we will show small but complete programs you can try out for yourself. If you do not already have access to a Java compiler and Java Virtual Machine (also called the Java Runtime Environment), you can quickly download the entire Java package, including excellent documentation, directly from the Sun website (http://java.sun.com/javase/). For work with this chapter, download the *Java Standard Edition Development Kit* (JDK), which also includes the Java Runtime Environment.

It's also a good idea to download the documentation (called JavaDocs) to your own computer, if you have the room on your disk. You can get to the same documentation on-line at the Sun website, but your access will be faster if the files are resident on your own computer.

To write programs in Java, you can use any editor or word processor you like. There are also several *integrated development environments* (IDEs) available. At first we recommend you simply use an editor with which you are already comfortable, for the IDEs have a learning curve of their own for you to deal with, and our focus here will be on the basics of the language.

JAVA TYPES

Every programming language defines a set of data types that it recognizes. In the case of early FORTRAN, the language only recognized integers and floating-point numbers. More modern languages recognize a wider range of data types, such as numbers of different levels of precision, true-or-false values, and strings of alphanumeric characters. Most modern languages also allow the programmer to define new types of data.

Java is an object-oriented language, which means that the Java language operates on software objects. The idea of a software object is a modern idea, and object orientation means that the programmer can define a new type of data element by defining a new class. Having defined a new class (e.g., automobile), the programmer can create an example object of the class (called an instance of a class; e.g., a Ford Mustang with a particular vehicle ID) and manipulate it as a unique object. This means that programs are not limited to computing numbers, strings of characters, etc. Programs can also compute automobiles, factory orders, concert schedules, etc. directly.

If this sounds magical, wait to read more in the classes and objects section coming later in this chapter. Rest assured that, in the end, it all boils down to bits (1s and 0s) in the computer. Object orientation is just a different way of naming and thinking about what's going on in the computer, and it's helpful because it usually makes thinking about the computation more natural. Also, object orientation often leads to software that is more easily used for multiple purposes, thus constantly expanding our resource of useful, tested programs.

But Java programmers need some basic data types to get started. These *Java primitive types* are not objects, but are simply the definitions of the varieties of data with which all Java programs can work. The primitive types fall into three categories:

1 integral types   integers and characters
2 floating-point types   fractional numbers
3 boolean type   true or false values

It may seem strange to call characters one of the integral types, but the reason is that each character is represented by an integer value. For instance, when you type an "A", the keyboard sends the integer value 65, the integer code for "A", to the computer. The code for "B" is 66, etc. Lowercase characters have different codes. For instance the integer code for "a" is 97, and the code for "b" is 98. So letters are just integers underneath, and software treats the bits as numbers or character codes depending on the context.

The Java primitive types, by category, are these:

1 integral types
    byte   8 bits wide   −128 to 127
    short   16 bits wide   −32768 to 32767
    int   32 bits wide   −2 billion to 2 billion
    long   64 bits wide   very small (-2^{63}) to very big ($2^{63}-1$) integers
    char   16 bits wide   Java uses "Unicode" character codes
2 floating-point types
    float   32 bits wide   +/− 3.4×10^{38} with 6–7 significant decimal digits
    double 64 bits wide   +/− 1.8×10^{308} with 14–15 significant decimal digits
3 boolean type
    boolean logical   true or false

Among the integer and floating-point types, the cost of computing with greater precision is that the higher-precision types require more space to store, and computations involve larger numbers of bits.

Here is an example Java program that uses only primitive data types:

```java
public class Primitive {
  public static void main( String[] args ) {
    int x;
    int y;
    int z;

    y = 7;
    z = 4;
    x = y + z;

    System.out.println( "x = " + x );
  }
}
```

Every program in Java is a class, and that is why the first line says that this is a public class (available for use by anyone) called "Primitive." The next line says that this is the start of a "method" called "main." Any Java program must have a "main" method declared exactly as this is. The line

```java
"public static void main( String[] args ) {"
```

is where the program starts. This line will be in all your programs. This line tells the *Java Virtual Machine* (JVM) where to start running your program.

"Public" means that anyone can run the program, "static" means that there is only one main method for the class, "void" means that the main method will not return any values, and "String[] args" means that if the user provided any "command line arguments," they are available to the program in an array of String variables called "args". Some of this probably doesn't make sense to you right now, so for now simply remember that every one of your programs must have a main method, and the first line of the main method must be written exactly as this example is written.

Notice that every statement in Java ends with a semicolon! Notice, too, that the Java language is "case-sensitive." The variable "x" is different from the variable "X." The class name of "Primitive" is different from a class name of "primitive."

The next three lines "declare" three variables of type `int`. The variables x, y, and z are each `int` variables, which means that each one requires 32 bits for storage, and each one represents an integer value. The JVM will reserve the required space for x, y, and z.

The next three lines assign the value of 7 to y, 4 to z, and the sum of 7 and 4 to x.

Finally, the last line displays the characters x = and the value of x, which is 11, on the "standard output device," usually the display. The result is:

```
x = 11
```

Notice the "curly braces" (i.e., { ... }) in the code. One pair of curly braces surrounds the "body" of the class `Primitive`, and one pair of curly braces inside `Primitive` surrounds the body of the method `main`. You must use curly braces to mark the beginning and end of a "code block" in Java. A code block is a "compound statement," and a code block can consist of variable declarations and statements. Classes, methods, loops (which we have not yet discussed), and control structures (which we have not yet discussed) all define code blocks, and blocks can be nested within one another to any level.

Use your favorite editor to type this code, and then save your work as file `Primitive.java`.

The next step is to compile your code using this command:

```
javac Primitive.java
```

When that is successful, you can run your program by typing:

```
java Primitive
```

Make sure all this works before continuing.

Aside from the Java primitive types, all data types in Java are classes. In other words, every class in Java represents a new data type. A programmer in effect creates a new Java data type every time the programmer creates a new class. The class `Primitive` above is a class, but it doesn't have any facilities for use by other programs, so it's not a good example of a reusable new data type. Soon we will show classes that do create new data types that can be useful to other programs, however.

Sometimes you will find it necessary to operate on objects instead of primitive types. This is because objects are **reference types**, and are handled differently internally than primitive types. For the purpose of converting variables of primitive types to reference types, Java provides a set of "wrapper classes" so that the programmer can always create an object having the same value as a corresponding variable of a primitive type. The Java wrapper classes corresponding to the primitive types are these:

Primitive	Wrapper Class
byte	Byte
short	Short
int	Integer
long	Long
char	Character
float	Float
double	Double
boolean	Boolean

For example, if the programmer needs an object corresponding to the integer 22148, the programmer can use this code:

```
Integer ix;
ix = new Integer( 22148 );
```

The first line declares that ix is a variable of type Integer. Since Integer is a class, not a primitive type, ix is an object. The JVM will reserve space for an Integer object, not just 32 bits for an int.

The second line says to create a new Integer object whose value is 22148, and assign that object to the variable ix.

Another built-in Java class that you will use very, very often is the class String. A String object consists of none, one, several or many characters which are treated as one object. For instance:

```
String myName;
myName = "Carl";
```

The first line declares that the variable myName is of type String. If the programmer prints the variable myName, all the characters in the word Carl will be printed:

```
System.out.println( "name: " + myName );
```

The plus sign in the println statement says to "concatenate" (combine together) the characters "name: " and "Carl". The result will be:

```
name: Carl
```

ARRAYS

A data structure is a way of organizing data, and arrays are among the simplest of data structures. An array is a data structure that holds multiple values of the same type. One speaks of an array of Strings, or an array of ints.

One declares an array by using square brackets, either after the type declaration or after the name:

```
int[] x; // either form declares an array of ints
int y[];
```

Declaring an array simply gives it a name. To create the elements of an array, one must also use the new key word, along with an integer within square brackets to indicate the number of elements in the array:

```
x = new int[15]; // 15 int elements, each set to 0
y = new int[10]; // 10 int elements, each set to 0
```

Once the array is created, its size cannot be changed.

Individual elements in an array receive default values of zero for numeric types, nulls for characters, and nulls for Strings and other objects.

By using a subscript, one can assign values to elements of an array, or read the value of an element. In Java, arrays are zero-based, which means that the first element of the array is referred to with a subscript of 0.

```
x[4] = 66; // assign the value 66 to the 5th element
c    = y[1];// read the value of the 2nd element into c
```

Each Java program's main method declares an array of Strings, by convention called args, for accepting any arguments that the user might supply from the command line. If the user types:

```
java myProg firstParam secondParam
```

the program `myProg` can retrieve the String "firstParam" from `args[0]`, and the String "secondParam" from `args[1]`.

JAVA OPERATORS

Operators are symbols in a language that stand for built-in functions. Java has a great many operators and, since this chapter will only serve to introduce the Java language, we will not discuss them all. Here are the operators we will discuss:

Operator	Function
=	assignment
+	add
-	subtract
*	multiply
/	divide
++	increment by 1
--	decrement by 1
&&	logical AND
||	logical OR
==	equal (notice that there are 2 equal signs)
!=	not equal
>	greater than
<	less than
>=	greater than or equal
<=	less than or equal

By assignment, we mean taking the value on the right side of the equal sign (sometimes called RS) and giving that value to the variable on the left side of the equal sign (sometimes called LS). If the value of k is 5, after the following statement is executed, the value of c will also be 5. Likewise, the value of k will remain 5 after execution:

```
c = k;
```

The arithmetic operators perform their expected functions. For example, if the value of a is 3, and the value of b is 5, after the following statement executes the value of x will be 15:

```
x = a * b;
```

In contrast to some other languages, Java has no operator for exponentiation. If a programmer wants to raise a number to some power, the program must perform the exponentiation either by repeatedly multiplying, or by using the `pow()` method of the `Math` class which is part of the built-in Java library.

The `++` and `--` operators are convenience operators that many programmers like because they save some typing. The following two statements have the same effect:

```
m = m + 1;
m++;
```

In either case, the value of m will increase by 1. The `--` operator works similarly, except that the value of the variable will decrease by 1.

The rest of the operators in our list are logical operators. We use logical operators to test the truth of conditions important to our programs. For example, if our program were going to find all the houses in a neighborhood whose assessed values were greater than $200,000, our program might have a statement like this in it:

```
if ( assessedValue > 200000 ) {
```

We will discuss the use of `if` statements in the section on Java control structures, so for now simply observe that the ">" operator allows one to test the truth of the condition that assessed value is greater than $200,000. If the value of the variable `assessedValue` at the time the statement executes is greater that `200000`, the logical operator ">" will return a value of `true`. Otherwise, it will return `false`.

We will discuss the other logical operators in the section on Java control structures. Remember, too, that we have not discussed all Java operators. Java also has operators for testing and shifting bit values, conditional statement execution, modulo arithmetic, and some other functions.

JAVA IDENTIFIERS

Every programming language has its rules for how to name elements of a program. In Java, names must always begin with a letter. Letters in Java include all lowercase and uppercase letters, as well as the underscore character "_" and the currency symbol "$".

After the first letter, any number of letters and/or digits may follow. A Java identifier may be of any length, and it is good programming practice to use names long enough to be self-descriptive. More experienced programmers generally use longer variable names, because longer names usually make programs much easier to read and maintain.

Java is a "case-sensitive" language. That means that Java recognizes uppercase and lowercase letters as different. The identifier `university` is different from `University`, and both are different from `UNIVERSITY`.

While one is not required to do so, standard programming practice is to begin all class names with an uppercase letter, and to begin all other names with a lowercase letter. Also, when an identifier consists of more than one word, the usual practice is to use what's called "camel case" capitalization (it's "humpy"). Here are some example variable names:

```
highWindWarning
wonLostRecord
mothersMaidenName
```

BASIC CONTROL STRUCTURES

All programming languages provide ways to alter the sequence of instructions that actually get executed when a program runs. This ability to select which logic to apply, or to choose an appropriate number of times to cycle through a section of code, is what makes programs flexible enough to be useful in the real world. Imagine a program to compute the average grades for students in a class, but imagine that the program requires all classes to have exactly the same number of students, and has no way to properly handle a missing grade! Such a rigid program would not be worth the trouble to write.

if

The most common control structure for selecting a block of code to execute is the `if` statement. The `if` statement can be used in its simple form, or in its extended `if-else` form. Here is an example of a simple if statement:

```
if(grade > 0) {
  sumOfGrades = sumOfGrades + grade;
  numberOfGrades++;
}
```

This statement says, if the variable `grade` is greater than 0, then add the grade value to the variable `sumOfGrades`, and increment the variable `numberOfGrades` by 1. Otherwise, do nothing. Either both statements following the if statement will be executed, or neither will be, because they are both within the curly brackets which follow the if. The curly brackets mark a *code block*.

If the tested condition is true, then the code block of the if statement will be executed. If the condition is false, the code block will be skipped.

Here is the syntax of the simple if statement:

```
if( <conditional expression> ) <statement>
```

The conditional expression must evaluate to either true or false. If the conditional expression is true, the following statement will be executed, but not otherwise. The <statement> can also be a ***compound statement***, which is another way of saying that <statement> can be a code block enclosed in curly braces. A compound statement or code block is enclosed in curly braces, and each statement inside must be terminated with a semicolon.

Here is an example of an if-else statement:

```
if( windSpeed > 20 ) {
  hoistSmallSail();
}
else {
  hoistLargeSail();
}
```

The if-else statement allows the program to select one of two mutually exclusive paths of execution. In this case, if the wind is strong, the program calls a method to hoist a small sail. Otherwise, the program calls a method to hoist a large sail. By the way, you can tell that hoistSmallSail() and hoistLargeSail() are methods because a pair of parentheses follows the name. A method is a named block of code, and we will talk about methods when we discuss classes and objects in more detail later.

Here is the syntax of the if-else statement:

```
if( <conditional expression> ) <statement_one>
else <statement_two>
```

If the conditional expression is true, statement_one will be executed. If the conditional statement is false, statement_two will be executed. As before, statement_one and statement_two can be compound statements, i.e., code blocks framed in curly braces.

for

Programs frequently must *iterate* or *loop* through a block of code repeatedly. Java has several control structures for this purpose, and one of the most commonly used control structures of this type is the for loop.

Suppose we want to compute the average grade in a class of students. We have the scores in a file called Students, and each line in the file contains a single score. Each score is the grade of one of the students (e.g., 89.5). We could write code such as this to read the scores from the file and compute the total of all the scores:

```
double total = 0.0;
BufferedReader in = new BufferedReader(
                    new FileReader( "Students" ) );

for ( int i = 1; i <= numberOfStudents; i++ ) {
    String score = in.readLine();
    total = total + Double.parseDouble( score );
}
```

The first line declares a thing called a `BufferedReader`, which is "wrapped around" a `FileReader` that opens the file called `Students`. We will discuss these sorts of input/output statements further in the section on Input and Output. This statement declares the variable `in` to be a BufferedReader associated with the file `Students`.

Notice that programming statements in Java can continue to a second, third, or more lines. The Java compiler will continue to interpret the lines as one statement until it encounters the semicolon, which marks the end of the statement.

The `for` statement begins with parentheses enclosing three expressions, which are separated by semicolons. The first expression defines initial conditions in the `for` loop. In this case, the expression declares an `int` called `i`, and sets the value of `i` to `1`.

The second expression in the `for` statement establishes a condition which will evaluate to either true or false. When the condition is true, the code block of the `for` statement will be executed. In this case, as long as the value of `i` is less than or equal to the number of students, the loop will execute.

The third expression in the `for` statement specifies what to change each time the loop is executed. This expression is sometimes called the "increment expression," because it is usually employed to change the value of the variable being tested in the second expression. That is the case here, because the third expression says to increment the value of the variable `i` each time the loop executes.

The *body* or code block of the `for` statement follows the three expressions within parentheses. In this case, the `readLine()` method of the `BufferedReader` reads the next line of the file into a `String` variable called `score`. Since the `BufferedReader` reads character strings, we must convert the characters into an internal floating-point number before we can do our math. The last line says use the `parseDouble()` method of the `Double` class to interpret the character string in `score` (e.g., `89.5`) as a double (a floating-point number which can include a fractional part). The `Double` class is one of Java's "wrapper classes," which we discussed in the section on data types.

In summary, this `for` loop will begin executing with the value of `i` set to 1. After each execution of the loop, the value of `i` will be incremented. The loop will continue to execute as long as the value of `i` is no greater than the number of students. When `i` becomes greater than the number of students, the conditional test in the second expression of the `for` statement will fail (will be false), and the program will "drop out" of the loop and continue at the next statement following the `for` loop body.

Here is the syntax of the `for` statement:

```
for( <initial>; <test condition>; <increment> ) <body>
```

The conditional expression must evaluate to either true or false. If the conditional expression is true, the body of the `for` loop will be executed, but not otherwise. The `<body>` is usually a *compound statement*, which is a code block enclosed in curly braces. Each statement within the body must be terminated with a semicolon.

while

Another structure to control looping (iteration) is the `while` statement. Suppose we don't know how many student scores are in the file of student scores. We can use a while statement to read the file until there are no more scores in the file to be read:

```
double total = 0.0;
BufferedReader in = new BufferedReader(
                  new FileReader( "Students" ) );

String score = in.readLine();

while( score != null ) {
    total = total + Double.parseDouble( score );
    score = in.readLine();
}
```

We use the same `BufferedReader` as before to read the file `Students`. After reading the first line in the file, the `while` statement checks to see if the variable `score` has a value of null. The variable `score` will be null only if there was nothing in the file to read. As long as `score` is not null, the body of the `while` statement will execute—it will "parse," or interpret, as a fractional number, whatever the `BufferedReader` just read, and then it will read the next line in the file.

The `while` statement syntax is very simple:

```
while( <loop condition> ) <statement>
```

Again, the statement can be a code block enclosed in curly braces. As long as the test condition remains true, the body of the `while` statement continues to execute. This is a very appropriate control structure when we do not know in advance how many times a code block must execute.

do-while

A variation of the `while` statement is the `do-while`. In the case of the `do-while` statement, the body of the loop executes before the code checks the loop condition. When a program must execute a block of code at least once, the `do-while` may be the best choice for controlling a loop. Here is code to use the `do-while` statement instead of the `while` statement for reading the file `Students`:

```
BufferedReader in = new BufferedReader(
                        new FileReader( "Students" ) );
String score;
do {
    score = in.readLine();
    total = total + Double.parseDouble( score );
} while( score != null )
```

At first glance, it looks like this version saves code. However, in this particular case, this code exposes us to danger. If the file should ever be empty, the first call to `parseDouble` will cause the program to fail with a run-time exception, because `Double.parseDouble` cannot parse a null value. In this application, we would do better to use the `while` instead of the `do-while`.

This is the syntax of the `do-while` loop:

```
do <loop body>
while( <loop condition> );
```

The loop body can be, and usually is, a code block framed by curly braces. As long as the loop condition remains true, the loop body will execute again and again. The `do-while` structure is particularly appropriate when you require the loop body to execute at least once every time the program runs.

switch

The last control structure we will discuss here is the `switch` statement. Like the `if` statement, the `switch` statement allows your program to select certain statements to execute under certain conditions. The `switch` statement is more complex, and one can always use a series of `if` statements instead of a `switch` statement, but `switch` is very appropriate and readable for some programming problems.

Suppose we have a group of students and want to assign them to different dorms depending upon whether they are freshmen, sophomores, juniors, or seniors. Let's assume that the variable `yearInSchool` is coded as an `int`, and is set to 1 for freshmen, 2 for sophomores, 3 for juniors, and 4 for seniors. We could then use this code to decide to which dorm each student should be assigned:

```
switch( yearInSchool ) {
    case 1: System.out.println( "Oberlies Hall" );
            break;
    case 2: System.out.println( "Kiriazides Hall" );
            break;
    case 3: System.out.println( "Glisson Dorm" );
            break;
    case 4: System.out.println( "Valk Hall" );
            break;
    default: System.out.println( "illegal year" );
}
```

If a student is a freshman, the student will be assigned to Oberlies Hall; if the student is a sophomore, the student will be assigned to Kiriazides Hall; etc.

Notice the break statements. The break statement says to exit the switch statement. If the break statement is missing, the execution of the switch statement will "fall through" to the next case. Sometimes you will want that to happen, but certainly not always. Forgetting to insert the break statement appropriately is a common programming error.

Here's an example using the switch statement to allow "falling through" from one condition to the next in a helpful way:

```
switch( dayOfChristmas ) {
    case 12: System.out.println( "Twelve drummers drumming" );
    case 11: System.out.println( "Eleven pipers piping" );
    case 10: System.out.println( "Ten lords a-leaping" );
    case  9: System.out.println( "Nine ladies dancing" );
    case  8: System.out.println( "Eight maids a-milking" );
    case  7: System.out.println( "Seven swans a-swimming" );
    case  6: System.out.println( "Six geese a-laying" );
    case  5: System.out.println( "Five golden rings" );
    case  4: System.out.println( "Four calling birds" );
    case  3: System.out.println( "Three French hens" );
    case  2: System.out.println( "Two turtle doves" );
    case  1: System.out.println( "And a partridge ... tree" );
            break;
    default: System.out.println( "?Day = " + dayOfChristmas );
}
```

Notice that in this example, the case statements proceed from highest to lowest, instead of the other way around. The cases can be ordered in any way that makes sense, even nonsequentially. The switch statement executes by taking the value of the integral expression inside the parentheses (assume that dayOfChristmas is an int). The switch statement then compares the value of the integral expression to each case value. When it finds a match, the code for that case begins to execute.

In this example, the switch statement helps us write the lyrics for the song *The Twelve Days of Christmas*. For instance, if the dayOfChristmas equals 3, execution will begin at case 3 and continue until it encounters the break at the end of case 1. The one break statement is necessary to avoid executing the default error message. The result will be the lyrics for the third day of Christmas:

```
Three French hens
Two turtle doves
And a partridge in a pear tree
```

Here is the syntax for the switch statement:

```
switch( <integral expression> ) {
  case value_one:    <statement_one>
  case value_two:    <statement_two>
  case value_three: <statement_three>
  . . .
  case value_n:      <statement_n>
  default:      <statement_default>
}
```

The integral expression must evaluate to an integer value. This usually means that the integral expression is an `int` or a `char` value. In particular, the expression cannot be a `String` (although that option would be nice to have sometimes).

The statements can be compound statements, and in a "switch" from other syntax, compound statements within a `switch` case need not be framed in curly brackets. However, if you like curly brackets, the Java compiler will accept curly brackets around the compound statements.

The `default` case is optional, but we believe a `default` case should always be included, if only to provide error checking. If your program expects the days of Christmas to vary between 1 and 12, it's good practice to put in a `default` statement which will let you know if the value of `dayOfChristmas` ever turns up as some value other than 1 through 12. Especially with more complex programs, such `default` code could save you many hours of debugging. Without the `default` statement, if none of the cases match the integral expression, the JVM simply skips over all the `switch` code. Having the `default` case will catch the anomalous condition and show you where the problem is.

Here is a complete program to print the words to the 12 verses of *The Twelve Days of Christmas*. The program uses a `while` loop to iterate through the 12 verses. Then it uses an `if-else` statement to decide whether this is the first verse or one of the later verses; that is necessary because the line about a partridge in a pear tree has the word "And" in it for the 2nd through 12th verses, but not for the 1st verse. The `\n` at the end of the lines having to do with a "partridge in a pear tree" is an example of an *escape sequence*. An escape sequence begins with a backslash, and the following character has special meaning for the Java compiler. The `\n` means to insert a linefeed, so that there will be a blank line between verses. There are other escape sequences for tabbing and other functions, too.

Finally, this program illustrates how to add comments to a program written in Java. Any typing that follows `//` on a line is treated as a comment; that is, the typing is ignored by the Java compiler. Also, any typing between the characters `/*` and `*/` is also a comment, and such comments can extend over multiple lines. If such a multiline comment begins with `/**`, it is a javadoc (Java documentation) comment, and will be included by the javadoc processor in the automatically generated documentation of the program. Javadoc comments can include special tags, such as `@author`, which the javadoc processor recognizes when it generates the HTML format of the documentation.

We will not be describing the javadoc processor in any more detail in this chapter, but you can read about javadoc comments here: **http://java.sun.com/j2se/javadoc/**. In our opinion, the javadoc processor is one of the magnificent contributions Java has made to programming practice. The javadoc processor uses comments within the programs themselves to generate attractive and complete documentation of every class. Wonderful!

As a matter of programming style, I like to put a comment following closing curly braces that tells me which block of code is being terminated. Particularly when many code blocks are nested within one another, such comments help me keep track of my curly brackets. This style is a personal preference, not a standard. Adopt it only if you wish.

```
/**
 * A program to print the words to the Twelve Days of Christmas
 * @author Carl Reynolds
 */
public class DaysOfChristmas {
  public static void main(String args[]) {

    int dayOfChristmas = 1; //start with the 1st day of Christmas

    while( dayOfChristmas <= 12 ) {
      if( dayOfChristmas == 1 )
      {
        System.out.println( "A partridge in a pear tree \n" );
      }//if
      else
      {
        switch( dayOfChristmas )
        {
            case 12: System.out.println( "Twelve drummers drumming" );
            case 11: System.out.println( "Eleven pipers piping" );
            case 10: System.out.println( "Ten lords a-leaping" );
            case  9: System.out.println( "Nine ladies dancing" );
            case  8: System.out.println( "Eight maids a-milking" );
            case  7: System.out.println( "Seven swans a-swimming" );
            case  6: System.out.println( "Six geese a-laying" );
            case  5: System.out.println( "Five golden rings" );
            case  4: System.out.println( "Four calling birds" );
            case  3: System.out.println( "Three French hens" );
            case  2: System.out.println( "Two turtle doves" );
                     System.out.println(
                                "And a partridge in a pear tree \n" );
                     break;
            default: System.out.println( "?Day = " + dayOfChristmas );
        }//switch
      }//else

      dayOfChristmas++;
    }//while

    System.out.println("The End" );
  }//main
}//class
```

OBJECT-ORIENTED PROGRAMMING

Java is an object-oriented language, which means that Java facilitates the writing of object-oriented programs. Object orientation is more a matter of how one thinks about programming than it is a particular programming technique. When one writes object-oriented code, one thinks of software "things" that are analogous to things in the outside world.

For instance, if our job is to write software for the State Thruway Authority for automated toll collection, we would think about the job differently depending upon whether we take the older "procedural" approach or the newer *object-oriented* (OO) approach.

Using the procedural approach, we would break the job down into subtasks, or subroutines, write the routines, and combine the routines with a main program into a sequence of activities to be performed. We might have a `carEntersThruway` procedure, and a `carExitsThruway` procedure, and we might keep information in a file about the cars using the Thruway.

Using the OO approach, we would think about the "things" in our problem domain, and create analogous software classes. For instance, we would probably have a `Vehicle` class, and we might have a `ThruwayInterchange` class, and a `VehicleOwner` class. We would give `Vehicles` characteristics that are important to our application, such as `licenseNumber`, `state`, `make`, `model`, and `color`. Since we need to track where vehicles enter and leave the Thruway, we might add `Vehicle` properties `enteredAtInterchange` and `exitedAtInterchange`. Likewise, the properties of a `VehicleOwner` might include `firstName`, `lastName`, `streetAddress`, `city`, `state`, and `zipCode`.

The logic of an OO program gets coded as "methods" of the objects. Instead of having an isolated or application-wide `carEntersThruway` procedure, as we might using the procedural approach, we can have similar code in a method of the `Vehicle` class. The logic may be the same, but in the OO approach we think of a `Vehicle` object having "behaviors" appropriate to the application. When a `Vehicle` enters the Thruway, we will call the `Vehicle`'s `enterThruway` method, and the `Vehicle` object will deal appropriately with that event.

The data one operates on and the logic one encodes may be the same for the procedural approach and the object-oriented approach, but the object-oriented approach organizes the work differently. When an object-oriented program is complete, a set of classes is the result. These classes, if well designed, can be reused and extended more easily so that future programming projects have a head start.

Putting the code inside classes also allows functionality to be *encapsulated*, which leads to more effective testing and more reliable use later on. The software classes exist as their own entities, with known properties (attributes), and well-defined methods. Using *inheritance*, the OO approach also offers a standard way to add functionality without changing at all the code that has already been written. There is less temptation to modify the classes that have already been defined, implemented and tested. The result is usually more stable and reliable code.

Object orientation is an advance in how programmers think about their work. The OO approach leads to software classes which more closely model the real world, and therefore make the application more natural to think about. In addition, building classes usually leads to code which is more easily reused. Both effects lead to better programming productivity.

CLASSES AND OBJECTS

People new to OO programming often have difficulty distinguishing what are called *classes* from what are called **instances**. A class is a specification, a blueprint, or maybe even a concept, like vehicle; an instance is a specific example of a class. From the class `Automobile`, one can build or identify particular cars. My Ford with vehicle ID `1FABP64T1JH100161` is said to be an instance of the class `Automobile`.

Often the word *object* is used as a synonym for the word instance. One also says that my Ford is an object of the class `Automobile`. This can be confusing, especially at first, because Java, like some other OO languages, also recognizes a class called `Object` (capital O). In fact, every class in Java inherits from the class `Object` (we will discuss inheritance soon); the class `Object` is the root of the Java class hierarchy. Though the use of the word in two senses can be confusing, generally one should understand the word "object" to mean "instance," unless the word "Object" is capitalized.

We say that <an instance> "is" <a class>. Some writers say that an "is-a" relationship exists between an instance and its class. For instance, my Ford is an `Automobile`.

OBJECT STATE AND BEHAVIOR

Grady Booch, a well-known writer on the topic of OO programming, has defined an object as something "that has state, behavior, and identity." In other words, an object has characteristics (which may change over time), an object can perform certain prespecified actions, and an object provides us a way to refer to it.

The state of an object is provided by variables. As the values of variables change, the state of the object changes. At any point in time, the values of the instance's variables provide its state. For example, the `speed` of my Ford varies over time. At any particular moment, the state of my Ford includes the speed at which it is currently moving.

The behavior of objects is provided by methods. A method is a programming procedure. In the case of my Ford, the `accelerate()` method allows my Ford to change speed. In the world around us, we observe that different members of the same class behave similarly; it's easy to distinguish a dog from a cat by the way the individual animals move. Likewise, we expect different instances of the same Java class to behave similarly, so methods are defined by procedures in the class, not in the individual instances. The class `Automobile` will have the definition of the `accelerate()` method, and any particular instance of `Automobile` will behave similarly by changing speed using the same method.

INHERITANCE

You may be thinking that one `accelerate()` method might not work for all instances of the class `Automobile`. May be the acceleration behavior a Ferrari should be modeled differently from the acceleration behavior of a Kia. If we want to model such differences, we can take advantage of the OO programming paradigm called inheritance.

One class can *inherit* from another, in which case the new class (called the *subclass* or *subordinant class* or *child class*) carries all the variables and methods of the higher-level class (called the *superclass* or *superior class* or *parent class*). In addition, the child class can add state variables unique to the child class, and add behavior methods unique to the child class. In addition, the child class can *override* methods of the parent class in order to give the child class different behavior, even though the name of the method implementing the behavior has the same name as the method of the parent class.

These sorts of considerations lead software developers to create a *class hierarchy*. The programmer defines the more general state variables and behavior methods in higher-level classes. Then, when writing the subordinant classes, the programmer uses the inherited state and behavior when it fits, and adds state variables, methods, and overriding methods to subordinant classes in order to implement differences between the superior and subordinant classes.

The beauty of this technique is that classes which are written and tested do not change. Existing software functionality can be reused. When the programmer requires new features in a class, the programmer can inherit from an existing, tested class, and write new software simply to meet the new requirements.

If one decides to implement the `accelerate()` method differently for different `Automobiles`, one would write the parent class `Automobile`, and then have subordinant classes inherit from `Automobile`. In our example, we might design several classes to inherit from `Automobile`, a class called `EconomyCar`, a class called `FamilyCar`, and a class called `SportsCar`. Each of these subordinant classes would inherit the `accelerate()` method from the `Automobile` class, and could override the inherited `accelerate()` method to change the acceleration behavior of instances of the subordinant class. If a subordinant class does not override the method of the superior class, instances of the subordinant class will respond to the method just as instances of the superior class do. If my Ford "is" a `FamilyCar`, my Ford also "is" an `Automobile`, because `FamilyCar` inherits from `Automobile`.

INSTANCE AND STATIC VARIABLES AND METHODS

One twist of complexity is that some state information and some behaviors belong to the class, while others belong to the instances of a class. For instance, we would maintain the `speed` of each Automobile as part of the state of each individual car (part of the state of each instance). On the other hand, we would maintain a `count` of the total number of `Automobiles` as part of the state of the class `Automobile`. It seems natural that speed should be associated with a particular car, but we need a central place to keep track of the total number of `Automobiles`.

Perhaps we're stretching the analogy a little bit, but imagine a Ford on the road. It has a `speed` we can measure, but after the Ford exits the factory, there is no easy way for the Ford to be kept apprised of the total number of `Automobiles` that have been built. If we want to know how many `Automobiles` have been built, we must go back to the factory and get the `count`. The factory is the class.

Variables like `speed`, which represent the state of an instance of a class, are called ***instance variables***. Variables like `count`, which are maintained by the class itself, are called ***static variables***. The word static means many things in computer science, and this use of the word static may be confusing. Other languages label the same idea with a different name; for example, Visual Basic calls variables of this kind "shared" variables, because they're shared by all instances of a class. That term may be more helpful as you learn, so when you see "static," think to yourself "shared," or "class."

Similarly, methods can be ***instance methods*** or ***static methods***. If two different instances of a class both call the instance method `accelerate()`, it will be as if there were two different copies of that method, and each instance had its own. (In reality, there will not be two copies of the code, but each instance will get its own "stack" for local variables, which will keep the execution of the two calls separate, as if the code existed in two places.) On the other hand, if two different instances of a class call the static method `getAutomobileCount()`, the two instances will be using exactly the same code, because there is only one copy, and that is shared.

Variables and methods will always be instance variables and methods, unless you specifically label them `static`. If you label a variable or method `static`, the variable or method will exist only at the level of the class, and will be shared among the instances.

Below is our example `Automobile` class. Notice that there is no `main` method in the `Automobile` class. This class cannot be executed directly. If we were to add a public `main` method, the class could be executed, and whatever the `main` method were coded to accomplish would be done. However, this `Automobile` class is intended to be a "factory" to create `Automobile` objects for use by other programs and classes, rather than to be a program to be run by itself. You can think of the `Automobile` class as creating a new data type—`Automobile`.

Notice also that in the class `Automobile` there is a method named `Automobile`; *the name of the method is the same as the name of the class*. The method named `Automobile` is the *constructor* for the class. Whenever another program needs an instance of an `Automobile`, the other program will use the `new` keyword to request a new `Automobile`. We can tell from the `Automobile` constructor that the constructor expects four parameters whenever a new `Automobile` is requested; these are the make, the model, the year, and the horsepower. The first two parameters are `String` values, and the last two are `ints`.

When another program asks for an instance of an `Automobile`, the constructor will create an `Automobile` object and return to the other program a *reference* to the new `Automobile`. A reference is an address. The other program can then use the reference to the new `Automobile` object to manipulate it.

```
    /**Class Automobile
*    Illustrating instance and static varibles
*    and methods
*   @author Carl Reynolds
*/
class Automobile {
  //static variable
  private static int count;  //count of automobiles

  //instance variables
  private String make;
  private String model;
  private int    year;
  private int    hp;
  private double speed;

  //Constructor
  Automobile( String mk, String mdl, int yr, int power ) {
    make  = mk;       //assign constructor parameters
    model = mdl;      // to private instance variables
    year  = yr;
    hp    = power;

    count++;          //add to count of Automobiles created
  }
```

```java
    //static method
    static int getCount() {
      return count;
    }

    //instance methods to set and get speed
    public void accelerate( double newSpeed ) {
      if( newSpeed > 70. ) speed = 70.;
      else speed = newSpeed;
    }

    public double getSpeed() { return speed; };

    //returns a text representation of an Automobile
    public String toString() {
      return year + " " + make + " " + model;
    }
}
```

Here is a class which uses the Automobile class:

```java
/**
 *   Class AutomobileFactory
 *   @author Carl Reynolds
 */
class AutomobileFactory {
  public static void main( String[] args ) {
    Automobile economy, family, sports;

    economy = new Automobile(
                    "Kia", "Rio", 2006, 110 );
    family  = new Automobile(
                    "VW", "Passat", 2002, 170 );
    sports  = new Automobile(
                    "Ford", "Mustang", 2005, 300 );
    System.out.println(
            Automobile.getCount() + " Automobiles" );
    System.out.println( economy );
    System.out.println( family );
    System.out.println( sports );
  }
}
```

The class `AutomobileFactory` can be executed directly, because it has a main method coded in the standard way. The main method declares three variables to be of type `Automobile` (notice you can declare several variables of the same type on one line, as we did here), and then it creates three `Automobile` objects by using the `new` keyword to invoke the constructor for the `Automobile` class three different times.

The first `println` statement calls the static method `getCount()` by specifying the class name `Automobile`, followed by a dot (period), followed by the method name `getCount()`. The `getCount()` method will return the number 3, because each time the constructor of the `Automobile` class generates a new `Automobile`, it increments its static `count` variable.

Finally, the three `println` statements at the end print a text representation of each `Automobile`. Such use of an object's name, such as `economy`, inside `println` causes the JVM to use the `toString()` method of the class. When that happens here, the result on the screen is this:

```
3 Automobiles
2006 Kia Rio
2002 VW Passat
2005 Ford Mustang
```

Inheritance

OO programming makes it easy to add functionality to software without rewriting the code one has already written and tested. Suppose we want to add distinctions between types of `Automobiles`. A Ferrari can go much faster than a Kia, so the `accelerate()` method should be different, and perhaps other behaviors should also be different for such different `Automobiles`.

We can add a new class called `SportsCar` that will inherit from `Automobile`, and we can give the `SportsCar` class a different `accelerate()` method. Here is the Java class for `SportsCar`:

```java
/**
 *   Class SportsCar
 *      Inherits from class Automobile
 *   @author Carl Reynolds
 */
class SportsCar extends Automobile {
  private double maxSpeed = 150.;

  //constructor
  SportsCar( String mk, String mdl, int yr, int power )
  {
    super( mk, mdl, yr, power );
  }

  //override of inherited accelerate() method
  public void accelerate( double newSpeed )
  {
    if( newSpeed > maxSpeed ) speed = maxSpeed;
    else speed = newSpeed;
  }
}
```

The `SportsCar` class extends the class `Automobile`; that means `SportsCar` inherits from `Automobile`. Any instance of a `SportsCar` will also be an `Automobile`, and except where there are differences between the code for `SportsCar` and the code for `Automobile`, an instance of a `SportsCar` will have exactly the same state variables and behavior as any instance of the class `Automobile`.

The `SportsCar` class must also have a constructor; it's called `SportsCar`. The constructor for `SportsCar` simply uses the constructor for `Automobile`, the superclass, by using the `super` key word to pass the same values for make, model, year, and power to the constructor for the `Automobile` class.

The only difference between instances of `SportsCar` and instances of `Automobile` will be the behavior provided by the `accelerate()` method. In the case of an `Automobile`, the maximum speed will be 70, but in the case of a `SportsCar`, the maximum speed will be 150. We say that the subclass `SportsCar` *overrides* the `accelerate()` method inherited from the superclass `Automobile`.

Everything else that is true about an `Automobile` object will be true about a `SportsCar` object. All will have instance variables to store make, model, year, horsepower and speed. Creating either a new

`Automobile` or a new `SportsCar` will increment the count of `Automobiles` maintained by the `Automobile` class.

We didn't have to change any of our existing code to enhance our work to treat sports cars differently from other automobiles!

POLYMORPHISM

The word polymorphism means "many forms." When a subclass overrides a method of a superior class, the behavior of the method will depend upon which type of object is being used in the program, an instance of the superior class or an instance of the subclass. This characteristic of OO programming is called polymorphism, and it is a powerful feature of the OO approach.

We will add some lines to our `AutomobileFactory` class to set the speed of a family car to 120 and set the speed of a sports car to 120. Looking back at the `accelerate()` method for the class `Automobile`, you will see that the maximum speed for an instance of the `Automobile` class is 70. Compare that with the `accelerate()` method for the `SportsCar` class; the top speed for a `SportsCar` is 150.

When we call the same `accelerate()` method for an instance of `Automobile` and an instance of `SportsCar`, the results are different. The `Automobile` speeds up to 70, and the `SportsCar` speeds up to 120. To show this, add code to the `AutomobileFactory` class:

```
/**
 *   Class AutomobileFactory
 *   @author Carl Reynolds
 */
class AutomobileFactory {
.
.
.

    family = new Automobile(
                    "VW", "Passat", 2002, 170 );
    sports = new SportsCar(
                    "Ford", "Mustang", 2005, 300 );

.
.
.

    //same method call to instances of 2 different classes
    family.accelerate(120. );
    sports.accelerate(120. );

    //polymorphism will cause the effects to be different
    System.out.println( family + " " + family.getSpeed() );
    System.out.println( sports + " " + sports.getSpeed() );
}
```

This will be the new output:

```
3 Automobiles
2006 Kia Rio
2002 VW Passat
2005 Ford Mustang
2002 VW Passat 70.0
2005 Ford Mustang 120.0
```

Polymorphism allows us to write programs in a more general way. We can reference the superior class as we write programs, and if the object being used by the program happens to belong to a subclass of the superior class, the methods in the subclass which override the corresponding methods in the superior class will insure that methods appropriate to the particular instance will be called. This is another way in which OO programming reduces the amount of code that must be written and tested, and also promotes reuse of existing code in new applications.

INTERFACES

In Java, we can also specify an *interface* to enforce a common set of behaviors among different classes. For example, think about the problem of sorting a group of Automobile objects. How should Automobiles be ordered? By year? Alphabetically by make? By horsepower? This problem arises frequently when we're working with objects, so the Java language specifies an interface that any new class can implement in order to facilitate sorting instances of the new class.

An interface consists of one or more *method signatures*, but it does not contain any code implementing any of the methods. (An interface can include constants as well as method signatures, but we will focus on the methods.) A method signature is like the first line of a method; the signature specifies what the method will return, the name of the method, and what arguments the method expects when it is called.

For example, Java provides the interface Comparable, and the Comparable interface specifies a single method called compareTo(). The compareTo() method expects an object as an argument (the object with which to compare the first instance) and it returns an int. The value of the returned int will be 0 if the two objects being compared are equal, -1 if the first object is "smaller" (should be ordered first), and +1 if the first object is "larger" (should be ordered second).

We can implement the interface Comparable in our Automobile class by adding this code to our class Automobile:

```
class Automobile implements Comparable<Automobile> {
  .

  .
public int compareTo( Automobile car )
  {
    return this.toString().compareTo( car.toString() );
  }
```

The new first line of our Automobile class now declares that the class Automobile will implement the interface Comparable. The <Automobile> syntax says that we will only be comparing an Automobile object with another Automobile. If, by some error of programming, our program tries to compare an Automobile object with a Thermostat object, the JVM will generate an error.

The new compareTo() method implements the Comparable interface for the class Automobile. We've taken a shortcut here which takes advantage of the toString() method we already have for Automobile. The phrase this.toString() will return a String object which represents this instance of an Automobile. The key word this always references the particular instance itself. The String returned will be of this form:

```
2002 VW Passat
```

The year will be followed by the make and the model of the Automobile. Likewise, the phrase car.toString() will return a String representing the other Automobile, such as this:

```
2006 Kia Rio
```

The String class has a compareTo() method that orders Strings in "ASCIIbetical" order, which is like alphabetical order, except that it follows the ASCII encoding values of characters. In ASCII the letters are coded in alphabetical order, but all uppercase letters come before any of the lower-case letters, and digits and symbols are included as well as letters. For our purposes of ordering Automobiles, we thought that the toString() representation of Automobiles sorted in ASCIIbetical order would be fine. Older cars will be ordered first, and among cars of the same year, cars will be sorted ASCIIbetically by make and model.

The interface idea is similar to the idea of a class, in that an interface creates a new data type. When the class Automobile implements the interface Comparable, instances of Automobile can also be treated as instances of Comparable. Just as good design of a class hierarchy can reduce programming and improve reliability, good interface design can also.

For instance, the sort() method of the Java Collections class will sort lists of Comparable objects. Our Automobile class implements Comparable, Java's String class implements Comparable, Java's Date class implements Comparable, etc. One sort() method will work for any group of objects whose class implements Comparable. That alone is a great example of code reuse.

It's easy to design and use your own interfaces, too. However, in this brief chapter we will not be discussing that topic.

ERROR HANDLING

Java uses Exceptions to represent error conditions.

Exception is actually a class in Java, and when a program creates an Exception, it creates a new object, which is an instance of the Exception class. An Exception object can have information about what went wrong, usually including an error message, and a "stack trace" showing which method created the error.

Having created an Exception object when something goes wrong, the program "throws" the Exception using the key word throw. The JVM will print an error message and stop execution when a program throws an Exception, unless the programmer has provided code to "catch" the exception and handle the error condition in the program. This approach to handling program errors is called "exception handling" for obvious reasons, and it's a relatively modern idea.

One advantage of handling errors this way is that code to handle error conditions will be segregated into code blocks separate from the main logic of the program. This makes it much easier to follow the intent of the programmer, both in the main logic and in the error handling code.

Java provides many subclasses of Exception so that different problems result in different classes of Exception objects being thrown. Some examples include FileNotFoundException, NullPointerException, and NumberFormatException.

Java recognizes two types of Exceptions, checked and unchecked. The names come from what the Java compiler does with them. The compiler "checks for" appropriate handling of checked Exceptions, but does not check for handling of unchecked Exceptions.

An unchecked Exception represents an error that is probably too serious for an application to correct. An example is the NullPointerException, which occurs when the program tries to access a variable which should contain a reference to an object, but which contains null instead. The compiler assumes that such an exception should cause the program to terminate with an error condition, so it does not check to see that the program has code to handle that error condition itself.

A checked exception such as FileNotFoundException represents an error condition from which the program potentially could recover. In the case of FileNotFoundException, for example, the program could prompt the operator for a new file name and try again. If the compiler recognizes that a method could encounter a checked exception, the compiler will require that the method either provide a handler for that exception or declare with its own throws declaration that it can itself generate the checked Exception.

The way to add exception handling to a Java program is to enclose program statements which might generate an Exception within a *try block*. A try block begins with the key word try and an open curly brace. At the end of the code being included in the try block is a close curly brace. Immediately following the try block will be one or more *catch blocks*. A catch block contains the code to handle the error.

Let's go back to our Automobile class and its accelerate() method. Instead of simply setting the speed of the Automobile to its maximum value when the argument to the accelerate() method is too large, we can have the Automobile class generate a special subclass of Exception appropriate to this application. Here is the code for our new ExcessiveSpeedException class:

```
public class ExcessiveSpeedException extends Exception {
  ExcessiveSpeedException( Automobile a ) {
    super( "New speed exceeds maximum speed of "
           + a.toString() );
  }
}
```

Our ExcessiveSpeedException inherits from Exception. The ExcessiveSpeedException constructor expects an Automobile object as an argument. To take advantage of the message attribute inherited from the superior class, it incorporates the toString() description of the Automobile into the message that it passes to the constructor of the superior Exception class.

Now we can rewrite the accelerate() method of Automobile as follows:

```
public void accelerate ( double newSpeed )
                            throws ExcessiveSpeedException {
if( newSpeed > 70. )
            throw new ExcessiveSpeedException( this );
speed = newSpeed;
}
```

The reference to this means that the particular instance of Automobile that generates the ExcessiveSpeedException will be passed to the ExcessiveSpeedException constructor. Notice that the method header for accelerate() now includes a declaration that the method can throw an ExcessiveSpeedException. If you forget to include the declaration, the compiler will require such a declaration when it sees that some statement within the method throws an ExcessiveSpeedException.

Finally, notice that we no longer require an else clause after the if statement. Once a method throws an exception, execution stops, except for whatever code is ready to catch the Exception. Therefore, we no longer need else to insure two non-overlapping paths of execution in response to the test in the if statement.

We can rewrite the AutomobileFactory class to handle the possible occurrence of an ExcessiveSpeedException.

```
   .
   .
   .
try {
    family.accelerate( 120. );
    sports.accelerate( 120. );
}
catch( ExcessiveSpeedException ex) {
    System.out.println( ex.getMessage() );
}
System.out.println( family + " " + family.getSpeed() );
System.out.println( sports + " " + sports.getSpeed() );
   }
```

In this case, the catch block simply reports the error, and the program continues on. With other errors, the catch block might try to correct the problem, ask the user for a decision, or simply terminate the program by calling System.exit().

The output from this version of AutomobileFactory looks like this:

```
3 Automobiles
2006 Kia Rio
2002 VW Passat
2005 Ford Mustang
New speed exceeds maximum speed of 2002 VW Passat
2002 VW Passat 0.0
2005 Ford Mustang 0.0
```

When `AutomobileFactory` tries to accelerate the VW to too great a speed, the `Automobile` class throws an `ExcessiveSpeedException` which stops execution of `accelerate()` and transfers control to the catch block. The catch block reports the problem by printing the message attribute of the `Exception` object. When the catch block completes, the program continues, but the speeds of both `Automobiles` remain 0.0, because the path of execution never set the speed of either one.

There can be more than one catch block; in fact, you can have several. Each one can specify a particular class of `Exception` to handle. That is important to segregating code for handling different kinds of problems. If a method throws a `FileNotFoundException`, it may be easy to fix by asking the operator to enter the file name again. On the other hand, if a read of the file fails and the method throws an `IOException`, it may be difficult for the program to recover. In the first case the catch block may "soldier on," and in the second case the catch block may simply report the error and then call `System.exit()`.

When more than one catch block follows a try block, the catch blocks should be ordered such that lower-level `Exception` classes occur before higher-level, more general classes of `Exceptions`. When a method throws an exception, the try block searches down the list of catch blocks until it finds a match between the `Exception` class that was thrown and the `Exception` class declared in the catch block. The first acceptable match will be invoked to handle the error. If the first catch block specifies objects of class `Exception`, the most general class, the first catch block will handle all `Exceptions`, regardless of whatever other catch blocks there may be. So, if a program wants to attempt to recover from a `FileNotFoundException` and terminate on any other failure, the catch block for the `FileNotFoundException` should come before the catch block for the class `Exception`.

There's one more option. After the try block and all the catch blocks, a programmer can add a *finally block*. A finally block contains code that will always be executed, whether an error occurs or not. A finally block is a good place to put general "clean-up" code, like the statement to close a database.

Here is the syntax for the `try/catch/finally` construction:

```
try {
   .
   . //main line logic goes here
   .
}
catch( SpecificException ex ) {
   .
   . //handle SpecificException
   .
}
catch( LessSpecificException ex ) {
   .
   . //handle LessSpecificException
   .
}
catch( Exception ex ) {
   .
   . //handle everything else that might happen
   .
}
finally {
   .
   . //tidy up — this code will always be executed
   .
}
//If code is successful, or exception is caught and
// handled, execution will continue here.
```

Java's error-handling mechanism is one of its great strengths. Exception handling with `try`/`catch`/`finally` is very robust and leads to very supportable code. Since one can easily add application-specific exception classes to support one's own work, this approach is also very extendable.

INPUT AND OUTPUT

Java programs read and write data by means of *streams*. A stream is a series of data elements that flows from some input device to the program, or from the program to some output device. The general approach to input and output (I/O) from a Java program is to:

```
Open the stream

While there is data to read or write
     read and process data, or write data
}

Close the stream
```

The stream classes for I/O are grouped together in a Java *package* called `java.io`. A package is just a collection of related classes. One can create packages of one's own classes, but we will not be describing that in this brief introduction to the language. The reason to mention the package name here is that a programmer must `import` a package in order to take advantage of the classes within it. In order to use the stream classes we will soon discuss, your program must have a statement at the very beginning, even before the class statement, that says,

```
import java.io.*;
```

The asterisk means to import all the classes in the package. If the programmer wants only one of the classes, the programmer can substitute the class name for the asterisk. Usually one simply types the line as we have shown it.

The stream classes in Java are divided into two great categories: `Reader/Writer` and `InputStream/OutputStream`. If the class is in the `Reader/Writer` category, it is a stream for reading and writing character data—letters, numbers, and symbols. If the class is in the `InputStream/OutputStream` category, it is a stream for reading and writing bytes—raw data, 8 bits at a time.

Students are sometimes confused thinking about the difference between character data and bytes. Are not bytes used to encode characters? Yes they are. In fact, we could get along with just the `InputStream/OutputStream` classes, and let programs be responsible for making sense of the data by converting the data to characters when that was appropriate.

However, often data sources consist of character data, and it is very convenient to have I/O classes for that common situation. If the information exists in the form of characters, a `Reader/Writer` will interpret the information correctly and return a set of characters to the program. This saves the programmer having to write a tedious conversion that would otherwise be necessary frequently.

If the information exists in some other form than characters, such as binary numbers in integer or floating-point format, as in an image file, then it will not make sense to interpret the bit patterns as characters. In that case, the programmer should use the `InputStream/OutputStream` classes, which will simply transfer the bytes. Then the program will be responsible for interpreting the bytes correctly.

One other situation calls for the use of `InputStream/OutputStream` classes, too. That is when one does not care what the data represent. This would be the case, for example, when the task is to copy a file. The program doing the copying does not need to know what the content of the file means; it just needs to copy each byte to a new file. In that case, using the `InputStream/OutputStream` classes instead of the `Reader/Writer` classes makes sense, even if the file to be copied consists of characters, because the `InputStream/OutputStream` classes will be more efficient—the step of translating bit patterns to characters will be skipped.

There are 50 classes in `java.io`, and we will describe only a few here. To read a file of character data, one would use a `BufferedReader` "wrapped around" a `FileReader`. The Java I/O design is very flexible, and this is a good example of that. A `FileReader` reads characters from a file, and by wrapping the `FileReader` with a `BufferedReader`, the I/O will be accomplished more efficiently by reading a group of characters at once. The `BufferedReader` also provides a method called `readLine()`, which allows the program to read a whole line at a time from a file into a `String` variable. Without the `BufferedReader`, a `FileReader` only has methods to read characters.

Here is a little program to read a file of character data and display it on the screen:

```java
import java.io.*;
  /**
   * A program that opens a character based file,
   * specified on the command line,
   * and shows its contents on standard output.
   *
   * @author Carl Reynolds
   */
public class ShowFile {
  public static void main( String args[] ) {
    BufferedReader in = null;
    String         line;

    // Make sure the number of arguments is correct
    if ( args.length != 1) {
      System.err.println( "Usage: ShowFile sourceFile" );
      System.exit(1);
    }

    // Attempt to open the file for reading
    try {
      in = new BufferedReader( new FileReader( args[0] ) );
    }
    catch ( FileNotFoundException e ) {
      System.err.println( "ShowFile: " + e.getMessage() );
      System.exit( 1 );
    }

    // Read and display
    try {
      while ( (line = in.readLine() ) != null ) {
        System.out.println( line );
      }
    }
    catch ( IOException e ) {
      System.err.println( "ShowFile: " + e.getMessage() );
      System.exit( 1 );
    }
    finally {
      // Close the file
      try{
        in.close();
      }
      catch( Exception e ) {}
    }
  }//main
} //ShowFile
```

This program checks the command line arguments in the array of Strings called `args` to make sure that the user provided a parameter for the file name. If the user provided exactly one argument, the program assumes this argument is the name of a file, and it attempts to open the file using a `BufferedReader` inside a `try` block.

If all goes well, the program enters a `while` loop calling the `readLine()` method of the `BufferedReader` to read a line of the file at a time into the `String` variable `line`, and then display the text using the `println()` method. The loop will terminate when `readLine()` returns a null value; that is the signal that the `BufferedReader` has encountered the *end-of-file* (EOF).

The program uses the `finally` block to close the file. Since the `close()` method can itself throw an `IOException`, the call to `close()` within the `finally` block must also be surrounded by a `try` block. If an error occurs here, however, this program simply ignores it; the `catch` block is empty of any code.

Our second example reads a file for the simple purpose of copying the bits in the file to a new file. For this purpose we use a `BufferedInputStream` wrapped around a `FileInputStream`. The program copies the bits literally, one byte at a time. This approach is highly efficient because there is no overhead of translating the bit patterns into characters.

```java
import java.io.*;
/**
* Copy files from the command line.
* @author Paul Tymann
* @author Carl Reynolds
*/
public class FileCopy {
  public static void main( String args[] ) {
    BufferedInputStream  in  = null;
    BufferedOutputStream out = null;
    int data;

    // Check command line arguments
    if ( args.length != 2 ) {
      System.out.println(
                  "Usage: FileCopy sourceFile destFile");
      System.exit(1);
    }

    try {
      // Open the input file.
      in = new BufferedInputStream(
                    new FileInputStream( args[0]) );
      // Open the output file.
      // If the output file exists, it will be overwritten.
      out = new BufferedOutputStream(
                    new FileOutputStream( args[1] ) );
    }
    catch ( FileNotFoundException e ) {
      System.err.println("FileCopy: " + e.getMessage() );
      System.exit( 1 );
    }
    // Now copy the files one byte at a time
    try {
      while ( (data = in.read() ) != -1) {
        out.write( data );
      }
    }
```

```
      catch ( IOException e ) {
        System.err.println( "FileCopy: " + e.getMessage() );
        System.exit( 1 );
      }
      finally {
        // Close the files.
        try {
          in.close();
          out.close();
        }
        catch( Exception e ) {}
      }
    }//main
  } //FileCopy
```

When the program opens the BufferedOutputStream, the new FileOutputStream opens an existing file for overwriting, or, if the output file does not exist, it creates a new output file for writing. There is a second parameter in the constructor for the FileOutputStream which would allow a program to append to an existing file, but we have not used that here.

With the read() method of the BufferedInputStream, either a byte of data is returned, or, if the program encounters the EOF, a binary −1 is returned. As long as the read() continues to return bytes, the program calls write() to copy the data. Though you see individual bytes being read and written, the transfer is much more efficient than you might think, because the InputStream and OutputStream are buffered.

SCANNER

Often we need to read information from the user of the program. We might prompt the user, for example, to ask them what kind of car they drive. We can ask the question of the user by displaying the question using System.out.println(). We have shown many examples of displaying information on the screen.

Java provides a class called Scanner that makes it easy to read information from the keyboard into the program. To create a scanner object for reading from the keyboard, we simply pass the standard input "stream" to the constructor for a new Scanner. For example, here is a snippet of code to create a new Scanner for reading from the keyboard, and then to use the Scanner to read a floating-point number:

```
...
    Scanner scanner = new Scanner(System.in);

    // Obtain input
    System.out.print("Enter balance: ");
    double balance = scanner.nextDouble();
...
```

The Scanner class has many methods, and you should consult the Java API documentation to see what they are, and what choices you have.

You can also use a Scanner to read from a file. To associate a Scanner with a file of text, just pass a FileReader object to the Scanner constructor:

```
sc = new Scanner(new FileReader( myFile.txt ) );
```

To read lines of text, you can use the nextLine() method of Scanner to transfer a line of text into a String variable. You can also use the hasNextLine() method to test to see whether there is something to read. Here's a snippet of code to loop, reading text for processing into a String called lineOfData.

```
String  lineOfData;
Scanner sc = new Scanner( myFile.txt );

while( sc.hasNextLine() ) {
  lineOfData = sc.nextLine();
  ...
}//while
```

When the program reaches the EOF, the hasNextLine() method will return false, and the program will exit the while loop.

PRINTWRITER

The PrintWriter is another very convenient I/O class; it makes writing text to a file as easy as writing text to the display. To create a PrintWriter that is associated with a file, you simply pass the name of the file to the constructor. Then you can write to the file simply using the print() and println() methods you have learned to use for writing to the display.

A PrintWriter can be used with any output stream, but a very common use is to make it very easy to write formatted text to a file. Here is a simple program that reads lines of text typed at the keyboard, and writes the same text into a file using a PrintWriter. Using the println() method, this program adds a line number at the front of each line as it writes the line to the file.

```
import java.io.*;       //PrintWriter is here
import java.util.*;  //Scanner is here

public class PrintToFile{

  public static void main( String[] args) {

    PrintWriter myWriter;
    Scanner     sc;
    String      lineOfData;
    String      fileName;
    int         lineNumber;

    try {
      System.out.print("Enter file name: " );

      sc       = new Scanner( System.in );
      fileName = sc.nextLine();
      myWriter = new PrintWriter( fileName );

      System.out.println( "Now enter lines of text." );
      System.out.println( "When you are done, " +
                  "type only Cntrl/z (EOF) on the line." );
      lineNumber = 1;
while( sc.hasNextLine() ) {
        lineOfData = sc.nextLine();
        myWriter.println( lineNumber + ". " + lineOfData );
        lineNumber++;
      }
      myWriter.close();
    }
    catch( IOException e ) {
```

```
        System.err.println( "I/O error: " + e.getMessage() );
    }
  }
}
```

SUMMARY

Java is a modern object-oriented programming language. This chapter discussed how to compile and run Java programs. We discussed the "primitive" data types in Java, as well as the frequently used "reference" types including `String` and `Array` types. We explained the use of control structures for selective code execution and iteration. These statements included the `if-else`, `for`, `while`, `do-while`, and `switch` statements.

Java takes advantage of the OO concept of classes, and the attendant principles of inheritance, encapsulation, and polymorphism. An instance of a class is called an object, and objects have state and behavior. Classes define both instance and static variables, which manifest the state of an object. Classes also define both instance and static methods, which endow objects with their characteristic behaviors. Java also provides the concept of an interface, which makes it possible to enforce similar behavior across different classes.

Error handling in Java is accomplished using `Exception` objects. When an error occurs, a program can throw an `Exception`, which can describe the problem. `Exceptions` can be caught within the application when the code generating the `Exception` is enclosed in a `try` block. Following the `try` block can be multiple `catch` blocks and a `finally` block. `Catch` blocks can specify which subclasses of `Exception` they will handle. Code in a `finally` block will always be executed, whether an error occurs in the `try` block or not. If the application does not catch an `Exception`, the `Exception` will propagate up to the JVM, which will handle the Exception by reporting it and terminating the program.

Input and output in Java occurs using streams. A stream is a sequence of data elements. The many types of streams available in Java can be classified into `Input/OutputStreams`, which handle raw binary data as bytes, and `Reader/Writer` streams which handle character data, and automatically perform translations to and from character encodings. For efficiency, good programming practice is to wrap a base stream object in a buffered stream to provide efficient buffering of I/O.

The `Scanner` class in Java is a handy class for reading text from the keyboard, a file, or other input stream. The `PrintWriter` class is another convenience class that facilitates the common task of writing formatted text to a file.

REVIEW QUESTIONS

5.1 Write a Java program that divides the number 74.3 by 12.6 and reports the result of the division. Store the dividend and divisor in variables named `dividend` and `divisor` before performing the division. What will be the type of these variables? What will be the type of the result? What is the quotient?

5.2 Write a Java program to compute the area of a circle whose radius is 5. For the value of PI, use 3.14. Now rewrite your program so that it uses the very precise value of PI available as a static constant in the `Math` class that comes with Java. Here is how you use the `Math` class constant:

```
double pi = Math.PI;
```

How much does your result change?

5.3 Write a Java program that prompts the user for a number, and then tells the user whether the number is an even multiple of 5. Use `Scanner` to read the number from the user, and use the modulo operator (%) to decide whether the number is a multiple of 5.

5.4 Write a Java program that asks a user to enter five `Strings`, one at a time. Have it save the `Strings` in an array of strings. Then have the program display the words in reverse order. Use a `for`, or a `while`, or a `do while` loop to read in the `Strings`, and another `for`, `while`, or `do while` loop to print them out.

5.5 Write a Java program that can categorize vehicles based on the number of wheels the vehicle has. Your program should prompt the user for the number of wheels on the vehicle, and then read the number into an `int` variable. If the user says the vehicle has 2 or 3 wheels, the program will report that it is a motorcycle, if it has 4 wheels the vehicle will be labeled a "car or light truck," if it has 6, 8, 10, 12, 14, 16, or 18 wheels, it will be categorized as a truck. Any other number of wheels will be reported as an error. Use a `switch` statement to compute the decision.

5.6   Write a Java class called `Vehicle`. The `Vehicle` class will have instance attributes for color, make, model, speed, number of occupants, and maximum number of occupants. The `Vehicle` class will also have a static variable called `vehicleCount` that can be used to track the number of vehicles in the application. The constructor for `Vehicle` should expect values for make, model, maximum number of occupants, and color, and it should set the vehicle speed to zero, the number of occupants to 1, and increment the count of vehicles each time the constructor is called. Each of the instance and static variables should have an accessor (`get`) method that will return the appropriate value, and all except the `vehicleCount` variable should also have a mutator (`set`) method so that the value can be modified. You should also give the `Vehicle` class an instance method called `changeSpeed`. The `changeSpeed` method should expect a floating-point value for the new speed, and it should return a floating-point value representing the difference between the new speed and the previous speed of the vehicle. Include a `public static void main(String[] args)` method that creates a few vehicles, sets some speeds, and reads some variable values, so that you can test your code by launching the class from the command line.

5.7   Write a `Skateboard` class that inherits from `Vehicle`. Override the `changeSpeed` method for the `Skateboard` class, so that instances of the `Skateboard` class can never exceed 10 mph. If a larger value is supplied, the method will simply set the speed of the `Skateboard` to 10.

5.8   Write a `Bus` class that inherits from `Vehicle`. An instance of the `Bus` class must always have a named driver. In the constructor for a `Bus`, make sure that your code expects and stores the name of the driver. Also, the `Bus` class should have accessor and mutator methods for returning and changing the name of the driver.

5.9   To the class `Vehicle`, add a `refuel` method that expects two parameters, `fuelQuantity` and `milesSinceLastFueling`. Also add instance variables to the `Vehicle` class for `totalMileage` and `totalFuelConsumed`. Further, add an accessor method called `fuelEconomy` that will return the total miles per gallon of the vehicle.
What will you do to make the `refuel` method work properly when invoked on an instance of `Skateboard`? Write a test class called `ManyVehicles` that creates a variety of different `Vehicles`, exercises all the methods you have created, and checks for proper execution. Try to set the speed of a `Skateboard` to 60, for example, or to refuel a `Skateboard`. Check that the fuel economy calculations are being performed correctly.

5.10 Write a class that extends `Exception` and is called `TooManyOccupantsException`. Have the `Vehicle` class mutator for number of occupants throw such an exception if the `numberOfOccupants` would exceed the maximum number of occupants for the vehicle. What will you need to change in your `ManyVehicles` test class?

5.11 Change your `ManyVehicles` class so that it reads from a text file called `Vehicles.txt` the specifications for the `Vehicles` to create. Use a `BufferedReader` or a `Scanner` to read the file. Using a `Scanner` is probably easier in this case. Here is a sample `Vehicles.txt` file. The first word in a line is the color, the second word in a line is the make, the third word is the model, and the fourth word is the maximum number of occupants:

```
red Ford F-150 3
silver BMW 328i 4
blue GM bus 32
gold Chrysler PTCruiser 4
orange WorldIndustries ProBoard 1
```

5.12 Write a Java program that iterates through the integers from 1 to 20, computing the square of each number and writing the information to a file called `squares.txt`. Use a `PrintWriter` to write the file of the first 20 integers and their squares. Arrange for two columns with a line of column headings at the top. You will find this easy to do using the `println()` method of the `PrintWriter`.

CHAPTER 6

Operating Systems

CAPABILITIES OF THE HARDWARE

"It ain't nuthin' but aarn," one of my (Reynold's) instructors at Hewlett Packard used to say. He was big man from Georgia with a strong accent, and by "aarn" he meant iron. The computing machinery itself, without any operating system, is as useful to the average person as a chunk of iron. Maybe it is less useful, for a sufficiently large piece of iron could at least serve as a boat mooring.

The precise list of things a particular computer can do directly is very short. The list is the "instruction set" of the computer. Modern computers have instruction sets of about 70 to 150 instructions.

The instructions the machine understands allow the machine to move bits from one memory location to another, or to move bits to/from memory from/to a register, or to shift the bits in a computer "word" (most computers today regard 32 bits as a "word") some number of positions left or right, or to compare the values of two words, or to complement the bit values of a word (change the ones to zeros, and vice versa), or to add two values. The machine can also compare two values, and skip an instruction if the values are different (or, using a complementary instruction, if the values are the same). There's also a jump instruction to allow the machine to execute an instruction elsewhere in the program.

Such primitive operations are a long way from doing anything really useful for people, and even at that, with nothing but the bare machine, one would have to know the bit code for each instruction, enter the sequence of instructions one bit at a time, and then press the start button! Early computers (even as recently as the early 1980s) usually had a "front panel" with rocker switches and lights to allow one to do just that.

If one were to write a program to act as a simple four-function integer (no decimals) calculator, with nothing but the bare machine, one would write something like the following.

1 Enable a read from the keyboard by using one of I/O instructions in the machine instruction set to ready the keyboard interface (the electronics behind the connector port to which the keyboard is attached) to accept a character from the keyboard.
2 Wait by entering a "loop," continuously testing the flag signal on the keyboard interface. If the flag is false, check it again, and again, and again, until it becomes true.

When the flag becomes "true," a character will have arrived at the keyboard interface from the keyboard. However, the character will arrive as the ASCII encoding of the character we know, not as a binary numeric value.

You can see the encodings of various characters by looking at a table of ASCII encodings. One reference is this: http://www.lookuptables.com/. If you consult the table, you will see that the character 0 is encoded as the bit pattern equivalent to the decimal number 48. The character 1 is encoded as 49; the number 2 as 50; and so on, up to character 9, which is encoded as 57. Likewise, the equal sign is encoded as 61, the plus sign as 43, etc.

If the user types a 3, it will arrive as the decimal value 51.

3 When the user types a character, the signal flag on the keyboard interface becomes true, and our program exits its endless loop testing the signal flag. Now the program can use another I/O instruction to read the character on the keyboard interface into a register of the *central processing unit* (CPU).

4 Check to see if the character now in the register is one of the characters we're interested in, i.e., a number, operation sign or equal sign. If the character is not one of those, ignore the character, and enable another read from the keyboard.

5 If the character is a number, see if the previous character was a number. If so, then this is the next digit in a multidigit number. In that case, multiply the previous number by 10, add the new number to it, and store the result in a known memory location.

Before you can add the new number, however, you must decode the ASCII and convert the character into a binary number. A commonly used "trick" is simply to subtract 48 from the coded value of the number (e.g., if the number is 3, subtracting 48 from 51, the encoding, returns the binary numeric value 3).

On the other hand, if this is the first digit in a number, just decode the ASCII and store the binary value in a memory location set aside by the program for one of the operands.

6 If the character is one of the operation signs, store the sign in a memory location set aside for storing the operator. The program will refer to this later, after the program receives an equal sign.

7 If the character is an equal sign, load the operands saved in memory into CPU registers, retrieve the operator character, and, depending on the operator, jump to the instruction(s) to perform the arithmetic operation on the contents of the registers. Then store the result back in the memory location for operand 1, construct the character string to send as the result, and send the result back to the display.

Here's how the program constructs the characters to send to the display:

a If the result is greater than 9, then the result will require more than one character, so divide the result by 10 until further division results in a number less than 1.

b Add 48 to the integer result to encode it as ASCII.

c Load the interface register in the computer with the character, and issue the I/O instruction to have the first character sent to the display.

d Wait (loop again) until the character is sent, and acknowledged by the display via the flag being set on the display interface.

e Having sent the most significant digit, subtract the appropriate value from the result and repeat the formatting and output operations until the entire character string result is sent to the display.

8 Reenable the keyboard interface to read the next character.

What a lot of work! And many programs need to read from the keyboard and write to the display! And many programs need to decode strings of numeric characters, and also to encode numbers into character strings! We don't want every programmer reinventing this code, and making similar mistakes over and over again. Obvious problems like this I/O programming and formatting prompted interest in common, efficient, debugged programs that different programmers could easily reuse.

At first such code came into use as libraries of standard "routines." Later, computer scientists created the first "resident monitors" or "operating systems" os which made it easier for programmers to use such shared code, and made use of the machine more efficient and secure.

The operating system of a computer is a program, often called the "kernel," which is always running on the computer, and which governs the execution of all the other programs that run on the computer. The operating system makes it much easier to write programs and execute them, because the operating system handles all the complex details, like performing I/O and formatting input and output.

Two or three key motivations lay behind the development of the first operating systems. The first was to make the computer much more easily useful. The second was to use what were at the time very expensive computing resources efficiently. The third was to provide security and reliability in computing.

In general, operating systems are programs written to run on the bare machine and provide services to user programs. The services operating systems provide include:

- Management of I/O
- Management of memory
- Scheduling of user processes (start, interrupt, and stop)
- A secure and reliable environment for programs and users

- A convenient interface for users
- Networking services
- Messaging and synchronization services between processes
- Utility "system software" such as editors, loaders, help, etc.

OPERATING SYSTEMS HISTORY

Batch Jobs

Early conceptions of computing revolved around computing "jobs." A computational job would be presented to the computer, the computer would process the job, and the computer would deliver an answer. The first operating systems made this sort of use easier, and were known as "batch" operating systems (1955–1965). A "resident monitor" (the operating system) provided the commonly needed routines to perform I/O to the devices of the day (most of the OS code consisted of device drivers), and to format data back and forth between encoded form and binary values. The resident monitor also provided a simpler user interface through *job control language* (JCL).

The user would embed JCL commands to the operating system in the sequence of program instructions and data presented to the computer as a "batch job." A user could prepare a payroll job, for example, using a deck of punched cards where the first card identified the job and the user, the next called for a particular compiler (probably FORTRAN), the next group of cards comprised the program source code, the next card called for the "loader" to assign particular addresses in memory, the next card called for the OS to run the program, and the following cards presented data on which the program would operate, probably the hours worked by each person that week.

Multiprogramming (mid-1960s on)

In the mid-1960s, operating systems were enhanced to provide *multiprogramming capability*. That meant that several programs could be loaded at the same time, and the operating system would switch among them to make sure the machine stayed as busy as possible. Computers were extremely expensive, so the OS was improved to make better use of the computer time. If one program was waiting for a magnetic tape to be mounted by the computer operator, another could be scheduled to run while the first waited. IBM's OS/360 was a good example of such a multiprogramming batch operating system.

Multiprogramming required some important advances. Because several programs could execute concurrently, I/O control of unshareable devices became even more important. For instance, printed output that interleaves lines of output from different programs is not very useful! So the OS provided more than just device drivers; the OS also provided locking mechanisms so that only one program at a time, for example, could send data to the printer.

"Interrupt systems" were added to the I/O hardware so that slow I/O tasks could be started without requiring all the jobs on the computer to wait. Once the I/O for a job was started, the system could schedule some other computation until the I/O task completed and generated an "interrupt," signaling readiness to continue with the first job.

With more than one program in memory, it also became important that one user was not able to address, even by accident, memory allocated to another program. Memory protection hardware, comprising "base" (starting address) and "limit" (maximum program size) registers along with address checking hardware, was added to the machines, and the operating system managed the contents of the memory protection registers.

With this new dependence of user programs on services provided by the operating system came the requirement that some instructions be reserved for use only by the operating system. For instance, only the OS should be allowed to change the contents of the base and limit memory protection registers. Only the OS should determine which print request goes to the printer at any particular time.

The solution was a hardware "mode" switch to provide a "user mode" context and a "privileged mode" context. (Other words for privileged mode include system mode, monitor mode, and kernel mode.) Certain instructions, such as loading the base and limit registers, and all I/O instructions, became "privileged instructions." Privileged instructions can only be executed when the computer is in privileged mode.

When the computer boots up, the hardware sets the computer to privileged mode and the operating system begins executing. As soon as the OS starts a user program executing, the OS sets the mode to user mode.

Any attempt by the user program to execute a privileged instruction is trapped by the hardware as an error, and causes a special interrupt to occur. When any interrupt occurs, the OS regains control and the mode switches back to privileged mode. In the case of the errant user program, the OS issues an error message, terminates the faulting program, and resumes computing with another process.

Timesharing (1970s and 1980s)

When computers were so extremely expensive, a vision of the future for many was that a central expensive computer would provide services to many users via remote terminals. Timesharing was developed as an extension of multiprogramming where the job commands came to the central computer via the terminal communication lines.

Timesharing required an important advance in program scheduling called the "timeslice." In round-robin fashion, each user program in turn received a small unit of time on the CPU. Since the central computer was so fast, each user had the illusion that they had the computer to themselves.

With timeslicing, the system clock became a source of important interrupts. At programmed intervals, the clock interrupts; the interrupt invokes the OS in privileged mode; the OS decides if the currently executing process should continue, or if its timeslice is up; then the OS either resumes the currently executing process or schedules another, as appropriate.

SINGLE-USER OS → NETWORK OS

With the advent of inexpensive personal computers, the vision of the future migrated from terminals connected to a powerful central host to small inexpensive computers distributed widely, and loosely connected by network services. Operating systems for such machines now incorporate all the features of large computer operating systems of the past.

In fact, operating systems such as UNIX, originally developed to support terminals connected to a central computer, have been moved to personal computer platforms. Microsoft's operating systems, on the other hand, have grown from single-user-only environments to fully featured operating systems that even include multiuser and multiprocessor support.

When computers on the network provide resources to other computers, such as a web server does, the computers are called *servers*. Networked computers that access the services and data of other machines on the network are called *clients*. Often a single computer may act as both client and server at different times.

MULTIPROCESSOR OPERATING SYSTEMS

Computers with multiple processors offer the potential of greater computational speed. With this potential comes complexity, however. The complexity surrounds the shared resources that must be managed properly in a multiprocessor environment.

For instance, there will be a Ready queue of processes to be run. Should there be a Ready queue of programs to run for each CPU? Should instead each CPU inspect the same Ready queue that all share? Should one CPU handle the scheduling for all the other CPUs? Or, should each CPU make its own scheduling decisions? What about shared I/O devices and device tables? What about shared memory and the allocation of processes to memory?

The simpler approach to a multiprocessor OS is to have one CPU be the "master" and have it make decisions on behalf of the other "slave" CPUs. This approach is called "asymmetric multiprocessing." For a small number of processors (say, 10 or fewer), asymmetric multiprocessing can work well. As the number of processors increases, however, the master becomes a bottleneck, for it must be consulted for all important resource allocation decisions.

A more sophisticated approach to multiprocessor support is called *symmetric multiprocessing* (SMP). With SMP there is only one copy of the OS code in the shared memory, and all processors execute it. There is only one set of system tables, which all processors share. SMP dynamically provides load balancing, but the trick to making SMP work is in synchronizing access among the processors to the shared resources.

With multiple CPUs, the OS does not have the luxury, as is the case in a single-processor system, of simply disabling interrupts while it completes uninterruptible work. With multiple CPUs, each has its own interrupt system, and synchronization can require additional hardware like an interprocessor bus with a locking protocol, and very careful analysis of other resource-locking mechanisms.

REAL-TIME OPERATING SYSTEMS

A small but important category of operating systems is called "real time." Real-time systems are constrained to execute within limited and defined time windows. A computer recording frequent readings from an instrument such as a frequency counter or voltmeter could be an example. Recording the values and reacting to them, if necessary, within a specified time is critical for real-time systems.

Real-time operating systems include special features that tailor them to critical real-world responsiveness. For instance, process scheduling is usually based strictly on priority rather than on some round-robin timesharing scheme. The highest-priority task is always the one that will be executing. For example, with a real-time system, when the valve controlling cooling water to the nuclear reactor needs adjustment, that task will get the CPU, and it will not have to share time with a word processor.

Some real-time systems also permit preallocation of disk space, either as part of the file system or independent of the file system. When a program writes to the disk, it will not incur the overhead of a general-purpose file and directory manager.

Memory management may be more wasteful but faster to execute in a real-time system. Rather than tailor the amount of memory allocated to a process, the OS may simply dispatch a process to a fixed, large block of main memory, thus reducing the setup time for the process.

In all these ways, real-time systems support fast interaction with instruments and devices in the outside world.

EMBEDDED SYSTEMS

By far the most common type (by simple count) of operating system today is the *embedded system*. Embedded systems lie within the automobiles, airplanes, thermostats, and other devices we use every day. It's easy to overlook the fact that they are there, but our day-to-day lives are ever more dependent on such systems to supervise the execution of the built-in programs for the microprocessors controlling everything from dishwashing to transportation.

MANAGEMENT OF INPUT AND OUTPUT

The early operating systems consisted largely of a collection of code for device drivers. One could argue that the most fundamental service of the operating system is to manage I/O, so that programmers can focus on higher-level activity, and so that shared I/O devices are shared properly.

Strictly speaking, the operating system (or any software doing I/O directly) interacts with the device's interface (or "controller," or "adapter"), rather than the device itself. Every I/O device such as a printer, disk, or mouse connects to an interface, often a separate printed circuit board, and the interface connects to (plugs into) a bus (an electronic connection path consisting of multiple lines) in the computer.

When information is sent out to a device, the information is passed to the device controller, and the controller is given a command by the computer to transfer the information to the device. The controller then does so. When the transfer is complete, the controller signals the computer that the task has been accomplished.

The controller itself represents a significant off-loading of detail for the computer. For example, the computer can tell the disk controller that it wants to write a set of bytes at a certain address (track and sector), and the controller will take care of commanding the disk read/write heads to move, and of actually causing the bits to be written in the right place.

In general, devices are classified as "character" or "block" devices. Roughly, these terms equate to "slow" or "fast," respectively. A character device like a keyboard or printer transfers one character, or byte, at a time. A block device like a disk or a tape drive transfers a whole buffer, some multiple number of bytes, at a time. On the other hand, some devices don't fit in this classification, such as a monitor with "memory mapped video."

Programmed I/O

Simple character-at-a-time (byte-at-a-time) I/O is sometimes called *programmed I/O* to distinguish it from *interrupt-driven I/O* or *direct memory access* (DMA), which we will discuss shortly. With programmed I/O, the driver checks to see if the device is available (not busy). If so, the driver will write a character to the buffer on the controller, and command the transfer to begin with a "set control; clear flag" (different computers may name these status bits differently). Set control tells the device to start, and clear flag makes the device appear busy. The driver then loops, testing for the flag to be set. When the byte is transferred, the controller will clear the control bit and set the flag bit. The driver will find the flag bit is set, and that will indicate that the transfer is complete and the device is again available to accept another character.

The unfortunate characteristic of programmed I/O is that the computer can spend a great deal of time waiting for a slow device. In the time it takes to process a character out to a 56K baud modem, for example, the computer could easily perform 200 to 1000 other instructions.

Interrupt-driven I/O

To avoid the waste of computing power using programmed I/O, virtually all operating systems today use interrupt-driven I/O. With interrupt-driven I/O, the program requesting the transfer is blocked (suspended) while the bytes are being transferred. The operating system copies the bytes to be transferred into system memory space so that the suspended program can be temporarily removed from memory, if necessary. Then the OS calls the "initiator" section of the device driver. The initiator moves the first byte into the controller's buffer, commands the controller to begin, and then returns to the OS. The OS then decides which process to execute while waiting for the I/O to complete.

When the character has been transferred, the controller generates a hardware *interrupt*. An interrupt causes the OS to take control. The OS saves the state (register contents, program counter value, etc.) of the currently executing program, and calls the "continuator" section of the driver for the interrupting device. If there are additional bytes to transfer, the continuator puts the next byte into the controller's buffer, commands the controller to begin again, and returns to the OS. The OS then restores the state and resumes execution of the other process.

When the last character has been transferred, the continuator will return to the OS, signaling that the suspended process can be restarted. Now the OS can choose among the available processes, and restart whichever one is of highest priority.

The key advantage of interrupt-driven I/O is that the CPU works on other processes while the controller transfers the data to the device. This is a very substantial improvement in the efficient use of computing resources, but it is still true that processing interrupts imposes overhead which can be substantial, especially when interrupts are frequent.

Direct Memory Access

A further improvement in efficiency is possible when the I/O device is relatively fast, like a disk drive or a tape drive. The computer design may include one or more *direct memory access* (DMA) controllers (or channels). A DMA controller is a computer within the computer that specializes in I/O, and its purpose is to drastically reduce the number of interrupts that the OS must service.

When DMA is used, the driver sets up the DMA transfer once, passing the address of the buffer to be transferred to the DMA controller and telling the DMA controller which device to transfer to/from. The driver then returns to the OS, and the OS begins executing another process. The DMA controller takes care of moving the information directly from/to memory and to/from the device. The only interrupt the OS sees is the one from the DMA controller when the entire transfer is complete.

Strictly speaking, DMA can be used with any device, but usually DMA is used only by drivers of fast devices that would otherwise generate many frequent interrupts. DMA channels are usually few in number, so their use is usually reserved for devices for which the DMA channels make the most difference.

Memory Mapped I/O

Most computers of the 1960s, 1970s, and 1980s had a special set of instructions for I/O, and many computers still do. With such architecture, reading from a buffer on an interface requires a different instruction than reading from a memory location. In one computer architecture, for instance, the I/O instruction to read from the interface in slot 7 is LIA 7, "load into the A-register from slot 7." The memory reference instruction to read from memory location 7 is LDA 7, "load into the A-register from memory location 7." The instructions LIA and LDA are different. LIA is a privileged instruction, available only in privileged mode, and LDA is not; any program can execute LDA.

In the 1980s the idea of memory-mapped I/O gained currency. With memory-mapped I/O, certain memory locations are reserved for reference to the control registers and buffers of the I/O interfaces. Communicating with the controllers becomes as easy as writing to and reading from memory.

Memory-mapped I/O offers several advantages. First, since I/O uses the same instructions as memory references, I/O programs (drivers) can be written entirely in a high-level language. Second, protection against issuing I/O commands in user mode can be effected using the memory protection hardware already required for enforcing bounds on a user program's access to memory. No special mechanism for detecting the privileged status of I/O commands is required.

A disadvantage of memory-mapped I/O becomes apparent when the computer design includes separate buses for memory and I/O. Since the controllers cannot "see" the transfers to memory, some mechanism is necessary to intercept reads and writes to I/O mapped-memory locations and pass them off to the I/O bus.

Another disadvantage of memory-mapped I/O is that most modern computers, in order to speed access to memory, use local "cache" memory to hold the contents of recently accessed memory locations. A cache holds a copy of what is in memory in a location closer to the CPU. If a driver needs to read the control flag register to learn if the interface is busy, and the contents of the memory location are cached, the driver may never see the device become available. Some additional mechanism must be added to provide for *selective* caching—a mechanism that avoids caching of I/O mapped addresses.

Some computers use both special I/O instructions and memory mapping. For instance, the PC architecture uses memory mapping for the transfer of buffers to I/O controllers, and also uses I/O instructions to write to the control registers of the interfaces.

PROCESSES AND SCHEDULING

The conceptualization of a running program has been refined as the field of computing has matured. Early on, one spoke of running a job, or program. The program would be loaded on the computer, and it would run to completion.

Later, computer scientists made the distinction between a program and a process. The program is the set of instructions that will be executed when the program runs, and a process is an instance of a running program. The difference is that the process maintains the state information about that execution of the program; it has certain values for variables, for example, and a program location counter value at any particular moment, and a certain section of the computer memory assigned to it.

In a multiprogramming environment (the name "multiprogramming" emerged before the widespread use of the term "process," for in today's language one would call it "multiprocessing"), the distinction between program and process becomes important. Two instances of an editor program, for example, may be simultaneously operating on different files. Therefore, two processes with different state information are executing the same program. It's important for the operating system to maintain the distinction between the two processes.

Later still, the concept of a process was broken into two concepts: the process and the "thread." The process is the set of resources assembled for the execution of the program (files, memory allocation, etc.), and the thread is a line of execution within the program.

Before programmers had access to threads, tasks that required multiple lines of execution would be written as separate processes that communicated with one another somehow (shared memory, messages, shared file, etc.). However, as we will show, setting up a new process is a fairly high-overhead task for an operating system, and the communication of messages between processes can itself require a significant programming effort and entail additional operating system overhead. These problems, which were encountered frequently, motivated the distinction between threads of execution within a process, and the process itself as a set of resources available to all threads.

Not all, but a significant number of, programs can take advantage of threads. A common example is a word processor that checks one's spelling as one types. One thread attends to the typing at the keyboard, and a second thread constantly checks to see if the words typed match any of the words in the dictionary. Both threads are part of the same process; they share access to the same files, the same user, the same memory, etc.

In the case of the word processor, the keyboard thread gets priority, so that the user feels the computer is quickly responsive to his or her typing. When the computer is waiting for more typing to occur, the "background" spell-checking thread can inspect the words for correct spelling. This approach to program design is referred to as *multithreading*.

Getting back to the concept of a process, let us consider what the operating system does when one "runs" a program. The operating system creates a table entry for each process running on the machine. Usually the entry is referred to as a *process control block* (PCB), but the name for the concept varies among operating systems.

The PCB is used to track all the information about the process, and it includes fields such as the program name, code location on the disk, priority, state (ready/waiting/running), open files, memory boundaries, parent process (the process which started the process), user ID, group ID, and storage for the register contents and program counter value when the process is interrupted. The PCB is a fairly large structure; a PCB for a single process in Linux is over 350 bytes in size.

When a program is run, the process does not necessarily execute immediately. First the OS creates the PCB, and then it adds the process to the Ready queue; the process enters the Ready state. The operating system will select one of the Ready processes to execute, and that process will enter the Running state.

A process in the Running state will continue to run until the process completes, the OS decides that a higher-priority process should run instead, the OS decides to give another process a chance to use the CPU for a while (i.e., the "time quantum," or "timeslice," expires on the running process), or the running program must pause to perform some I/O, wait for some resource to become available (e.g., a shared file), or receive a message or signal from another process.

How is it that, "the OS decides to give another process a chance to use the CPU?" There's only one CPU, and the executing process has control. It seems an impossibility that the OS could have any influence at all, once it turns the CPU over to the executing process.

The answer to this conundrum is the system clock. The OS programs the computer's clock to generate an interrupt at set intervals. For example, the SunOS has the clock interrupt at 10 ms intervals, so 100 times per second the clock generates an interrupt, just like an I/O device.

When the clock interrupts, the hardware shifts to monitor mode automatically, and the instruction stored in the memory location associated with the clock device "vectors" to the OS code that handles "clock tick processing." At every clock tick, the OS will check to see if the time quantum of the executing program has expired, if any I/O device has "timed out," and if any process priorities need adjustment (some scheduling algorithms use such time-based adjustments). It will also update the system time-of-day clock to keep it accurate. When the OS completes its clock tick processing, it will again put the computer in user mode and transfer control of the CPU to the appropriate user process.

Besides being in the Ready or Running state, a process can also be in the Waiting (or Blocked) state. Some OSs have more than one waiting state as a way to segregate processes waiting for different conditions, such as waiting for I/O, waiting for child processes to complete, waiting for memory, etc. The SunOS recognizes five states: Running, Runnable in Memory (i.e., Ready), Runnable Swapped (i.e., Ready, but the code is on the disk at the moment because the process was removed from memory in favor of another process), Sleeping in Memory (i.e., Waiting), and Sleeping Swapped (i.e., Waiting for some event like an I/O completion, and the code is on the disk so that another process can occupy the memory).

When a process moves out of the Waiting state, it does not go directly to the Running state. Instead, when the event for which it was waiting occurs, a Waiting process becomes Ready. The OS then chooses from among the Ready processes one process to run.

THREADS

Modern operating systems often provide the thread model for execution control. Threads allow multiple lines of execution within a single process. This is much like multiple processes, but without the overhead of managing multiple PCBs, and with the built-in facility for sharing memory and other resources among threads of the same process. Instead of a PCB, a thread requires a much smaller thread table entry, primarily to provide storage for register and program counter contents when the OS switches among executing threads.

In an operating system that supports threads ("kernel threads," which we will discuss shortly), the object that gets scheduled, and which gains control of the CPU, is the thread. The process is still important, but as a collection of resources. Threads are what get executed, and threads are what enter the states of Ready, Running, and Waiting.

Since threads resemble processes, some operating systems refer to threads as "lightweight processes" (e.g., SunOS). And just as OSs came to be described as multiprogrammed when they began to support multiple processes simultaneously, OSs that support threads are described as "multithreaded."

Threads are useful because many applications benefit from separating the whole job into semi-independent parts. Earlier we mentioned the word-processor/spell-checker example. Another example could be a time-and-attendance application where one thread does a quick check of the employee ID as the employee enters or leaves the plant, and another thread updates the payroll database in the background. In this threaded design, the quick gate-check thread can keep people moving through the gates, even if the more complex database thread takes a little more time.

Web servers are almost universally multithreaded. The main server thread waits for a request to arrive, and, when one does, it creates a new "worker thread" which then handles the request and provides the reply. The main server's only job is to recognize a request and then to create a thread to do the work of responding. This multithreaded approach keeps the web server responsive to new requests. Multithreading is efficient compared to the alternative of using multiple processes, because creating a new thread requires about one hundredth the time that creating a new process requires.

Another advantage of threads appears when the computer contains multiple CPUs. In that case, different threads can be executed on different CPUs, with the potential for completely parallel execution and great speed improvement.

Threads can be provided as "user threads" or "kernel threads." Threads provided by the OS are kernel threads. If the OS itself does not support threading, it is possible to implement threading using a user thread library that executes as a user process. For example, the POSIX thread package is a user thread package available for UNIX computers.

Kernel threads have the advantages associated with the OS itself being aware of the threads. For instance, since the OS does the scheduling of the threads, if one thread must wait for some reason (e.g., for I/O to complete), the OS can schedule another thread from the same process. Likewise, when one thread exhausts its timeslice, the OS can choose another thread from the same process to receive the next timeslice.

User threads have some advantages, too. Since the OS has no knowledge itself of the threads, the OS does not get involved with thread creation and scheduling. This lack of OS involvement means less overhead, so creating threads and switching among threads can be more efficient with user threads.

The disadvantages of user threads are the reverse of the advantages of kernel threads. When one thread must wait, the OS will block the entire process, for the OS has no knowledge of the different threads within the user process. Likewise, a user thread may claim all of its process' CPU time, to the exclusion of the other threads. When the user thread package transfers control to a thread, the user thread package has no way to interrupt the executing thread after some timeslice, because the user thread package does not gain control on a clock tick as the OS does.

In the case of Java and some other languages, threads are provided as part of the language. The implementation of the Java Virtual Machine determines how the Java Thread class is mapped to the thread model of the OS. The Java programmer is protected from having to know the details of the underlying threading model of the computer.

SYNCHRONIZATION

Often processes or threads must share access to the same information. For instance, imagine an application where one thread, the server thread, adds requests to a list of pending tasks, and another thread, the worker thread, reads from the list, removes the task from the list, and executes the task. Appreciate, too, that "adding a request to a list" will require more than one machine instruction to accomplish; the list object must be referenced, the address of the last element must be calculated, and some reference to the new task must be calculated (perhaps the address of a String buffer) and stored in the appropriate list memory location. In addition, such an application will almost always limit the number of elements in the list so that a flood of requests will not simply swamp the computer and leave no time or memory for processing requests. So the server thread will also include a check to see if the number of pending requests is already at its maximum value; if so, the server thread will wait until the worker thread can complete at least one of the tasks.

On the other side, imagine the worker thread taking tasks off the list. Again, removing a task from the list will require multiple machine instructions. The worker thread will also be checking to see if the list is empty, for there may be no work to do. In that case, the worker thread will wait until some task is added to the list by the server thread.

Since an interrupt can occur between any two machine instructions, and since the operating system may choose to execute any ready thread at any moment, it is possible that the server thread will be interrupted as it adds a task to the list, and that the worker thread will be scheduled to execute next. Without some control to insure that items are added to and removed from the list at appropriate times and as whole items, it's possible that the coordination will fail.

For instance, suppose the server thread finds the address of the last element of the list and then is interrupted. After the OS services the interrupt, the OS schedules the worker thread, which removes a task from the list and completes processing. In fact, the worker may continue to execute and remove several tasks from the list before the OS intervenes to schedule another thread. When the server thread eventually regains the CPU, it will continue from the point it was interrupted, and store a reference to a new task in the location it previously computed. Now, however, the address is incorrect. Depending on the situation, one of several possible errors will occur, but the application will surely fail, and it will fail in a way that cannot be reliably reproduced. Such errors can be devilish to debug.

The section of code that must be executed in isolation in order to avoid corruption is called the "critical section." Guaranteeing correct execution of the critical sections requires that "mutual exclusion" be enforced when the critical sections are executing. The code of a cooperating thread that is not in the critical section (and often most of the code is not in the critical section) is called the "remainder section."

Since operating systems themselves are often also implemented as multiple threads, coordination between executing threads or processes is important both to people writing operating systems ("systems programmers") and applications programmers. This synchronization problem occupied a great deal of computer science research during the 1960s, 1970s, and 1980s. Several solutions have been developed.

Dekker offered the first software solution to the problem in 1965, and a simplification by Peterson was published in 1981. These solutions involved shared variables and employed "busy waiting" (i.e., the waiting process or thread had to wait continually check to see if the condition had changed). While these papers were groundbreaking, one would not use this approach today. For one thing, these approaches are limited to situations where only two processes are cooperating, and for another, the busy wait is wasteful of CPU time.

A hardware approach to synchronization is relatively simple, but does have the limitation that it, too, requires a busy wait. All that is necessary is a single machine instruction that tests some condition and also sets the condition in the same instruction execution cycle. Since it can't be interrupted, such a "test-and-set" instruction can be used for coordination. In pseudocode, here is what a test-and-set instruction does:

```
boolean testAndSet( boolean lock ) {
    if( !lock ) {
        lock = true;
        return true;
    }
    else return false;
}
```

This code says:

The routine name is testAndSet, and
it will return either 'true' or 'false' (a boolean value).
testAndSet operates on a variable we will call 'lock',
and 'lock' can have the value 'true' or 'false' (it's a boolean variable).

If `lock` is not true (`!lock`), then
make `lock` true, and return the value `true` to the calling program.
Otherwise, return the value `false` to the calling program.

Some boolean variable called `lock` is used to lock or unlock the resource. If the resource is not locked at the time of the call, the instruction will lock it and return `true` meaning, "It's OK to proceed." If the resource is locked at the time of the call, the instruction will return `false` meaning, "You must wait."

If such an instruction is part of the machine instruction set, code like this can take advantage of it:

```
boolean thisLock;
. . .
while( !testAndSet( thisLock ) ) { /* Do nothing */ }
/* Now do whatever needs to be done in isolation */
. . .
/* Now free the lock */
thisLock = false;
. . .
/* Carry on */
. . .
```

This code says:

While `testAndSet` returns `false` (`!testAndSet`), do nothing.
When `testAndSet` returns `true`,
do whatever needs to be done in the critical section.
(Note that the locking variable is now set `true`, and competing
processes using the same `testAndSet` routine will have to wait.)
When the critical section is complete,
indicate that by changing `thisLock`, the locking variable, to `false`.'

Because the test-and-set instruction requires a busy wait, it often is not the best choice of synchronization mechanism. However, this approach is quite useful for coordinating threads in an operating system on a multiprocessor machine. The effect of the busy wait is much less onerous when the waiting thread has its own processor, and the wait is not likely to be long.

There are other variations on the test-and-set instruction idea. A 'swap' or 'exchange' instruction that atomically (without interruption) exchanges the values of two arguments can be used the same way. Here is pseudocode for a `swap` instruction:

```
void swap(boolean a, boolean b) {
    boolean temp = a;
    a = b;
    b = temp;
}
```

This code says:

Given two boolean values (`a` and `b` can each be either `true` or `false`),
exchange the two values, using the variable `temp` for temporary storage."
(The `void` means that this routine does not return any value. It simply swaps `a` and `b`.)

Application code such as the following uses the `swap` instruction:

```
boolean lock;          // shared data; initialized to 'false'

boolean key = true; // not shared; used for this thread only
. . .
//Wait until key becomes false, which means lock was false
while ( key ) swap(lock, key);
      /* critical section */
...
/* Now free the lock */
lock = false;
...
/* remainder section */
. . .
```

This code says:

> While the variable key is true, swap the values of key and lock.
> (When key becomes false, it will mean that lock was false,
> and because key was true before, lock will now be true.)
> When key becomes false, execute the critical section.
> When the critical section is complete, release the lock by setting it back to false.

The swap instruction has the same applications and limitations as the test-and-set.

SEMAPHORES

In 1965 one of the most prolific contributors to computer science proposed the construct of a "semaphore" which could be used to provide mutual exclusion and to avoid the requirement for busy waiting. Edgar Dijkstra proposed that the operating system execute a short series of instructions atomically to provide such a service. The operating system can execute several instructions atomically, because the operating system can turn the interrupt system off while the code for a semaphore is being executed.

Basically, the semaphore is a short section of code that operates on an integer variable. A semaphore offers two operations. Dijkstra (from the Netherlands) called these operations "proberen" (P, or test) and "verhogen" (V, or increment). As time has passed, other names for these methods have included "wait," "down," and "sleep" for P, and "signal," "up," and "wake" for V. Multiple names for the same operations can make it difficult to read different accounts of semaphores, but the idea is simple.

When a process or thread invokes the P operation, the semaphore P method decrements the integer, and if the value is now less than 0, the operating system blocks the process. Later, some other process will invoke the V operation using the same semaphore. The V operation will increment the value of the integer, and if the integer value is now equal to or greater than zero, the process that was blocked will be unblocked.

The semaphore construct is very flexible. Its integer value can be initialized to allow for a variety of uses. Most often it is initialized to 1, which allows the first process access via the P operation, and blocks any other process until the first process completes its critical section and executes the V operation.

A semaphore also may be initialized to 0, which will cause the first process that executes a P operation to block. Some other process will have to execute a V operation on the same semaphore before the first process will be unblocked. Programmers can use this mechanism to insure that one of two processes always executes first.

A semaphore also may be initialized to some number greater than 1, say 3. That would allow the first three attempts to execute the P operation to succeed without blocking. To show how this might be useful, here is an example of two cooperating programs where one produces a series of n items to be consumed by the other (this is the "producer–consumer" problem, much like the "server thread–worker thread" example we discussed earlier).

```
// 'empty', 'full', and 'mutex' are all semaphore objects
empty = n     // n = the maximum number of items
              //      permitted to be waiting to be consumed
full  = 0
mutex = 1

/* Producer: */

while( true ) {         // while( true ) means continue looping forever
    . . .
    produce an item
    . . .
    P(empty);
    P(mutex);
    . . .
    send item to consumer
    . . .
    V(mutex);
    V(full);
}

/* Consumer: */

while( true ) {
    P( full )
    P( mutex );
    . . .
    consume an item
    . . .
    V( mutex );
    V( empty );
    . . .
}
```

When the producer has an item ready to give to the consumer, the producer executes a P operation on the empty semaphore. As long as there are fewer than the maximum permitted items waiting to be consumed, the producer does not block. Then the producer executes a P operation on the mutex semaphore. The mutex semaphore is there to make sure that the producer and consumer cannot simultaneously add and consume items, for that would lead to elusive errors of synchronization. When the producer succeeds and produces a new item, the producer executes a V operation on the mutex semaphore to release control of the group of items to be consumed, and a V operation on the full semaphore. The full semaphore keeps a count of the items waiting to be consumed, and the consumer will test that semaphore with a P operation before trying to consume an item.

When the consumer is ready to do something with the items provided by the producer, the consumer executes a P operation on the full semaphore to be sure that something is there to consume. If so, the consumer does not block, and instead goes on to test the mutex semaphore using the P operation. If the P operation on the mutex semaphore does not block, it means that the consumer has exclusive access to the set of items ready to be consumed. After the consumer removes an item from the set, the consumer releases the mutex semaphore by executing a V operation on the mutex. The consumer then increments the count of additional items permitted to be in the set of items to be consumed, by executing a V operation on the empty semaphore.

Semaphores are simple and powerful, but it can be difficult to design more complex interactions between processes using semaphores. For instance, suppose a number of threads share read and write access to a file.

Perhaps the designer wants to avoid the situation where a writer changes something while a reader is reading. It's fairly easy to use three semaphores to design the application so that as long as any reader is active with the file or waiting to be active, no writer is permitted to make any changes.

On the other hand, suppose the designer wants to avoid having a writer change the file contents while a reader is reading, but also wants to give a writer priority over waiting readers so that readers will get the latest information. To implement this writers-first policy requires five semaphores and very careful thinking about how to use them.

MONITORS

In the mid 1970s, researchers Hoare and Brinch Hansen proposed the monitor idea. A properly written monitor can simplify the coordination of processes or threads. Monitors are either built into the programming language, as with Java, or if the application language does not provide monitors, they are specially written.

A monitor is a special object, or "abstract data type," that can insure that only one process or thread is active in it at one time. A process enters the monitor by calling one of the monitor's methods. Once a process enters the monitor, no other process can enter until the first process exits the monitor. If another process calls one of the monitor's methods while a process is active within the monitor, the second process blocks, waiting for the first process to exit the monitor.

Since the monitor insures mutual exclusion by virtue of the fact that only one process may be active within it, the programmer using the monitor can dispense with worrying about semaphores or other mechanisms to assure mutual exclusion. In fact, the first lines of code in a monitor's method may use a semaphore internally to enforce the mutual exclusion, but the programmer need not be concerned with the mechanism.

In addition to insuring mutual exclusion, a monitor can be used to synchronize access by different threads or processes by using "condition variables" to allow a process to wait, if some condition necessary for success is absent at the time it is active in the monitor. Condition variables also allow the waiting process to be restarted when the condition changes. The two operations defined for condition variables are usually called 'wait' and signal (to reactivate).

For instance, suppose a consumer process using a monitor finds there is nothing to consume at this moment. The monitor would provide a condition variable, perhaps called itemsReady, on which the process could wait.

When a process is waiting on a condition variable within the monitor, another process may enter. In fact, if another process has been waiting for the monitor, as soon as the active process in the monitor waits for a condition variable, the process that has been waiting will gain access to the monitor and become the monitor's active process.

At some point, some cooperating process will change the condition on which another process has been waiting. For instance, a producer process will create an item that the consumer can process. When a process makes such a change, the active process will signal the condition variable. A signal will cause the monitor to reactivate one of the processes waiting (there may be more than one process waiting) on that condition variable.

Signals are not counters, as semaphores are. If a signal occurs and no process is waiting on that condition variable, nothing happens. The signal is like the old tree falling in the forest. The noise makes no difference if no one is there to hear it.

Suppose that a monitor called PC (for Producer–Consumer) is available to support a set of processes that cooperate producing items (e.g., product orders) and consuming them (e.g., making entries in shipment schedules for different distribution centers). The monitor has two methods, addOrder and retrieveOrder; addOrder takes an Order as an argument, and retrieveOrder returns an Order. The application code becomes very simple:

Producer:

```
while( true ) {
    Order newOrder = createOrder( orderNumber );
    PC.addOrder( newOrder );
}
```

Consumer:

```
while( true ) {
    Order thisOrder = PC.retrieveOrder( );
    distributeOrder( thisOrder );
}
```

The complexity of guaranteeing mutual exclusion and proper coordination is hidden in the monitor's code. While a monitor may require some thought to create, it greatly simplifies the rest of the code for the cooperating processes.

Java provides a simple and general-purpose monitor feature. Every object in Java has an associated monitor that is entered by a thread when the thread enters code that is *synchronized* on the object. If a thread attempts to enter synchronized code, and another thread already occupies the object's monitor, the thread blocks.

A block of code may be explicitly labeled as synchronized with this Java syntax:

```
synchronized( someObject ) {
    . . .
    /* Code executed within the monitor of someObject */
    . . .
}
```

As a convenience, a class in Java can also declare some of its methods to be synchronized. Such a declaration is the same as synchronizing on *this* particular instance of the class. Thus, when one thread is executing any one of the synchronized methods of the class, no other thread will be allowed to execute any synchronized method of that instance of the class, whether the same synchronized method or a different one.

Java monitors differ from the classical monitor idea in that Java monitors do not support condition variables. However, a thread can decide to wait while in the monitor, and give up the lock on the monitor while waiting, by using the synchronizing object's `wait()` method. Likewise, a thread waiting in the monitor can be awakened when another thread in the monitor uses the object's `notify()` method.

Here is an example of a class that could be used to implement a producer–consumer relationship between threads in Java. As long as the producer and consumer reference the same instance of the class PC, their interaction will occur correctly because the `putMessage` and `getMessage` methods are synchronized:

```
import java.util.*;
  public class PC {
    static final int MAXQUEUE = 5;
    private List messages = new ArrayList();
      // called by Producer
  public synchronized void putMessage(){
    while ( messages.size() >= MAXQUEUE )
      try {
        wait();
      }catch(InterruptedException e){}
    messages.add(new java.util.Date().toString());
    notify();
  }

  // called by Consumer
  public synchronized String getMessage(){
    while ( messages.size() == 0 )
      try {notify();
          wait();
      }catch(InterruptedException e){}
    String message = (String)messages.remove(0);
    notify();
    return message;
  }
}
}
```

Here is code called PC_demo, along with code for `Producer` and `Consumer` thread classes, that exercises the PC class as a monitor to synchronize activities:

```
public class PC_demo {
    public static void main(String args[]) {
        PC      monitor = new PC();
    Producer producer = new Producer( monitor );
    Consumer consumer = new Consumer( monitor );
    consumer.start();
    producer.start();
    }
}


public class Producer extends Thread {
    PC monitor;
    static final int MAXQUEUE = 5;

    Producer( PC theMonitor ) {
        monitor = theMonitor;
    }

    public void run() {
      while ( true ) {
        monitor.putMessage();
        try { Thread.sleep( 1000 );
        }catch(InterruptedException e){}
      }
    }
}


public class Consumer extends Thread {
    PC monitor;

    Consumer( PC theMonitor ) {
        monitor = theMonitor;
    }

    public void run() {
      while ( true ) {
        String newMessage = monitor.getMessage();
        System.out.println( newMessage );
      }
    }
}
```

Since every object in Java has an associated monitor, using a monitor in Java is very convenient. The trick is to be sure that all the cooperating threads are synchronizing on the same object. A frequent error by beginners is to have multiple threads synchronizing on different objects, which of course leads to failure of synchronization. In the example above, the class PC_demo creates an instance of the monitor, and then passes that same particular instance to both the Consumer and the Producer in the constructors of the Consumer and the Producer. This insures that the Consumer and Producer are synchronizing on the same object.

DEADLOCK

In the multiprocessing, multithreaded environment, conditions can occur which produce a deadlock, a conflict of needs and allocations that stops all computing. For instance, suppose processes A and B share access to files X and Y, and assume the usual case that when a process opens a file for writing, the operating system gives that process an exclusive lock on the file. Process A opens file X for writing, and then tries to open file Y for writing. Process A cannot open file Y, however, because process B has file Y open for writing, so process A blocks. Then process B tries to open file X for writing. However, process B cannot succeed because process A already has file X open. Now both processes are blocked indefinitely. A deadlock has occurred; the processes are locked in a *deadly embrace*.

Four conditions are necessary for deadlock to occur:

1 Mutual exclusion
2 Hold and wait
3 No preemption
4 Circular wait

By mutual exclusion, we mean that resources are allocated exclusively to one process or another (and throughout this discussion you can substitute "thread" for "process"). If, in the example at the start of this section, the files had been opened in shared mode, mutual exclusion would not apply, and the deadlock would not occur.

By hold and wait, we mean that a process can continue to hold exclusive access to a resource even as it waits to acquire another. If either process in the example had been compelled to release any file it had locked when it requested exclusive access to another file, the deadlock would not occur.

By no preemption, we mean that the operating system will not force the release of a resource from a blocked process in order to satisfy a demand by another process. If, in the example, the operating system had forced blocked process A to release its control of file X in order to grant access to file X to process B, the deadlock would not occur.

By circular wait, we mean that there exists some chain of processes waiting for resources such that one process waits for another, which waits for another, etc., until the last process waits for the first again. In the example, there are only two processes, and each waits for the other, so the circular wait is a short chain and easy to discern. If, on the other hand, process B blocked waiting for some resource held by process C, and C could eventually complete and release the resource required by process B, there would be no circular wait, and the deadlock would not occur.

Deadlock prevention

Deadlocks may be prevented by insuring that at least one of the conditions necessary for deadlock cannot occur. While this sounds straightforward at first, applying this idea is often impractical.

Suppose one decides to do away with mutually exclusive access to resources? What if two processes use the printer at the same time? Some real-time systems allow such things to occur because the operating system is so simplified and streamlined for real-time performance that no provision is made for exclusive access to I/O devices. The result is that the lines of output from two simultaneously executing processes get intermingled, leading to unintelligible output on the printer. In the general case, one does not have the option of doing away with mutual exclusion.

Suppose one decides to do away with hold and wait? An alternative is to require a process to request in advance all the resources it will need during the course of its execution. If it receives all the resources it needs, it proceeds; if it cannot reserve everything at once, it blocks until it can. This approach can work, but at the cost of reduced efficiency. Suppose a long-running process requires a printer only at the end of its run; the printer will be unavailable to other processes in the meantime. Some systems, especially older mainframe systems, employ this design, but most modern systems do not, for reasons of efficiency.

Suppose one decides to do away with no preemption? Alternatives providing for preemption run into the same problems as alternatives doing away with mutual exclusion. For example, it usually won't make sense to take a printer away from a process that has blocked because it's waiting for a file. The resulting intermingling of output will fail the needs of both processes.

Suppose one decides to do away with circular wait? There is a workable alternative for doing away with circular wait. The solution is to apply a numerical ordering to all the resources, and to require processes to lock resources in numerical order. For instance, suppose these resources are given this numerical ordering (the order is arbitrary):

1 File X
2 File Y
3 Printer
4 Tape drive
5 CD-ROM drive
6 Plotter

If a process needs to have exclusive access to file X and file Y, it must lock the files in that order. Likewise, if a process first locks the printer, it may not then lock either file. Having locked the printer, however, the process could still go on to lock the CD-ROM drive.

It can be shown rather easily that such a scheme will prevent circular wait. The difficulty in a general-purpose operating system is to enforce such a discipline among all the application programs. In addition, if the more abstract resources such as entries in various system tables, and individual records in files, are considered resources, the complexity of the ordering becomes much greater.

Because of these implementation problems, general-purpose operating systems do not provide such a facility for deadlock prevention. However, this principle can be of great practical value to application developers who work with complex, multithreaded applications. The application developer can impose their own ordering on the shared resources of the application (files, timers, database tables, etc.) and insure that threads or processes within the application access the resources in order. Doing so can insure that the application never deadlocks.

Deadlock avoidance

Since deadlock prevention is not, in general, practical, another approach is to have the operating system maintain a vigilance that will avoid situations where deadlock is possible. In 1965, Edgar Dijkstra published the "banker's algorithm" for deadlock avoidance.

The banker's algorithm behaves as a banker might in considering whether to grant loans. If granting a new loan would put the bank at risk of failing, should too many borrowers make demands on the bank's resources, the banker will deny the loan. Thus does the banker avoid difficulty.

The banker's algorithm requires that each process declare at the start the maximum number of resources of each type (e.g., how many printers, how many tape drives, etc.) it will require over the course of its execution. Then, whenever a process requests exclusive access to new resources, the OS simulates granting the request, and checks to see that there is some way for all processes to complete, even assuming that each process immediately requests its maximum requirement of all resources. If the check is favorable, that means that the system will remain in a "safe state," and the OS grants the resource request. Otherwise, the OS blocks the requesting process.

As appealing as the banker's blgorithm may be, it is not usually applied in practice, for several reasons. Many times, processes do not know in advance what their maximum requirement for resources will be; it depends on the results of the computation or the dynamic needs of the application. The number of processes is not fixed, either; processes can be added to the mix at any moment, rendering previous calculations of the safe state invalid. Likewise, the number of resources may change, as when a device fails or goes off-line (e.g., a printer runs out of paper).

Deadlock detection

Some systems or subsystems (e.g., database systems) implement deadlock detection. This is different from deadlock prevention and deadlock avoidance, which we have discussed and concluded are impractical in general purpose systems. On the other hand, deadlock detection can be implemented with beneficial results in some systems.

Deadlock detection works by having a deadlock detection routine run either periodically, or in response to some circumstance (e.g., low CPU utilization), to determine if a deadlock exists. Such a routine will inspect the resources allocated to each process, and examine all the pending requests by processes for additional resources.

If there is some way for all processes to have their pending requests satisfied and run to completion, then deadlock does not exist. Otherwise, deadlock does exist, and some action must be taken to break the deadlock.

The deadlock detection algorithm works by maintaining several data structures. First, the algorithm maintains a vector with the count of available resources of each type. This vector is called `Available`. If a system has seven printers, two CD-ROM drives, and six plotters, and all devices are allocated to one or another process (none is available), then the vector

```
Available = [0, 0, 0]
```

A matrix called `Allocated` records the counts of resources of each type already allocated to each active process. In a particular case of five active processes, where all of the resources listed in the previous paragraph have been allocated, the matrix `Allocated` might look like this:

Allocated			
	P	**CD**	**Plot**
P0	0	1	0
P1	2	0	0
P2	3	0	3
P2	2	1	1
P2	0	0	2

A matrix called `Requests` maintains the counts of all pending resource requests, at this particular moment, by each process. Suppose this is the matrix `Requests` for the same set of five processes at a particular instant:

Requests			
	P	**CD**	**Plot**
P0	0	0	0
P1	2	0	2
P2	0	0	0
P3	1	0	0
P4	0	0	2

With this information, the system can determine whether deadlock has occurred. All it needs to do is determine whether there is some way all processes can have their requests met, and then continue to execute. If there is some way all processes can complete, then there is no deadlock.

In this case, no resources are available; all resources are already allocated. However, P0 and P2 are not requesting any more resources. Suppose P0 and P2 run to completion; P0 will release one CD-ROM drive, and P2 will release three printers and three plotters. At that point `Available = [3, 1, 3]`. Now the requests of P1 for two more printers and two more plotters can be satisfied; P1 can complete; and P1 can return the two printers it already has, plus the two more it requested. Now `Available = [5, 1, 3]`. It's obvious that similar reasoning shows that the requests of the remaining processes can be satisfied, and therefore there is no deadlock *at this time*.

Suppose, however, that one small change is made to the matrix `Requests`. Suppose that P2 has a pending request for one plotter. Now the matrix `Requests` looks like this:

Requests			
	P	**CD**	**Plot**
P0	0	0	0
P1	2	0	2
P2	0	0	1
P3	1	0	0
P4	0	0	2

P0 can still proceed as in our earlier analysis, and when it completes it will return one CD ROM drive. Then `Available = [0, 1, 0]`. Unfortunately, there is no way to satisfy the requests of any other process, and P1, P2, P3, and P4 are deadlocked.

Deadlock recovery

Once the system detects a deadlock, the next question is what to do about it. Some resource could be preempted from one of the processes, but the operating system probably will not know the consequences of such an action.

One of the processes could be terminated, but again the consequences will probably be unknown. What if the deadlocked process had just withdrawn $1000 from a savings account, and was now blocked as it attempted to deposit that money in a checking account? One wouldn't want to terminate the process; nor would one want to restart it.

An exception might be if one of the processes were a compiler or some other process whose computation could be restarted from the beginning. Since such a process could be safely restarted, it could be terminated in order to free resources. Such action might or might not, depending on the circumstances, remove the deadlock.

Most database systems have the ability to roll back transactions that fail, and a database management system may provide for rollback in the face of deadlocked access to database tables and rows. In fact, modern database management systems are the most likely application area to find implementations of deadlock detection and recovery.

In the end, it may be best for the system to simply announce that a deadlock has occurred and let the operator take some action the operator thinks appropriate.

Deadlock detection is potentially expensive of computing time, especially if run frequently, and the question of what action to take when a deadlock occurs is usually too difficult to automate. As a result, general-purpose operating systems almost never try to manage deadlock. On the other hand, database management systems often do try to detect deadlocks and recover from them within the narrower purview of database management.

SCHEDULING

One of the very most important tasks of an operating system is to schedule processes and threads for execution. In the early days of computing, the programmer would load the program into memory somehow (front panel switches, paper tape, etc.), and then press the start button. Very soon the task of starting, interrupting, and restarting processes became the bailiwick of the OS.

The question of which task to schedule for execution at any moment has been the subject of much research and considerable design effort. The answer depends in part on the type of operating system. If the system is a batch system, the scheduling plan should optimize throughput (the number of jobs completed per hour), CPU utilization, and/or "turnaround time" (the average elapsed time between the submission of a job and its completion).

If the system is an interactive system, the scheduler should provide responsiveness and the impression of fairness to all users. Interactive systems often have less well-defined boundaries of jobs, so the criteria mentioned for batch systems are not as relevant. A more important criterion is *response time* to the user, the time delay between input from the user and some response back from the process.

If the system is a real-time system, with important constraints on execution time, the scheduler will be judged by the consistency with which applications meet their deadlines, and the predictability of performance. Some real-time systems are *hard* real-time systems, meaning that important absolute limits bound performance requirements (imagine a system that coordinates process equipment in a chemical plant). Other real-time systems are *soft* real-time systems, meaning the highest priority processes should execute as fast as possible, but absolute limits on processing time do not exist.

An important way in which schedulers differ is in whether or not the scheduler is preemptive. A preemptive scheduler can interrupt an executing process and switch to a different one. Such a change is called a "context switch," and entails a substantial amount of system overhead in changing the contents of registers, memory maps, and cache memory.

First come first served (FCFS)

Early batch systems used a simple FCFS (FCFS—also called FIFO, for first in first out) scheduling system. With FCFS, the first process to the system is scheduled, and it runs to completion or until it is blocked (e.g., for I/O). When a job completes or blocks, the next process on the waiting queue of processes is allowed to execute. As a process becomes unblocked, it goes to the end of the FCFS queue as if it had just arrived.

While simple to implement, FCFS does not perform as well as other algorithms on the measures of turnaround time and throughput, particularly when some processes are much more "compute-bound" (need extended time with the CPU for computation) and others are more "I/O-bound" (use less CPU time, but require many interruptions for I/O).

Shortest job first (SJF)

With SJF, the operating system always chooses the shortest job to execute first. The merit of this plan is that such a scheme will insure the minimum average turnaround time and the maximum average throughput (in terms of jobs per hour).

The challenge is to know in advance which job is the shortest! The usual solution to this problem of estimation is to require the user to declare the maximum execution time of the job. Since shorter jobs get executed first, the user is motivated to provide an estimate that is only as large as necessary. However, if the job exceeds the estimate provided by the user, the job is simply terminated, and the user learns to estimate more accurately in the future.

Shortest remaining job first (SRJF)

SRJF is a preemptive version of SJF. When a new process becomes ready, the operating system inspects both the newly ready process and the currently executing process, and chooses the process with the least time remaining to run. If the new process will complete more quickly than the one that was interrupted, the new process is scheduled to execute.

Round robin (RR)

Round robin scheduling is frequently used in interactive systems. As the name implies, each process is given a share of time with the CPU, and then the next process gets a turn. RR scheduling came into widespread use with timesharing systems, beginning in the mid 1960s.

Each unit of time allocation is called a "timeslice" or "quantum." RR schedulers can be tuned by changing the value of the quantum. If the quantum is sufficiently large, the system effectively becomes FCFS. With a smaller quantum, the system interleaves ready processes giving the illusion of simultaneous computation. If the value of the quantum is too small, the overhead of context switching among the processes can hurt overall system throughput (however measured). Most RR schedulers use a quantum value of 20 to 50 ms (Tanenbaum, Andrew, *Modern Operating Systems*, Saddle River, NJ, Prentice Hall, 2001).

Priority based

Scheduling based strictly on process priorities is characteristic of real-time systems. The ready process with the highest priority is always the process chosen to execute. Usually real-time schedulers are also preemptive, so any time a higher priority process becomes ready, a context switch occurs and the higher priority process is dispatched.

Priority-based scheduling is also used in other contexts. For instance, a system may use priority-based scheduling, but decrement a process's priority for every quantum of CPU time the process is granted. This is one way to implement a RR scheme, but using priorities instead of position in a queue to choose the process to execute.

More commonly today, a system will implement multiple queues with different queue priorities, and then schedule processes from the highest priority queue that has processes ready to run. The scheduling rule within a particular queue may be RR or something else.

Starvation (withholding of CPU access) is always a possibility with any priority-based scheme. A system that is at saturation (i.e., full capacity) will not be successful with any priority system. Imagine an airport commanded to handle more air traffic than it can accommodate. One can give priority for landing to those short of fuel, but if, in a given period of time, there are more airplanes to land than the airport can accommodate, very soon all the aircraft in the sky will be short of fuel.

Multilevel queues

A simple example of multiple queues with different priorities is a system where processes are classified as interactive "foreground" processes and batch "background" processes. As long as there are foreground processes ready to run, the system uses RR to share the CPU among the foreground processes. Only when all the foreground processes terminate or are blocked does the system choose a process from among the background processes to run. To keep things simple and minimize context-switching overheads, the system might use FCFS to schedule the background tasks.

Multilevel feedback queues

A more complex and dynamic use of multiple queues of different priorities uses experience with the executing processes to move interactive processes to a higher-priority queue, and batch or CPU-bound processes to a lower-priority queue. A process which proves to be a heavy user of the CPU gets moved to a background queue, and a process which blocks often for I/O (and is likely, therefore, to be an interactive process) gets moved to a foreground queue. Foreground queues will use RR schedulers, and higher-priority foreground queues will use smaller timeslices. Background queues may be scheduled FCFS and background processes, when finally scheduled, may enjoy longer intervals of CPU time, so that once the low-priority jobs get the CPU, they can finish.

Any specific implementation of a scheduler is usually based on a combination of scheduling strategies. For instance, traditional UNIX scheduling used multiple queues. System functions like swapping processes and manipulating files ran in higher-priority queues, and user programs ran in the user process queue. User process priorities were adjusted once a second. Processes that proved to be CPU-bound had their priorities lowered, and processes that proved to be I/O-bound had their priorities raised. The effect was to give preference to interactive processes, which were I/O-bound serving users at terminals (Stallings, William, *Operating Systems: Internals and Design Principles*, 5ed, Saddle River, NJ, Prentice Hall, 2005).

On the other hand, Hewlett Packard's Real-Time Executive (RTE) of the 1980s used a strictly priority-based real-time scheduler. There were 32,767 different priority levels (something of an over-supply of priority levels!), and whichever ready process had the highest priority was the one that was dispatched.

MEMORY MANAGEMENT

The operating system is responsible for assigning to processes memory in which to execute. In fact, the operating system is responsible for managing a whole array of memories in support of processes, principally main memory, cache memory, and disk memory.

To set the stage for this discussion, recall that the computer must have a prepared sequence of machine language instructions before a program can be executed. The programmer writes in source code and submits the source code to the compiler. The compiler translates the source code to machine language, but since the compiler has no way of knowing which address in any particular computer is the first available address (lower memory may be occupied by operating-system code or another process), the compiler starts putting variables and instructions at address zero. The file the compiler creates is called a *relocatable* file, because the addresses in the file still need to be adjusted (relocated) before the code can be executed.

One approach to adjusting the relocatable addresses is to have the loader add the offset of the first available memory location to all the addresses in the relocatable file. For example, if the compiler creates variable X at location 100, and the first available memory for a user program is at location 1112, then the loader can adjust the address of X in the *executable* file (machine code file) to be 1112 + 100.

In early computers without multiprogramming capability, a process executable, or "image," was first created by the loader. Then the image was loaded into memory, executed, terminated, and removed from memory. One could execute a second program only after the first was completed.

MEMORY MANAGEMENT WITH MULTIPROGRAMMING

With multiprogramming came more sophisticated memory management. More than one program could be in memory at one time, and it became important that an executing process did not change the contents of memory devoted to the operating system itself, or of memory belonging to another process.

The solution in the mid-1960s and 1970s was to use two registers whose contents would be set by the operating system just prior to turning execution over to the user process. One register was called the "base" or "relocation" register, and it held the starting address of the memory allocated to the process. The other register was called the "limit" register, and it held the maximum size of the program.

Each time a process accessed memory, the computer hardware (called the *memory management unit* (MMU)) would check the address to make sure it was less than the limit register contents. If not, the MMU would *trap* the error and generate an interrupt (an interrupt caused by software is called a trap) that would activate the operating system in kernel mode. Then the OS could deal with the problem, probably by generating a *memory protection* error and terminating the offending process.

On the other hand, in the usual case where the address was within legal range, the MMU hardware would add the contents of the relocation register to the address. The sum would then be the correct physical address for the program executing on this machine at this time, and the access would proceed. Having an MMU with a relocation register meant that a program could be loaded into one part of memory at time 1, and into a different part of memory at time 2. The only change between times would be to the contents of the relocation register.

The *part of memory* concept became more sophisticated over time. Initially, memory was divided into partitions of fixed sizes when the operating system was installed or generated (called a *system generation* or "sysgen"). A program could run in any partition big enough to accommodate it.

Later, operating systems gained the feature of being able to support dynamic memory partitions of varying sizes. This complicated the operating system's task of tracking and controlling memory usage, but it increased flexibility. The operating system would maintain a list or bit-map of memory allocations and free memory. When a program became ready to run, the operating system would find a big enough block of memory to accommodate the program, and then dispatch the program to that chunk of memory.

In a dynamic multiprogramming environment, with processes of different sizes starting and terminating all the time, it became important to make wise choices about how to allocate memory. It was all too easy to end up with processes scattered throughout memory, with small unallocated blocks of memory between, and no blocks of memory large enough to run another program. For example, a ready program might require 12K of space, and there might be more than that much unused memory, but the unused memory might be scattered widely, with no one block being 12K or larger.

Unusable memory scattered between allocated partitions is called "external fragmentation." On the other hand, unused memory within an allocated block is called "internal fragmentation." Internal fragmentation results because the OS allocates memory in rather large units, usually in "pages" of 1024 to 4096 memory addresses at a time. Almost always the last page allocated to a process is not entirely used, and so the unused portion constitutes internal fragmentation.

Unused memory blocks are called "holes," and much research was devoted to finding the most efficient way to allocate memory to processes. The "best fit" approach sought the smallest hole that was big enough for the new process. As desirable as that approach sounds, it did require the OS to look at every hole, or to keep the holes in order sorted by size, so that it could find the best fitting hole for a new process.

Another approach was called "first fit," and, as it sounds, first fit accepted the first hole that was large enough, regardless of whether there might be another hole that fit even better. The thought in favor of first fit was that it would execute more quickly.

Believe it or not, another contending algorithm was "worst-fit." The argument for worst fit was that it would leave the largest remaining hole, and hence might reduce the problem of external fragmentation. As a matter of fact, the research showed worst fit lived up to its name, and was worse than best fit and first fit.

TIMESHARING AND SWAPPING

Timesharing systems exposed the need to move a partially complete process out of main memory when the process was forced to wait for the impossibly slow (in computer time) user at a terminal. Even an actively typing user might cause the process to wait for the equivalent of 1000 instructions between typed characters.

The solution was called "swapping." When a process blocked for I/O, it became eligible to be swapped to the disk. If another process were ready to use the memory allocated to the blocked process, the OS simply copied the entire contents of the blocked process's memory, as well as the CPU register contents, to a temporary "scratch" or "swap" area on the disk.

Since the process state at the time of the swap included the values of the registers and the values of the variables, the OS had to save the image of the executing process. Later, when the I/O completed, the OS could decide to bring the swapped process back into memory, and it was essential that the interrupted image be brought back. The OS could not bring in an original copy of the program from the original executable file, because the original executable file would not have the current values for the registers or variables.

Most general-purpose operating systems today continue to use swapping as part of a more sophisticated virtual memory management capability.

VIRTUAL MEMORY

The concept of *virtual memory* further separated the concepts of logical address and physical address. The logical address is the address as known to the program and the programmer; the physical address is the actual address known to the computer memory hardware. The relocation register was the first mechanism we discussed by which a logical address (the relocatable address) was converted into a different physical address.

Virtual memory completely separates the concepts of logical and physical memory. Logical addresses can be much, much greater than the maximum physical memory. With virtual memory, an entire program need not be in memory during execution, only the part of the program currently executing. Also, memory allocated to a program need not be contiguous, and instead can be scattered about, wherever available memory exists.

Many advantages attend virtual memory and justify its complexity. Most importantly, programmers can ignore physical memory limitations. This greatly simplifies software development. Virtual memory also allows a greater degree of multiprogramming, which can improve CPU utilization. More processes can be in memory ready to run, because each process can occupy much less memory than its full program size would otherwise require. Virtual memory also facilitates sharing of memory between processes, for purposes of sharing either code or data.

Virtual memory is implemented using demand paging or segmentation, or both. By far the more common approach is demand paging.

Paging

A paging system divides main memory, physical memory, into blocks called frames. The size of a frame is some power of 2 (for reasons that will become clear), and systems have implemented frames of sizes from 512 bytes to 64K. A typical size is 4K (1024 addresses in a system with a 32-bit, or 4-byte, word size).

A paging system divides logical memory into "pages" of the same size as the frames. When the operating system needs to allocate memory to a process, it selects one or more empty frames, and maps the process pages to the frames by means of a "page table."

The page table for a process has an entry for each page in the process' logical address space. When the process requires access to memory, the system inspects the logical address to determine which page it references. Then the system consults the page table entry for that logical page to learn what frame in physical memory the process is referencing. Finally, the system executes the reference to the proper physical memory location in the appropriate frame.

Making the frame and page size a power of 2 speeds the process, because it means that the logical address can be conveniently split into two fields, a "page number" and an "offset." The page number can become a quick index into the process page table, and the offset remains simply the address of the reference within the page/frame.

For instance, if a 32-bit system (addresses are 32 bits long) has a frame size of 4K, it means that 12 bits of the address are required for the offset within the page ($2^{12} = 4096$ bytes on a page). The low-order (least significant) 12 bits of the address become the offset, and the high-order (most significant) 20 bits become the page number.

Suppose the process references memory location 1424. Since that number is less than 4096, the reference is to page 0, the first page. The number 1424 represented as a 32-bit binary number is the following (for readability, the address is broken into bytes, and the page number field is underlined):

00000000 00000000 00000101 10010000

Notice that the high-order 20 bits are all zeros, so this logical address is on page 0, the first page.

Suppose instead that the process references memory location 10304. Since the page size is 4096, this reference is to a location on the third page, page 2 (remember that the first page was page 0). The number 10304 in binary is the following:

```
00000000  00000000  00101000  01000000
```

The high-order 20 bits now create the binary number 2, so this reference is to page 2. The offset within the page is given by the low-order 12 bits as 2112 (the sum of 2048 and 64 from bits 11 and 6; remember, the first bit is bit 0). Multiplying the page number (2) by the page size (4096) gives 8192, and adding the offset of 2112 gives 10304, the original address. Isn't that clever?

Now imagine how this works with a page table. The page address becomes an index into the page table. The entry in the page table contains the physical frame number. The system simply substitutes the contents of the page table entry, which is the physical frame number, for the page field of the address, and the result is a complete physical address.

Suppose that the frame allocated for page 2 (the third page) of the process is frame 9. The page table entry for page 2 would be the following (remember, there are only 20 bits for the frame address):

```
00000000  00000000  1001
```

Now the memory reference to location 10304 will result in the frame address of 9 being substituted for the page address of 2, and the resulting physical address will be this address, which is located in frame 9:

```
00000000  00000000  10011000  01000000
```

The physical address is 38976, in the 10th frame (again, the first frame is frame 0). Figure 6-1 shows a representation of the page table for a process. Note that the pages of memory allocated to the process need not be contiguous. The operating system can assign any free frame of memory to a process simply by including the frame in the page table for the process.

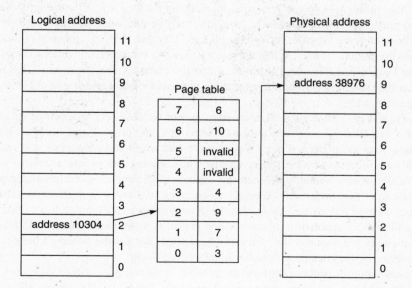

Figure 6-1   Mapping logical address 10304 to physical address 38976 using the page table.

Virtual Memory using Paging

A virtual memory operating system that uses paging will map into the process's page table only those pages of logical memory necessary for the process at a particular time. When a process starts, the OS will map in some number of pages to start. This number of pages is determined by an algorithm that takes into account the number of other processes running, the amount of physical memory in the machine, and other factors.

In addition to a frame number, a page table entry also includes several important status bits. In particular, a bit will indicate whether the page mapping is "valid." When the OS maps in several frames for a process, the process's code and data are copied into the frames, the frame numbers are written into the several page table entries, and the valid bits for those entries are set to "valid." Other entries in the page table, for which no mapping to frames has been made, will have the valid bit set to "invalid."

As long as the process continues to reference memory that is mapped through the page table, the process continues to execute. However, when the process references a memory location that is not mapped through the page table, the fact that the valid bit for that page is set to "invalid" will cause the reference to generate a "page fault." A page fault causes a trap to the operating system, and the operating system must handle the page fault by:

1 Locating the required page of code or data from the process image
2 Finding an unused memory frame
3 Copying the required code or data to the frame
4 Adding a mapping of the new frame to the process's page table
5 Setting the valid bit in the new page table entry to valid
6 Restarting the instruction which faulted

The processing of a page fault can also be more complex, as when all memory is allocated, and some previously allocated page mapping must be replaced. Also, because of the wait for disk I/O in reading the process image into memory, it's likely that another process will be scheduled while the disk I/O completes.

Virtual Memory Problems and Solutions

It's fine that each process has a page table mapping its logical address space to physical memory. However, there are additional problems to solve in real systems, in order to make virtual memory systems work well.

First, every reference to memory first requires a reference to the page table, which is also in memory. Right away, even when there is no page fault, using a page table cuts the speed of access to memory by a factor of 2.

A solution to this problem is to use an *associative memory* called a *translation lookaside buffer* (TLB). An associative memory is a small, expensive, "magic" piece of hardware that can perform a whole set of comparisons (usually 64 or fewer) at once. As a process is executing, the TLB, which is part of the MMU, maintains the recently accessed page table entries. When the process makes a reference to memory, the MMU submits the page number to the TLB, which immediately returns either the frame for that page, or a "TLB miss." If the TLB reports a miss, then the system must read the page table in memory, and replace one of the entries in the TLB with the new page table entry.

Virtual memory, and particularly the TLB speedup, works because real programs display the property of *locality*. That is, for extended portions of a process's execution, the process will access a small subset of its logical address space. Real programs use loops, for example, and arrays and collections, and real programs make reference repeatedly to addresses in the same vicinity. Thus, having immediate access to a relatively small number of pages of the process's total logical address space is sufficient to maintain efficiency of execution.

A second problem is that page tables themselves become very bulky in modern systems. Our example, which was realistic, showed 20 bits being used for the page number in a 32-bit address. That means that each process has a logical address space of over one million pages. If a page table entry is 32 bits (typical today), then 4 Mbytes of memory are required for each running process, just for the process's page table! Imagine the problem with the newer 64-bit machines—even imagining is difficult!

One widely used solution is the multilevel page table, a nested page table. To return to our example, suppose we break the 20-bit page address into two 10-bit fields. Ten bits will represent 1024 entities. The first 10-bit field will be an index into the "top-level" page table, and the second 10-bit field will be an index into a "second-level" page table. There can be 1024 second-level page tables, each with 1024 entries, so all one million pages in the logical address space can still be mapped.

However, almost no program requires the full million-page logical address space. The beauty of the multilevel page table is that the OS does not need to devote space to page table entries that will never be used. Each second-level page table can represent 1024 pages, and if each page is 4K, then each second-level page table can represent 4 Mbytes of address space.

For example, as I write, *Microsoft Word* is using almost 11 Mbytes of memory. That much memory could be mapped with only three second-level page tables. The sum of entries from the top-level page table and three second-level page tables is 4096. If each entry is 32 bits (4 bytes), then the page table space required for *Word* is 16K, not the 4 Mbytes required to represent the entire logical address space. Depending on the actual locations being referenced, the OS may in fact require more than the minimum number of second-level page tables to manage the mappings, but the improvement in memory utilization by means of the nested page table is still apt to be two orders of magnitude.

With the introduction of 64-bit computers, a new solution to the problem of large page tables is being implemented. This approach is called the *inverted page table*. The page table as we have discussed it so far has one entry for each page of logical memory. Flipping this idea on its head, the inverted page table has one entry for each frame of physical memory. And, instead of storing a physical frame number, the inverted page table stores a logical page number.

Since the number of frames of physical memory is likely to be much smaller than the number of pages of logical memory in a 64-bit computer (with 4K pages, 2^{52} = way too many logical pages to contemplate—millions of billions), the page table size remains reasonable.

Each entry in the inverted page table contains a process identifier and a logical page number. When a process accesses memory, the system scans the inverted page table looking for a match of process ID and logical page number. Since each entry in the inverted page table corresponds to a physical frame, when the system finds a match, the index into the inverted page table becomes the frame number for the actual memory reference. For instance, if a match occurs in the 53rd entry (entry 52, since the first entry is entry 0) of the inverted page table, then the frame for physical memory is frame 52. The system adds the offset within the page to the frame number of 52, and the physical address is complete.

The inverted page table keeps the size of the page table reasonable. Note, too, that there is only one page table for the whole system—not one page table per process. The only problem is that searching through the page table for a match on process ID and logical page number can require many memory references itself. Once again, the TLB delivers a workable solution. Programs still show strong locality, so the TLB continues to resolve most address lookups at high speed. TLB misses do require a lengthy search, but engineering means making sensible tradeoffs.

Finally on the subject of page tables, page table entries have additional status bits associated with them. Earlier we mentioned the valid bit, used for signaling whether the page was in memory or not. In addition, read and write permission bits allow the system to provide protection to the contents of memory, page by page.

There are also bits to indicate whether the page has been accessed and whether it has been modified. When it comes time to replace the mapping of one page with another, the accessed bit allows the OS to replace a page that isn't being accessed very often instead of one which is.

The modified bit also helps during page replacement decisions. Other things being equal, it makes more sense to replace a page that has not been modified, because the contents of memory don't need to be written to disk as the page is replaced; nothing has been changed. On the other hand, a modified, or "dirty," page will need to be written to disk to store the changes before its memory can be reallocated.

Page Replacement Algorithms

When a process needs a page that is not yet mapped into memory, and another page must be replaced to accommodate that, the OS must decide which page to sacrifice. Much research and experimentation have gone into creating efficient algorithms for replacing pages in memory. As an example, we will discuss the "clock" or "second chance" algorithm.

The clock algorithm uses the Referenced bits in the page table, and a pointer into the page table. Every read or write to a page of memory sets the Referenced bit for the page to 1. On every clock tick interrupt to the system, the OS clears the Referenced bit in every page table entry. The system also maintains a pointer, the "clock hand," that points to one of the page table entries, and the system treats the page table as a circular list of pages.

When a page fault occurs and one of the mapped pages must be replaced, the system checks the page table entry pointed to by the clock hand. If the Referenced bit for that page is 0, it means that the page has not been referenced since the last clock tick. In that case, that page of memory is written to the disk, if necessary (if it's "dirty"), and that frame of memory is reallocated for the new page.

On the other hand, if the Referenced bit for the page pointed to by the clock hand is 1, it means that the page has been accessed recently. Since recently accessed pages are more likely to be accessed in the near future, it would be unwise to replace a recently used page. So the clock algorithm sets the Reference bit for the page to 0, and moves to the next entry in the list. It continues in this manner until it finds an entry whose Referenced bit is 0, and in that case it reallocates the frame for new use with the new page.

The clock algorithm is also called the "second chance" algorithm because sometimes a page comes up for a second chance to be sacrificed. If the Referenced bits are set for all pages, then the pointer eventually will point to the page it started with. Since it cleared the Referenced bit for this page the first time around, on the second chance the page will be selected for replacement.

FILE SYSTEMS

The file system is one of the most visible facilities of an operating system. Since the early days of operating systems, the OS has provided a permanent means to store information. A file collects related information together and provides access to the information via the name of the file. Over time, many file *types* have been developed to suit different purposes.

Just as files organize information, file directories organize files. Today it seems almost beyond question that file directories should be of "tree" form, but that wasn't always true.

File Types

A widely used file type is the fixed-length record file. The file consists of *records*, or rows, each of which contains values for each of the *fields* of a record. This form was natural, especially in the days of punched cards. When one visualized a record, one saw in one's mind's eye a punched card. The card's 80 columns were divided into sets of columns (fields), where the values of the fields were punched. Such a conception of information storage seems natural for many purposes. Imagine your holiday greeting card list as a fixed-length record file, where each record represents a person, and each person record has a field for name, for street address, for city, etc.

An advantage of fixed-length record files is that the system can easily calculate exactly where information exists. If the user requests the 3rd field from the 57th record, simple arithmetic will provide the exact location of the information.

A problem with fixed-length record files is that often field values are naturally of varying length, and to make the file a fixed-length record file, the designer must make each field big enough to accommodate the largest value. Since most records do not need all the space, space will be wasted most of the time.

Another file type is the variable-length record file. In this case, each record consists of the same set of fields, but the fields can be of varying length (including zero length). While a variable-length record file fits the use of storage to the data, its format must provide the information about the size of each field in each record. This wastes some space, and it adds an overhead during reading and writing.

A special type of file is an "indexed-sequential file." Its special structure is designed to promote fast searches of a large file. The records in the main file are sorted by the value of the "key" field. In addition, the file system associates with the main file a much smaller file of pointers to records in the main file.

Suppose the indexed-sequential file contains records for a million people, and suppose that the key field, the field that uniquely identifies each record, is a *social security number* (SSN) field. The records in the file are ordered by SSN. Without indexing, finding any particular person would require, on average, reading 500,000 records (half of them).

However, now suppose that the associated indexing file has 1000 entries; each entry consists only of a SSN and a pointer to the record in the main file with that SSN. To find a person, the system will read the indexing file to find the indexing record with a value for SSN that is largest, but still less than or equal to the SSN being sought. Using the pointer from the indexing record, the system can now read the main file starting from a point near the record being sought. On average, the system will make 500 reads of the indexing file followed by 500 reads of the main file (one million records divided among 1000 index values means 1000 records per index, and on average the system must read half of them). So, indexing reduces the number of reads from 500,000 to 1000—improvement by a factor of 500.

Files may contain information in both character form (ASCII, UNICODE, or EBCDIC) and binary form. Executable files, for example, are binary files in the special format required by the operating system. Executable files are process images ready to be brought in from the disk, stored in memory, and executed.

UNIX takes the unique approach that any file is just a stream of bytes. If there's any structure to the information in the file, it's up to the application program to create the structure, and later to interpret it. In some applications this shifts some responsibility away from the file system manager to the application, but it is a simple, consistent conception.

File System Units

The file system relies on the disk hardware, of course. Disks almost always transfer multiples of a 512-byte *sector*. Even if your program tries to read a street address that is no more than 25 characters long, the disk will actually return to the operating system at least one sector, and somewhere within will be the street address. The sector is the unit of storage for the disk hardware.

Usually the file system has a larger unit of storage than the sector. This minimum storage allocation for a file is called a *block* or *cluster*. Even a file consisting of a single character will require one cluster of space on the disk. The file system tracks free clusters, and allocates clusters of space to files as necessary. The wasted space within a file due to unused space in the last cluster is internal fragmentation with respect to the file system.

Directories and Directory Entries

Today almost all operating systems represent the file system organization as a tree of directories and subdirectories. The directory entry for a file will contain information such as the file name, permissions, time of last access, time of last modification, owner, file size, and location of the data on the disk.

When a file is opened by a process, information from the directory is copied to an in-memory data structure often called a *file control block* or an *open file descriptor*. In addition to the information from the directory entry, the file control block may have information about read and write locks on the file, and the current state of the file (open or closed, for reading or writing).

An interesting approach taken by UNIX was to make directories files. A directory is just a file that contains information about files. This sort of stunningly simple consistency is part of the charm of UNIX for its admirers.

File Space Allocation

There are several general approaches to allocating file space. One is *contiguous* allocation. With this conceptually simple approach, the file system allocates adjacent blocks or clusters for the entire file. Contiguous allocation has the merits that writing to and reading from the file are fast, because all the information is in the same place on the disk. Some real-time systems and high-speed data acquisition systems use contiguous file allocation for the reason of speed.

One of the problems with contiguous allocation is that external fragmentation of the file system becomes a problem very quickly. The system must deliver a potentially large set of blocks to any new file, and the free space between existing files may be unusable because each is, in itself, too small. Another problem is that extending a file can be impossible due to lack of available space between allocations.

Another type of allocation is *linked* allocation of file space. Each block in a file is linked to the next and the previous with pointers. This removes any requirement for contiguous allocation, eliminates external fragmentation as a cause of wasted space, and permits extending files at any time. The starting block of a file is all the system needs to know, and from there the system can follow the links between blocks. Free space can be maintained likewise in a linked list of blocks.

There are some disadvantages of linked allocation. First, access to random records in the file is not possible directly. If an application needs the 57th record in a file using linked allocation, the system will have to read through the first 56 records to get to the 57th. It's also true that the pointers take up some space in the file system; that's overhead, although bits on the disk are cheap these days. Finally, if the blocks of a file really are scattered all over the disk, accessing the file contents will be slowed by all the mechanical delays of positioning the read/write heads again and again.

Windows uses linked file allocation, and the "defragmentation" exercise brings the dispersed blocks of files together so that access will be faster. When the linked blocks are in fact adjacent to one another, reads and writes occur faster.

A third approach to file allocation is *indexed* allocation, championed by UNIX. With indexed allocation, the file directory entry has pointers to the blocks containing the information in the file. The blocks need not be contiguous, and files can be extended by adding blocks at any time. Another advantage of indexed allocation is that the locations of all the blocks in the file can be determined from the directory entry, so random access is possible. A disadvantage is that any corruption of the directory entry can make it impossible to recover the information in the file.

In UNIX a file directory entry is called an i-node or inode, for index-node. Among other things, the inode contains pointers to the file blocks, permissions, ownership information, and times of last access and modification.

Since directories are just files in UNIX, each directory has an inode, too. When a program opens a file like /usr/work.txt, the system locates the inode for the root directory (almost always set to inode 2), and then reads the blocks of the root directory looking for something called "usr." When it finds "usr," it will also find the inode for "usr." Then it can read the file that is the directory "usr" and look for something called "work.txt." When it finds "work.txt," it will also find the inode for "work.txt." From the inode of "work.txt" the system will find pointers to all the blocks of the file.

Journaling File Systems

Some newer file systems incorporate *logging* or *journaling* of file system transactions. A transaction is a series of changes that must either all be successful, or none be successful.

For example, if one moves a file from one location to another (cut and paste), the new file directory entry must be written and the old file directory entry must be erased. Both actions must occur, or neither must occur.

A journaling file system first writes any intended changes to a "write-ahead" log file. Then it makes the required changes to the file system. If the changes to the file system fail for some reason (e.g., a total system failure at just the wrong moment), the file system can either recover the changes by redoing the transaction, or roll back the changes to the original state.

The Windows *NT File System* (NTFS) incorporates journaling features, and so does Sun's UFS and Apple's Mac OS X. There are also several journaling file systems available for Linux.

SUMMARY

Operating systems are programs designed to make the use of the computer hardware easier, more efficient, and more secure. They manage the scheduling of processes, the allocation of memory and other resources to processes, and all input and output of data. In addition, operating systems provide a file system for managing programs and data, and various system software utilities for facilitating program development and execution.

There are several varieties of operating systems, including interactive, batch, and real time. Each is designed to best meet the peculiar requirements of its intended use.

Most modern operating systems support the concept of threads in addition to processes. A process represents a set of resources such as memory, open files, common variables, network connections, etc., and a thread represents a particular path of code execution. Threading allows for easy sharing of resources among the threads, which are essentially separate cooperating tasks.

Multiprogramming, multiprocessing, and multithreading require careful consideration of thread and process synchronization techniques. These same operating system advances also introduce the possibility of deadlock. For process synchronization, most operating systems provide semaphores, a simple, effective construct first proposed by Edgar Dijkstra in 1965.

The four conditions necessary for deadlock to occur are: mutual exclusion, hold and wait, no preemption, and circular wait. Avoiding deadlocks, or detecting and correcting them, turns out to be costly of performance and difficult to implement in the general case. We discussed various mechanisms for preventing deadlocks, and we discussed the banker's algorithm for deadlock avoidance.

Today most general-purpose operating systems employ paged virtual memory. A page is a unit of logical address space, and a frame is a same-size unit of physical memory. By means of a page table data structure, which maps pages to frames, the operating system maps logical addresses to physical addresses. The advantages of virtual memory include a very large logical address space, and a higher degree of multiprogramming.

The file system is a very visible feature of any operating system. We discussed various file management systems, including systems based on linked allocation of file blocks and systems based on indexed allocation of file blocks. Newer file systems are incorporating journaling of transactions in order to better insure file system stability.

REVIEW QUESTIONS

6.1   What is the advantage of managing I/O with interrupts? If an active typist is typing 30 words per minute into a word processor, and the computer operates at one million machine instructions per second, how many machine instructions can be executed in the time it takes a character to be typed on the keyboard?

6.2   Explain why a DMA channel would or would not be useful in a computer without an interrupt-based I/O system.

6.3   What scheduling concept was critical to the development of timesharing computers, and has remained an important part of scheduling for interactive computer systems?

6.4   Categorize the following programs as system software or application software, and explain your categorization:
   • Java Virtual Machine
   • Excel
   • PowerPoint
   • C compiler
   • C library
   • Oracle database management system
   • Employee payroll system
   • Web browser
   • Media player
   • Control panel
   • E-mail client

6.5   Why is it that threads are faster to create than processes?

6.6   What advantage do kernel threads provide over user threads? Give an example of a user thread package.

6.7   When a process is multithreaded, which of these resources are shared among the threads, and which are private to each thread?
   • Memory
   • Program counter
   • Global variables
   • Open files
   • Register contents
   • Stack/local/automatic variables

6.8   List four events that transfer control to the operating system in privileged mode.

6.9   How can a semaphore be used to insure that Process First will complete before Process Second executes?

6.10 Describe how transaction logging might apply to a file system, and give an example of a file system that employs transaction logging.

6.11 If a memory access requires 100 nanoseconds, and the computer uses a page table and virtual memory, how long does it take to read a word of program memory?

6.12 If we add a TLB to the computer in the previous question, and 80 percent of the time the page table entry is in the TLB (i.e., the required memory access results in a "hit" in the TLB 80 percent of the time), on average, how long does it take to read a word of program memory?

6.13 A paging system uses pages with 1024 addresses per page. Given the following page table:

Page	Frame
0	4
1	10
2	6
3	7
4	5

What are the physical addresses corresponding to the following logical addresses?

Logical address
    0
  430
2071
4129
5209

6.14 Why do virtual memory systems include a modified bit in the page table entry?

6.15 Why would fixed-length record files be a good choice for storing data from database tables?

6.16 How would you expect process scheduling policies to be different on batch computing systems and interactive systems?

6.17 How would you measure the success of a batch operating system? Would you measure the success of an interactive system like Unix or Windows the same way? If not, how would you measure the success of an interactive operating system?

CHAPTER 7

Networking

INTRODUCTION

If you were to ask someone what invention of the 20th century had the most impact on the way in which people live their lives, a person might answer by saying, "computers." Clearly the computer and the application of computing technology have had a significant impact on the lives of people. One of the technologies that has benefited from computing technology is communications. Today we take for granted the fact that almost all of the computing devices that we own are often connected together, exchange information, and function cooperatively to make our lives easier.

A *computer network* is a group of computers that use common protocols to exchange information and share resources. The computers in a network communicate in a variety of ways. Some of the computers may communicate using electromagnetic signals transmitted over traditional copper wires or light being sent through fiber-optic cables. Others may communicate using radio, satellite, or microwaves. Two computers can communicate even if they are not directly connected. They can utilize a third computer to relay information.

In the context of a computer network, a *protocol* is a formal description of the message formats and the rules the machines in the network follow to exchange messages. Think about using a telephone to communicate with a friend. There are two aspects to the call: establishing the connection that makes it possible to talk, and the rules, or the protocol, you use once the connection is established.

Establishing the telephone connection consists first of dialing the number. Then the person you called answers, "Hello," and then you say, "Hi, this is George." Your connection is established.

The protocol following a connection on the phone is for one person to speak, and then the other. If two people speak at once, we expect both to stop speaking, and then listen for the other to begin again, after a short interval. Computer protocols are sometimes quite analogous to such human behavior.

Computer networks can be classified based on their size. A small network that connects computers contained in a single room, floor, or a single building is called a *local area network* (LAN). LANs have become very commonplace, and you may have a LAN in your home. A LAN is typically owned by an individual and connects computers that are relatively close together.

A *wide area network* (WAN) covers a large geographical distance. For example a WAN may span several cities, several states, or an entire country. A WAN, unlike a LAN, is typically owned and maintained by an organization and has the capacity to carry large amounts of data.

To understand the difference between a LAN and a WAN, consider for a moment the pipes that carry water to your house. Inside a typical home, water is carried in pipes that are from one-half to three-quarters of an inch in diameter. The pipes are part of the house, and if one springs a leak, the owner of the house is responsible for fixing the problem. The pipes buried under the street that supply the water to your house, however, are owned by the town in which you live and if they spring a leak, the town is responsible for making the repair.

Furthermore these pipes are typically much larger (some may be more than a foot in diameter), and because they connect many homes, have the capacity to deliver more water than the pipes in your home.

Computer networks that most people use on a daily basis appear to span the globe. In reality, most computer networks consist of smaller networks, which are in turn connected together to form larger networks. An internetwork, or *Internet*, is formed when two networks are connected together. In an internet the networks are not connected directly, but instead are connected using a computer that is connected to each of the individual networks. This common machine is referred to as a *gateway* or *router*, and passes information between the two networks.

In this chapter we will take a look at computer networks. We will learn how they are organized, how they work, and some of the applications they can provide.

REFERENCE MODEL

As with any complicated technology, networks are often divided into a number of layers in order to make it easier to understand how they work and to make them easier to build. Each layer is responsible for a different part of the communication process. One of the advantages of using layers is that in order to use a layer you do not need to understand how it works inside, you simply need to know what services it provides and how to ask for them. For example, consider making a call on a cell phone. You only need to know how to make the call and how to speak into the phone. You do not have to understand the technical mechanisms that convert your voice into a form suitable for transmission using public airwaves.

Several reference models have been developed to define a standard way to split the functionality of a network into a series of layers. This layered approach has resulted in casual talk of "the network protocol **stack**." The reference model most commonly used in networking was developed by the *International Standards Organization* (ISO) and is called the *Open Systems Interconnection* (OSI) model, or the ISO OSI model (How's that for acronym reuse!?). The OSI model consists of seven layers as shown in Fig. 7-1.

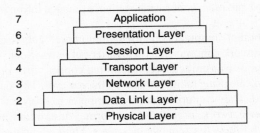

7	Application
6	Presentation Layer
5	Session Layer
4	Transport Layer
3	Network Layer
2	Data Link Layer
1	Physical Layer

Figure 7-1   ISO OSI reference model.

The physical layer is responsible for the transmission of a bit stream between two or more machines. You could think of the physical layer as a pipe through which individual bits flow. The basic objective of the physical layers is to make sure that when a "1" is sent, the other side receives a "1." The physical layer defines a medium through which messages can be sent.

The services provided by the physical layer are not that different from the services provided by the post office. When you send a letter using standard first-class mail, the post office promises that it will attempt to deliver the letter, but it provides no guarantees. In most cases the letter will arrive at the intended destination, but there are times when the letter may be lost. In those cases where you require reliable mail delivery, you might send a letter using a higher-level service like registered mail.

The data link layer uses the physical layer to provide reliable point-to-point delivery within a network. While the underlying physical layer may not be entirely error free, the data link layer transforms the connection into a facility that appears free of errors. It does this by means of error checking and retry mechanisms built into the protocol.

Note that the term point-to-point means that the machines involved in the communication are directly connected. As long as the two computers are directly connected, one to the other, with no intervening computers, the data link layer provides a service similar to that when you send a letter via registered mail.

In addition to reliable transmission, the data link layer, unlike the physical layer, provides structure to the messages that are being transmitted. The physical layer is concerned only with the delivery of the individual bits that make up the messages, and does not care about the structure of those messages. The data link layer, on the other hand, often divides messages into frames and adds additional information to the frames to provide synchronization and flow control. By synchronization we mean that the sender and receiver must agree on the start and end of each frame, and by flow control we mean that the receiver must have a mechanism for pacing the sender, so that the sender does not flood the receiver with data at a pace faster than the receiver can accept it.

The network layer is concerned with end-to-end communication between computers that are not necessarily directly connected one to another. When machines that wish to communicate are not directly connected, they must rely on other machines that are directly connected to relay their messages. The network layer is the lowest layer of networking protocol with a focus on exchanging messages by means of relaying communications between intervening computers.

For example, you have probably passed notes in class. If the person to whom you want to pass the note is on the other side of the classroom, you have to rely on the people sitting between you to pass the message. It may be the case that you know that your message will be safely exchanged between yourself and the person sitting next to you (i.e., point-to-point communication), but once the message is in the hands of the next person in the chain, it may be lost.

We can also use the analogy of passing notes in a classroom to illustrate one of the most important services provided by the network layer: routing. You may realize that there are several paths by which your message could make its way to your friend. Some of these paths may be faster than others, or some may be more reliable. Routing refers to the process of identifying the possible paths that you may use to transmit your message, and selecting the best path based on criteria that you specify. Routing is a service provided by the network layer.

The network layer usually does not make any guarantee of the end-to-end correctness of the message transmission. Because computers on the network can fail at any time, and new computers can be added to the network at any time, it is possible for frame routes to change in midmessage. As a result, frames of a message can arrive out of order, or frames can be duplicated, or frames can be lost.

In most cases, we care that the entire message be transmitted correctly, so another layer of protocol provides that guarantee. Ensuring not only that the message will be successfully passed between pairs of computers, but also that the message will be received correctly at the destination, is the job of the transport layer protocol. The transport protocol keeps track of the sequencing of frames in a message, and insures that regardless of whatever bad things may happen during transmission, the receiver will get all the frames, in the correct order, without duplications.

The OSI model provides three higher layers: the session, presentation, and application layers. While the OSI model distinguishes the services to be provided by each of these layers, this portion of the OSI model has never been widely adopted in practice.

Instead, the highest layers of the protocol stack have been joined together as the *application layer*. The rationale has been that once the message has been reliably transmitted between computers, possibly via a world wide web of computer connections, understanding the meaning of the message, and reacting appropriately, is the responsibility of whatever application program received the message. This approach has become known as the internet reference model, and it is shown in Fig. 7-2. The internet reference model is the most widely used model in practice.

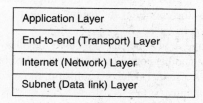

Figure 7-2   Internet reference model.

The internet model contains only four layers, yet the widely used internet model also can be mapped to the more general OSI model:

1 The subnet (data link) layer of the internet model takes on the responsibility of both the physical and data link layers of the OSI model. In most computers, this layer is implemented by the firmware on the network interface card and the corresponding drivers in the operating system.

2 The internet (network) layer of the internet model provides computer-to-computer delivery using the *internet protocol* (IP), and it corresponds to the network layer of the OSI model.

3 The end-to-end (transport) layer of the internet model maps to the transport layer of the OSI model. The internet model implements reliable end-to-end communication over many intervening networks using the *transaction control protocol* (TCP). TCP insures that, even if parts of a message travel by different routes to the destination, the message will be reassembled in the correct sequence, and presented without duplication, omission, or corruption of data.

4 Finally, the application layer of the internet model subsumes the session, presentation, and application layers of the OSI model. As the name implies, application programs have responsibility for the application software layer. For instance, web browser applications have responsibility for formatting and displaying the data sent to them from distant web servers.

Why has the internet model persisted in practice instead of being replaced by the more general and more layered OSI model? A big part of the answer is that the internet model was implemented first, and users found that its model, though simpler, was successful. By the time the OSI model was widely promulgated, the internet model was already in wide use. The advantages of a more elaborate layering of services were not persuasive to those already successful with the existing protocols. Nevertheless, the OSI model persists as the best general description of networking services, and is frequently referenced in textbooks and research relating to networks.

For our further discussion of the operation of different network layers and protocols, we will use the four-layer internet model because it is the model in wide use. Our goal in this chapter is to discuss how networking is actually implemented today.

SUBNET (DATA-LINK) LAYER

The responsibility of the subnet layer is to send and receive streams of bits between one machine and another. Computers transmit information by sending signals in the form of electromagnetic energy using some transmission medium. Computers that are connected using copper wires as the transmission medium will send signals in the form of electrical signals. Computers that are connected using fiber-optic cable will transmit signals in the form of light. Computers connected wirelessly broadcast and receive radio signals. Hardware at the physical layer generates signals of the appropriate type for the medium of transmission.

Because of the layering architecture of the networking protocols, one subnet approach may be substituted for another. Thus, my laptop computer can use a wired *Ethernet* connection if one is available, or can instead use a wireless connection if a *Wi-Fi* network serves the location where I wish to compute.

Most wired networks today use the Ethernet data link. Ethernet protocols were first developed at Xerox's Palo Alto Research Center in the 1970s. Today the descendent Ethernet data link is standardized in the IEEE 802.3 standard. The Ethernet protocol is interesting in its simplicity and its similarity to human speech interaction in groups.

Ethernet uses a CSMA/CD protocol. The full description is carrier sense, multiple access/collision detection. Each computer on an Ethernet network attaches to the same wire. This is referred to as a "bus" architecture; each computer can listen to all signals on the wire; that's the multiple access part. When a computer wants to send information, the protocol requires the computer to "listen" to what's on the wire, waiting for a quiet time, before broadcasting; that's the carrier sense part.

When a computer sends its message, it also listens to its own message. If the sender hears a jumbled mess instead of a clear message, it knows that another computer must have started broadcasting at exactly the same time; that's the collision detection part. When a sender detects a collision, the sender stops, and then waits a randomly chosen interval of time before trying again.

Doesn't this sound like what humans do in group conversation? When a person wants to speak, the person listens for a break in the conversation, and then begins. If the speaker hears interference from another voice, both people stop talking, and wait an interval of time before trying again to speak: CSMA/CD.

The Wi-Fi connections popular today use standards specified in IEEE 802.11. IEEE 802.11 is actually a family of standards using different encoding and transmitting techniques, and different speeds, with a common protocol. Wi-Fi uses CSMA/CA, where CSMA still stands for carrier sense multiple access, but CA stands for collision avoidance.

With wireless networks, it can be harder to detect collisions. If two computers are sharing a common Wi-Fi network, for example, both may be able to contact the access point, but one may not be able to detect the other, making collision detection difficult, even though simultaneous messages are garbled at the access point. Also, the radio environment may be naturally noisy, with cell phones and microwave ovens in the vicinity, for example, so collisions may be difficult to distinguish from normal noise.

For these reasons, 802.11 standards adopt the CA approach where a sender first waits for the clear radio channel, and then sends a short *request-to-send* (RTS) message to the destination computer. When the receiver replies with a *clear-to-send* (CTS) message, the sender proceeds. This approach results in fewer collisions and less wasted time on retransmissions.

Many other data-link standards exist. FDDI is a standard for computers linked with fiber-optic connections instead of wires. Token Ring is a standard that IBM popularized in the 1980s. Because the network protocols are layered, improvements in techniques for link-level connections can be adopted without disrupting the protocols that provide higher-level services.

INTERNET (NETWORK) LAYER PROTOCOL

An important higher-level service is that for the routing of messages between networks. When I send a message from my computer to my friend in the UK, the message must pass through many networks. Starting from my home network, the message must go to my *internet service provider* (ISP), which maintains connections with other ISPs and networks to enable my worldwide access. The routing of a message is the responsibility of the internet (network) layer protocol.

The internet layer protocol is responsible for transporting a "packet" of data from one computer to another over possibly many intervening networks. When one computer sends a message to another, the internet layer protocol breaks the message into pieces (packets), and appends a header to each packet that identifies the destination computer as well as the source. The internet layer then passes the packet, called a *datagram*, to the data-link layer to be broadcast onto the local network.

If the message is destined for a computer not attached to the local network, the router that connects the local network to another network will read the message. The router will rebroadcast the packet on the other network, and by such process repeating, the message will find its way through myriad intervening networks to its destination.

The most popular network layer protocol is *internet protocol* (IP). Each computer attached to the internet has a unique IP address. Most IP addresses today are 32 bits long (called IP version 4). With the enormous growth in the use of the Internet, network experts see the need in the future for a larger address field in order to accommodate a much larger number of computers on the internet. A new standard IP address called IP version 6 has an address field 128 bits long. Over time, more computers will begin using IPv6. In any case, the IP protocol identifies both the source and destination computers by their IP addresses.

You may be surprised that the IP protocol, on which we all depend, is specifically an *unreliable protocol*! IP simply builds datagrams and gives them to the link layer to send. The only error checking in the IP protocol uses a checksum in order to insure the header information has integrity. The checksum is a simple mathematical function of the bits in the header. Each receiver recomputes the checksum to make sure the checksum in the header matches. If the header is corrupted, the receiver simply discards the datagram! IP provides no checking whatever of the data in the datagram, so even if the header is intact, the data may be corrupted.

Also, it's possible that a data link, router, or a computer will fail at a time when datagrams are being sent. Such failures will result in loss of the datagrams, and nothing in the IP protocol will do anything to recover such losses. Further, since failures in the network can result in dynamic changes to routes between networks, datagrams sent later may actually arrive sooner than datagrams sent earlier.

Most of the time these problems don't occur. In fact, experiments over wired networks show amazing reliability most of the time. Error-testing devices often measure the bit error rate of networks in bits per billion sent! That's on the order of one to several errors per hour on a busy network. Nevertheless, to insure that datagrams all arrive, uncorrupted, in order, without duplication of datagrams, requires a higher-level protocol designed to insure reliable communication over the inherently unreliable IP network layer. The end-to-end (transport) layer protocol performs this magic every day.

END-TO-END (TRANSPORT) LAYER PROTOCOL

The transport layer protocol of the internet is transmission control protocol (TCP). TCP uses the IP layer to send messages through the internet, and TCP adds a whole set of services that together insure that complete messages always arrive, uncorrupted, in order, without duplication of data, at the intended destination, regardless of hardware or network failures or changes during the time the many datagrams comprising the message are being sent.

TCP is a *connection-oriented* protocol, which means that the two computers first establish a connection with one another before either begins sending data. To do this, one computer, the *server*, reserves a *port* for communication. Some writers call this the "passive open" of a connection, for nothing happens outside of the server; the server simply makes itself ready to communicate.

When another computer, the *client*, wishes to communicate with the server, the client contacts the server requesting a connection. This step is sometimes called the "active open." To do so, the client must identify the server, and must know in advance the port on which the server is "listening."

Since each computer has thousands of ports available, you may be wondering how the typical client application could possibly guess on which port to call the server? The answer is that the use of a small number of ports is standardized, and those port numbers are well known. For instance, web servers listen on port 80, so all of those visits you make to websites are really contacts with web server programs listening on port 80 of the web server computer.

After the client contacts the server, the client waits for an acknowledgement from the server of the client's request to open a connection. When the client receives one, the client acknowledges back to the server that the client has received the server's acknowledgement. At this time, both computers have established a connection on which to communicate.

This three-step connection establishment protocol may remind you of how people use telephones. We dial the other person (the server, or object of connection), we hear the other person pick up the phone and say, "Hello," (akin to the server's acknowledgement of the client's open request), and we identify ourselves in confirmation, "Hi. This is Carl," (confirming the server's acknowledgement). Once we have established the connection with one another, we proceed to exchange information with each other.

Once the TCP connection is established, the client and server begin to exchange messages and data. The TCP protocol uses sequence numbers to indicate the order in which pieces of the total message go together. Both the client and server exchange *initial sequence numbers* (ISNs) during the connection establishment exchange. One number is used for messages from the client to the server, and one is used for messages in the other direction.

When the client sends a message, the client labels the message with a sequence number. The client expects the server to acknowledge receipt of the message by responding with a sequence number one greater than the one sent.

If the client does not receive confirmation of a message it sent within a set period of time, the client assumes that the message was lost, and the client sends the same message, with the same sequence number, again.

On the server side, the server can use the sequence numbers to determine if it receives the same message twice. If a client mistakenly sends a message twice when the server already received the message, the server can simply discard the duplicate message.

Since different pieces of a message may travel by different routes to the destination, it's possible for component pieces of a message to arrive out of order. The sequence numbers on messages make it possible to put the pieces into correct order before delivering the full message to the application (e.g., the web server or the web browser).

Both the header and the data in a TCP packet are protected with a checksum. This allows the TCP protocol to insure that data in the message have not been corrupted. As you can imagine by now, if the destination computer detects corrupted data in a packet, it can simply ask the sender to resend data corresponding to a particular sequence number.

We have simplified the discussion of sequence numbering somewhat in hopes of making it easier to understand conceptually. In practice, every byte in a TCP message is sequenced. The message header in a TCP packet has the starting sequence number, and the receiver will increment that number by the number of bytes in the message. The receiver will expect the next packet to start with the incremented number plus one. The sequence numbering scheme insures correct sequencing of bytes in the message, efficient resending of corrupted or lost packets, and correct disposal of duplicate packets.

Yet another service of the TCP protocol is regulating the speed of senders. Data communications people refer to this as *flow control*. With every message and acknowledgement, each computer informs the other of the number of bytes it is ready to receive. This number of bytes is known as the *data window*. If a fast sender starts to overrun a slower receiver, the acknowledgement for a packet will soon show a zero for the data window. The sender will stop transmitting until it receives another packet from the receiver announcing that it has room in its data window again.

To the application programs on both sides of the connection, TCP presents a *byte stream* of the data, very much like a file. Applications can write to and read from a TCP connection very much as they would write and read files.

APPLICATION LAYER

The application layer is everything above the transport, network, and data-link layers. Application programs such as web browsers, file transfer programs, web servers, distributed databases, and electronic mail use the *application program interface* (API) of the network protocol stack, and libraries of common networking routines, to access other computers over the network. The Java language also has many built-in classes that make network programming much easier.

PUTTING IT ALL TOGETHER

To put it all together, envision this. A web server is in the middle of sending a file containing HTML text to a web browser. The web server has just read the next line of the file, so it writes the line to the TCP socket the server opened for communication with the browser. To the web server, this write operation is very much like writing to a file.

When the TCP software receives the buffer of text, it builds a header for a TCP packet that, among other details, includes the source and destination IP addresses and port numbers of the two computers, and the sequence number information. The TCP software also computes the checksum for the header and data of the TCP packet, and writes the checksum into the header. When the header is complete, the TCP software passes the original line from the file, prefixed with the TCP header, as a single buffer (a buffer is a series of bytes) to the IP protocol.

The IP software may separate the full TCP buffer into several smaller series of bytes. For each IP packet, the IP software builds an IP header that includes the source and destination IP addresses, and a variety of other details. The IP software calculates a checksum for the IP header, and inserts that number in the checksum field of the IP header. As the IP software constructs each IP packet, the IP software passes each packet to the data link software, which in most cases today means the driver for the network interface. However, if the destination IP address is not on the local network, the command to the data link layer tells the data link layer to send the message to the local *router*, or gateway, computer.

The data link software will build an appropriate data link header of its own, whose format depends on the type of data link, and write the bits to the destination computer. At this point, the destination computer is either another computer on the local network, or a router attached to the local network.

When the IP packet arrives at the router, the router's data link software will remove the data-link-level header, and forward the IP packet to the IP software. The IP software in the router will check the IP header checksum, and consult its tables to decide where to forward the message in order best to move the message toward its destination. The IP software will pass the IP packet back to the data link layer of the router, with instructions to send the packet over the adjoining network to the appropriate computer, or to the next router.

Eventually the destination computer will be a local computer on a network served by the last router in the chain. When the data link software at the destination computer receives the message, the data link software will strip the data link header from the IP packet, and pass the IP packet to the IP software. The IP software will verify the IP header checksum, reassemble the IP packet, if necessary, strip the IP header off the TCP packet, and pass the TCP packet to the TCP software.

The TCP software will check the sequence number and verify the TCP checksum. If everything is in order, the TCP software will remove the TCP header and transfer the line of HTML text to the waiting application program, in this case a web browser.

THE WORLD WIDE WEB, HTTP, AND HTML

What we now call "the Internet" started with a US military project called ARPAnet. ARPA stands for Advanced Research Projects Agency, which is part of the US Department of Defense. Work on ARPAnet began in the late 1960s, with the goals of creating a universal and fault-tolerant mechanism for linking computers in a wide network.

Packet switching, now the primary messaging technique of the Internet, was a new concept at the time, and the ARPAnet developed its protocols around packet switching. A small team of seven people at Bolt, Beranek, and Newman (BBN), a research organization based in Cambridge, MA, developed the initial protocols and had a working network connecting Stanford, UCLA, UC Santa Barbara, and the University of Utah by the end of 1969.

In 1971, one of the researchers sent the first e-mail message over the network, and in 1973, the file transfer protocol allowed a file to be moved from one computer to another over the network. These were major advances—those who did not live through this period can hardly imagine how exciting these advances were! Work on core network protocols continued as well, and the TCP/IP protocols became standard in 1983.

In 1985, the National Science Foundation took over the nonmilitary portions of the ARPAnet, and renamed it the NSFnet. The NSFnet supported the NSF's supercomputer centers at Princeton, UC San Diego, Cornell, University of Illinois, and University of Pittsburgh, as well as other major academic computing centers. The NSFnet became an international network, with connections to Canada, Europe, Central and South America, and the Pacific Rim. During this time, the NSF permitted only noncommercial use of the NSFnet. For a good technical description of the Internet, it's still worth reading Ed Krol's memo *A Hitchhiker's Guide to the Internet* from 1989 (http://rfc.sunsite.dk/rfc/rfc1118.html).

In 1989, Tim Berners-Lee of CERN, the European Laboratory for Particle Physics, proposed a project to develop "browsers" for users' workstations and a mechanism to allow users to add content that could be universally accessible over the Internet. The idea was to provide universal readership of information collectively available on the network.

This idea of the *world wide web* (WWW) was arguably even more important than the technical miracles worked by those who developed the protocols and applications of the ARPAnet and NSFnet. The WWW was conceived as a client–server arrangement, with *browser* applications that could present information, regardless of the origin of the information, running on the client computers. The server applications would be responsible for extracting information and sending it to the client applications.

At the heart of the WWW was a new protocol called *hypertext transport protocol* (HTTP). The idea behind hypertext is that text need not be sequential. A reader should be able to follow links to related information, and back, in whatever sequence suits the needs of the reader.

By the end of 1989, the small team at CERN had created HTTP and demonstrated the first WWW servers and a browser. Tim Berners-Lee and his associates wrote the Internet standard RFC1738 to define the *uniform resource locator* (URL) for use with HTTP (1994), and also wrote the Internet standard RFC1945 defining revision 1.0 of HTTP (1996).

The WWW made the Internet useful to nontechnical people. Besides e-mail and file transfers, nontechnical users could easily access a rapidly growing body of content made available very inexpensively by many different providers. In 1995, the NSF turned the NSFnet over to private organizations, and commercial use of the Internet began.

HTTP remains at the heart of the WWW. It is a simple application-level protocol, which means that it is a protocol used by programs at the application level. The TCP/IP protocols have no knowledge of HTTP or of URLs. HTTP is simply a language understood by application programs, particularly web server and browser applications. According to RFC1945, HTTP has "the lightness and speed necessary for distributed, collaborative, hypermedia information systems."

HTTP is a simple request/response protocol. When a web server program is listening for messages on port 80 of its computer, the server will respond to a HTTP request from a client computer. The two basic forms of request are GET and POST. Both are requests of the server, but the POST allows the client to enclose data in the body of its request. The server replies with an HTTP RESPONSE.

The GET request is simply a request for information. Usually a GET is for information on a web page, but it can also be for a file, such as a download of a program the user is interested in using. A GET request is usually a single line, and might look like this:

```
GET /pub/www/TheProject.html HTTP/1.0
```

or:

```
GET http://www.w3.org/pub/www/TheProject.html HTTP/1.0
```

The RESPONSE will include a status line and the data requested. The RESPONSE might look like this:

```
HTTP/1.0 200 OK
<HTML>
<HEAD>
<TITLE>Project Home Page</TITLE>
</HEAD>
<BODY>
[content of the web page, marked with HTML tags--see below]
</BODY>
</HTML>
```

When the client must provide data in order for the server to perform the requested action, the client uses a POST request. The POST protocol provides for the data to be contained in the body of the POST request. A POST request providing Carl for field fn and Reynolds for field ln might look like this:

```
POST /servelet/SomePhoneBook HTTP/1.0
Content-Length: 19
Content-Type: application/x-www-form-urlencoded
fn=Carl&ln=Reynolds
```

The simplicity of the WWW protocol is one of the reasons for its success. It is quite easy to implement both web servers and browsers. In fact, today computer science students often write a simple web server as a programming exercise.

Another reason for the success of the WWW is that Tim Berners-Lee and the others made all their code freely available to all. They encouraged the participation of academic and commercial parties, and the resulting collaboration brought millions of people to the WWW.

The related technology of the *hypertext markup language* (HTML) also allows people with limited technical understanding to format information to be made available over a web server. HTML is a text formatting language that browser programs understand. To ready a file for presentation as a web page, the author "marks up" the text with HTML "tags" which tell the browser how to present the information.

Many students today, from all disciplines, create their own web pages, having learned enough HTML on their own to do an adequate job, or having purchased an inexpensive program to help them do it. There are many books and web pages available to help web authors learn HTML, so we will not provide a full tutorial here. However we will show an example web page that demonstrates the general use and form of HTML.

There are 80 to 100 "tags" in HTML that tell the browser what to do with the text on the page. For instance, the <P> tag marks the beginning of a paragraph. Each tag has a closing form, which is the same as the opening form, except that a forward slash precedes the tag. The closing tag for a paragraph is </P>. One can use uppercase and lowercase interchangeably for the tags; <P> and <p> will work equally well.

Many of the tags have attributes one can set to modify their effect. One sets the attribute value by including the attribute name in the opening tag, following the attribute name with the equal sign, and following that with the value of the attribute in quotation marks. For instance:

```
<H1 ALIGN="center">Carl Reynolds' Home Page</H1>
```

This line will cause the text to be in the size of a large heading (H1), and the text will be centered on the line.

One can add comments to a HTML file by starting with the four characters `<!--` and ending with the three characters `-->`. For instance:

```
<!-- Any browser will ignore this comment -->
```

One of the beauties of the HTML standard is that it is pretty forgiving of errors. If a browser does not understand the HTML on a page, the browser simply displays what it can. The browser will not "crash" or issue cryptic error messages; the browser will simply do the best it can. So, all is not lost if the author forgets to include the closing form for a paragraph, for example.

As an example, Figure 7-3 is a simplification of the home page of one of the authors.

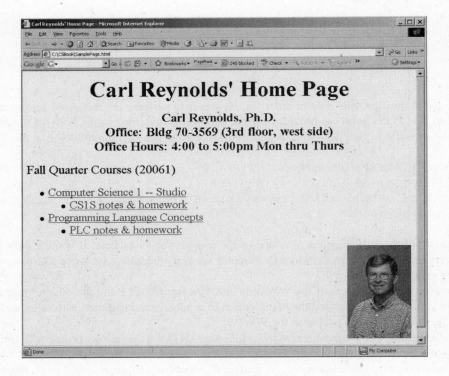

Figure 7-3   Carl Reynolds' home page.

And here is the file of HTML that created the page:

```
<!-- DOCTYPE tells the browser what version of HTML is being used -->
<!DOCTYPE HTML PUBLIC "-//W3C//DTD HTML 4.0//EN">
<HTML> <!-- Start of HTML document -->
<HEAD> <!-- Heading -->
<TITLE>Carl Reynolds' Home Page</TITLE>
</HEAD>

<!-- Start of the BODY, and set the background color to light blue -->
<BODY BGCOLOR="#F6FFFF">
<!-- H1 is a large heading, and center it on the page -->
<H1 ALIGN=center>Carl Reynolds' Home Page
</H1>
<!-- H3 is a smaller heading, and center these lines, too -->
<H3 ALIGN=center>Carl Reynolds, Ph.D.
<!-- BR is a line break, or line feed -->
<BR>Office: Bldg 70-3569 (3rd floor, west side)
<BR>Office Hours: 4:00 to 5:00pm Mon thru Thurs
</H3>

<!-- P is a paragraph marker -->
<P><BIG>Fall Quarter Courses (20061)</BIG> <!-- use big font -->
  <UL TYPE=disc> <!-- "Unordered List"; use a "disc" as bullet type -->
              <!-- LI is the tag for "List Item" -->
              <!-- A is an "anchor", or hypertext link to a URL -->
    <LI><A HREF="http://www.cs.rit.edu/~cs1s/">
                                        Computer Science 1 — Studio</A>
        <UL TYPE=disc>
        <LI><A HREF="http://www.cs.rit.edu/~chr/cs1s/CourseNotes/">
                                CS1S notes & homework</A>
        </ul>
    </li>
    <LI><A HREF="http://www.cs.rit.edu/~chr/plc/plcHomePage.htm">
                                Programming Language Concepts</A>
        <UL TYPE=disc>
        <LI><A HREF="http://www.cs.rit.edu/~chr/plc/CourseNotes/">
                                PLC notes & homework</A>
        </ul>
    </li>
  </UL>
</p>

<!-- Insert an image on the right side of the page -->
<!-- Find it in directory Images below the working directory -->
<P><IMG SRC="Images/CHR.gif" ALIGN=right>
</p>

</BODY> <!-- End of the BODY section -->
</HTML> <!-- End of the page -->
```

SUMMARY

The widespread networking of computers is a relatively recent phenomenon, and it may also be the aspect of the computer revolution that has most changed human life. Networks can be described as LANs, which are local to a building or campus, and WANs, which span wide, or even global, distances. The technical challenges are somewhat different between LANs and WANs, but the distinction between the two is not always clear.

When several networks are themselves connected together, the result is an internet. The world wide web we have come to know and depend upon is not one network, but many connected together, and hence is called the internet. A computer on a LAN connects to the wider internet through a gateway or router computer, which connects the LAN to the internet.

Computers communicate over a network by conforming to network protocols. Protocols are required at more than one level. At the hardware level, the computers must use the same signaling technology, the same medium of connection, the same speed of transmission, etc. At higher levels, the computers must agree on what the signals mean, and when to take turns sending and receiving. One describes and implements network protocols as multiple layers of software and hardware. The resulting set of software and hardware is often described as the network stack.

The OSI reference model is the standard network protocol model, and it has seven layers. The internet reference model is simpler, with four layers. For historical and pragmatic reasons, the internet model is the one in wide use, and that is the model we described in detail.

The link level consists of the interface card and operating system driver for the physical connection between computers. Common links today are Ethernet and Wi-Fi (wireless). Both have been standardized as IEEE standards.

The network-level protocol of the internet is IP, or internet protocol. IP is the protocol that is responsible for moving datagrams from one computer to another, possibly distant computer, over multiple intervening networks. IP does not provide a guaranteed service. Most of the time datagrams get delivered efficiently, but IP provides no guarantees that packets will arrive uncorrupted, in order, and without duplication.

The transport-level protocol of the internet is TCP. TCP is a connection-oriented protocol that adds reliability to the underlying, unreliable, network protocol. After first establishing a connection with a remote computer, TCP provides guaranteed delivery of complete, uncorrupted messages.

The application-level protocol over the internet is provided by the applications that take advantage of the network. There is no internet standard application-level protocol.

The technical advances in networking and protocols have had even greater impact on every day life since Tim Berners-Lee and his colleagues developed the HTTP protocol and the HTML language, beginning around 1990. Their vision of client browsers on workstations providing easy universal access to information made available by millions of servers has made the internet the "data superhighway."

REVIEW QUESTIONS

7.1 Explain how an IP packet might become duplicated and arrive twice at its destination.

7.2 Some researchers in networking complain that networking protocols have become "ossified." What do they mean by that, and why might that be so? Who benefits from "ossified" protocols?

7.3 Using Google or some other source, find a list of other "well-known ports" in networking besides port 80.

7.4 Most internet communications use the TCP protocol, but some do not. Some communications use only the IP protocol. Another name for the IP protocol is *user datagram protocol* (UDP). Why would an application choose to use UDP? Can you think of a category of applications that might prefer UDP?

7.5 IPv6 uses addresses that are 16 bytes long (128 bits). How many addresses is that per person in the world?

7.6 What classes does Java provide to make network programming easier? Which classes are for TCP communications? Which classes are for UDP communications?

7.7 It's hard to imagine today how hot the competition was between different vendors of proposed networking standards in the 1980s. Today most wired LANs are implemented using 802.3 Ethernet protocols. General Motors strongly backed a competitive standard called *manufacturing automation protocol* (MAP) that became IEEE standard 802.4. Do some research to answer these questions: Why did GM favor 802.4 over 802.3? Why did most of the world end up choosing 802.3?

7.8 The HTTP protocol is essentially a protocol providing for file transfer between the server and the client. Therefore, the HTTP protocol is said to be "stateless;" i.e., the server receives a request, and the server satisfies the request with a file transfer, regardless of what has happened before with this client. This statelessness has been a challenge to those developing applications to be delivered over the web. For instance, a banking application will need to keep track of the account number of the individual making inquiries, even though the individual makes repeated inquiries and updates using several different screens (web pages). How is application state maintained in such applications?

CHAPTER 8

Database

THE UBIQUITOUS DATABASE

Today databases are ubiquitous. Almost every application we encounter has a database foundation. When we buy something on-line, when we renew our driver's license, when we inquire about a flight schedule, when we look up the sports scores, we are using applications that rely on databases. Databases provide efficiency, security and flexibility of data storage, and are employed in applications ranging from library card catalogs to machine automation in factories. This was not always so.

Soon after computers entered the second generation of the modern era (i.e., the late 1950s), the availability of high-level programming languages and large storage capacities (usually magnetic tape) led to larger and larger collections of data. The data were stored in files—collections of data records—and it soon became clear that this approach presented a number of difficulties.

First, larger files took longer to search. Recall from our discussion of algorithms that a sequential search operates in O(n) time. Therefore, the larger the file, the more time a search for any particular item requires. That may not be a problem when you're keeping track of the birthdays of your friends, but if you're keeping a record of every MasterCard purchase transaction for millions of customers, the slow retrieval of information by serial search becomes prohibitive.

Other problems appeared as well. For instance, if you store the billing address of the customer in each record of each sale, you waste a lot of space storing data redundantly. Suppose that a customer changes their address; you have to rewrite all the transactions on record, using the new address. You might decide to solve this problem by putting the billing addresses in a separate file. That would save space in the transaction file, but now in order to compute a customer's bill, you must search serially through two files.

DATABASE TYPES

Starting in the late 1960s, database systems were developed to deal with these and other problems. Two early types of databases were the *hierarchical* and *networking* types. IBM offered DL/1, a hierarchical database, and various other hardware and software companies offered networking databases on the CODASYL (Conference On DAta SYstems Language, Database Task Group) model. IDMS was a particularly successful CODASYL database.

The hierarchical and networking database structures organized files together to provide more rapid access to the information, better security, and easier updates. However, the structures were complex, tied to the implementation details of the file system, and fairly rigid.

In 1970, E. F. Codd (Edgar, "Ted," an Englishman who moved to the US after serving in WWII) of IBM proposed the relational database model. The relational model relied heavily on mathematical theory. At the time, it may have sounded "dreamy," as data were simply to be stored in tables (called "relations"). Each relation/table would maintain information about one entity type (type of thing), and entities would be related to one another by virtue of information stored in the tables, rather than by external pointers or other devices.

Codd also proposed a language for data access that was based on set theory (in the 1980s IBM would bring structured query language (SQL) to the world). To many professionals at the time, Codd's proposals seemed impossible to implement efficiently.

However, in the 1980s, Oracle became the first company to offer a commercial implementation of a relational database, and IBM began selling its relational database called DB2. Today the relational data model is predominant, and that is the model on which this chapter will focus.

With the advent of object-oriented programming, new data management designs called object-relational or object-oriented database management have been developed. These systems promise convenience and congruity of operation with OO programming techniques. While they have not yet become widely successful, they may become so in the future.

ADVANTAGES OF USING A DATABASE

The primary motivation for using a database is speed of access. Assuming proper database design, access to individual pieces of information can be essentially instantaneous, regardless of the number of data records or the size of the database. The experience of instantaneously finding exactly the record in which you are interested, from among millions, can be a stunning one.

Access speed can be essentially zero and constant, regardless of n, the number of records. This can be expressed as $O(k)$, where k is a constant of a small value. Such performance becomes possible because the database management system stores data about the data (metadata) as well as the data itself.

Metadata also makes data stored in a database *self-describing*. This means that programs accessing the data don't need to know so many details regarding how the data are stored. If a program reads from an ordinary file, it must know about data types, formats, and the order of fields. However, when a program reads from a database, it often needs only specify what information it requires.

A database also allows for efficient utilization of storage space. One of the consequences of good database design is that duplication of data is minimized. When mass storage devices were more expensive, this virtue was more important, but minimizing redundancy is still helpful in promoting efficiency, avoiding errors, and protecting against corruption of data.

Database management systems (DBMS) also promote data security in a variety of ways. For instance, data backup and recovery facilities are always built into the DBMS, and data can be copied to a backup medium, even as the database continues to operate.

Database systems also support the concept of a *transaction*. A transaction is a group of related changes to the data, where all changes must occur, or else none must occur. The familiar example is removing funds from a savings account and depositing those funds in a checking account. We want both the withdrawal and the deposit to succeed, but if the withdrawal succeeds and the deposit fails, we want the withdrawal to be "rolled back" and the money put back into the savings account. The two changes constitute a single transaction which must either succeed in its entirety, or be rolled back to have no effects whatsoever. Database systems allow changes to the data to be grouped into transactions that are either "committed" upon full success, or entirely "rolled back" upon any failure.

DBMSs also promote data security by organizing use by multiple users. Imagine an enterprise like Amazon.com where many users from all over the world interrogate the database of available titles, and place orders, simultaneously. The DBMS coordinates multiuser access so as to preserve data integrity. Changes made by one user will not interfere with the use of the database by another. The DBMS manages potential conflicts by providing temporary locks on the data when necessary.

For all these reasons, database systems have become ubiquitous. As we will see, the use of database systems has been facilitated, too, by a set of language standards called SQL. It is difficult to imagine any substantial application today that does not include a database, or provide a direct link to an existing database.

MODELING THE DATA DOMAIN

Before creating a relational database, the designer goes through a process called data modeling. The modeling phase identifies the "entities" which will be of interest, the "attributes" of each entity type, and the "relationships" between different entity types.

For instance, in developing a database for a college, entity types would include students, professors, dormitory buildings, classroom buildings, majors, courses, etc. Attributes of a student would include name, address, dorm, room number, major, advisor, etc. One relationship between entity types would be the advisor/advisee relationship between a professor and a student.

Entities are the "things," the "nouns," the database will store. Often entity types correspond to classes of real-world objects, such as professors, cars, and buildings. Sometimes entity types correspond to more abstract objects, like a college within a university, an order for an on-line bookstore, and a privilege afforded a group of users. A big part of data modeling is deciding which entity types to model.

For those familiar with object-oriented programming concepts, an entity type is similar to a class. Each individual entity of an entity type (think of an instance of a class) will be characterized by a set of attribute values. Attributes are the "adjectives" or descriptors of the entities the database will store. For instance, extending the example from two paragraphs above, a particular student could have the attributes "Bill Smith," "Akron, OH," "Fisher Dorm," 323, "Computer Science," "Professor Findley," etc.

The structure of a database is described by its "schema." As we will see later, in order to convert the data model to a relational database schema, each entity instance of an entity type must be unique. Something in the set of attributes must make each entity different from all other entities of the same type. Returning to the example in the previous paragraph, we expect only one Bill Smith, and if there are two or more, we will find a way to make the different Bill Smith entities unique. We will assign a "key" to each entity of the student entity type such that we can distinguish each student.

Having selected the entity types to include in the database, the data modeler then specifies the relationships among the entities. For instance, we mentioned previously the advisor/advisee relationship between professors and students. One of the important decisions to make is whether the relationship will be 1:1 (one-to-one), 1:N (one-to-many), or N:M (many-to-many). These ratios are called *cardinality ratios*.

In the case of the advisor/advisee relationship, the designer might decide the relationship is 1:N, with 1 advisor advising N students. On the other hand, if the school assigns multiple advisors to each student (for instance, one for the student's major field and one for student life questions), the relationship could be defined as N:M, multiple advisors for each student, and multiple students for each advisor.

Another pair of decisions related to the cardinality ratio of a relationship is the specification of minimum cardinalities. Must a student have an advisor? If so, then the minimum cardinality on the professor side of the advisor/advisee relationship must be 1. If not, then the minimum cardinality on the professor side of the relationship will be 0; a student entity may exist who is not associated with any advisor.

Likewise, must every professor be an advisor? If so, then the minimum cardinality on the student side of the advisor/advisee relationship must be 1. If not, then the minimum cardinality on the student side will be 0; a professor entity can exist with no associated advisees.

Other relationships might be 1:1. Imagine an entity type called Parking Permit, and that the policy is to allow each student one and only one parking permit. The relationship between student and parking permit could be called "parks/permit-to-park," and the relationship is 1:1. The minimum cardinality on the student side would probably be 1, since otherwise it would mean the database tracks parking permits that are not issued to anyone. The minimum cardinality on the parking permit side would probably be 0, since some students probably will not have cars to park.

A many-to-many, N:M, relationship would exist between students and courses. We could call this relationship "takes/is-taken-by." Each student will take many courses, and many students will take each course. The minimum cardinality for both sides of the relationship will be 1, because each student will certainly take some courses and - each course will be attended by some students. On the other hand, if we keep courses in the database that are no longer actively taught for some reason, then the minimum cardinality on the student side of the takes/is-taken-by relationship will be 0.

Figure 8-1 shows a data model for the entities and relationships we have been discussing, using one of many standard approaches for graphically representing the entity-relationship diagram. Figure 8-1 was created using Microsoft Visio.

The rectangles represent entities, and the label in the upper portion of an entity rectangle specifies the identifier, or key, for the entity type. For dormitories, for example, the dorm name is the identifier; the name of the dorm distinguishes the record of one dorm from that of another. The labels in the lower portion of the entity rectangles represent the other attributes of the entity. The dorm entity includes information for each dorm about the total number of rooms in the dorm, the number of vacant rooms in the dorm, and the room rental rate for the dorm.

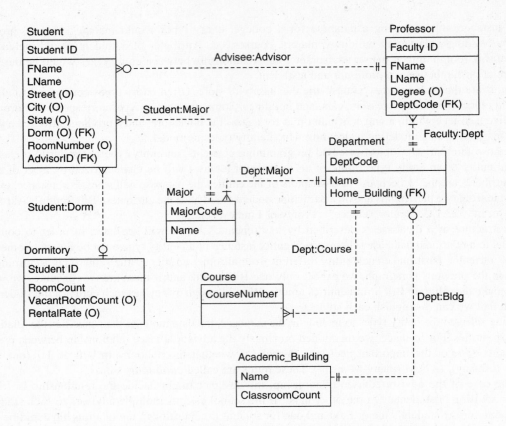

Figure 8-1   Example entity-relationship (E-R) diagram.

The lines represent relationships between entities, and the marks at the ends of the lines represent the cardinalities. A circle at the end of a line means that the relationship is optional with respect to that entity; a bar at the end of a line means that only one instance of that entity type may participate in an instance of the relationship; and a "crows foot" means that many instances of that entity type may participate in an instance of the relationship.

For instance, a single department offers one or many courses; every department offers at least one course. Also, a dorm may be associated with one or many students, and a student may be associated with no dorm, or with one dorm. Some students are commuters who will not be associated with a dorm, but if a student is associated with a dorm, the student is associated with at most one dorm.

These processes of defining entities, their attributes, and the relationships among entities are effective for most entities and relationships. There are a few more special cases, however, that come up often enough to require some additional discussion.

Some entities belong in the database only if another entity is already part of the database. For instance, we would include dependents of a professor in the database only if the professor were already included. If a professor leaves the university, the professor's information would be removed from the database, and it would no longer make sense to store information about the professor's dependents, either. An entity type such as "Dependent" is called a "weak entity." A weak entity is modeled like other entity types, except that it is identified as being dependent upon a "strong entity" in the database.

A particular type of weak entity is the "ID-dependent entity." An ID-dependent entity is a weak entity, such that the ID of the associated strong entity is also part of the identifier of the ID-dependent entity. Imagine the strong entity "Building" and the ID-dependent entity "Room". Attributes of a room may include size, seating capacity, number of windows, etc., but a room only makes sense in the context of a building, and the identity of a room will include the building name as well as the room number.

Another application of ID-dependent entities occurs when attributes are "multivalued." For instance, a professor may have more than one degree, or more than one telephone number. We model such multivalued attributes as ID-dependent entity types, and we specify 1:N relationships between the strong entity and the ID-dependent entities.

Relationships may also be *recursive*. That is, a relationship can exist among instances of the same entity type. For example, we might want to model the relationship between students who room together. In that case, we would define a recursive N:M student:roommate relationship to model the fact that students may room with one or more others. If all rooms permitted only two roommates, the relationship could be 1:1, but probably some suites allow for three, four, or more roommates, so the relationship between student and roommates will be N:M, and we will call it "rooms-with". The minimum cardinality on either side can be 0, if we have some students who will room alone.

Finally, some entity types can represent subclasses and superclasses. For instance, students may be either undergraduate or graduate students. We would model "student" as the superclass, and we would model "undergraduate" and "graduate" as subclasses. Attributes of student would include those attributes relevant to all students, such as name, address, etc. Attributes of undergraduate entities would include those attributes relevant only to undergraduates, such as student life advisor (assuming graduate students have no such advisor assigned).

Figure 8-2 illustrates weak and ID-dependent entities, multivalued attributes, and superclass and subclass entities.

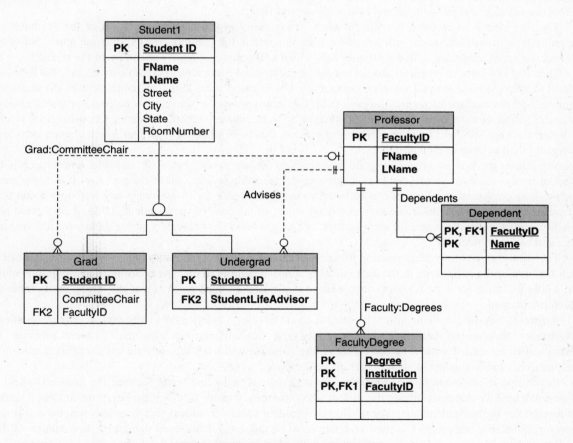

Figure 8-2   E-R diagram special cases.

In Fig. 8-2, the Dependents table is an id-dependent weak entity. The identifier for that table includes the key for the related strong entity Faculty, plus the name of the dependent (spouse's name, child's name, etc.). The FacultyDegrees entity represents a multivalued attribute. A single faculty member may have multiple degrees from multiple institutions, and this entity allows us to represent that fact. Finally, the Student entity shows two subcategories of students, grads and undergrads. An undergrad will have a faculty member serving as his or her Student Life Advisor, and a grad may (or may not) have a faculty member serving as the chair of his or her thesis committee.

BUILDING A RELATIONAL DATABASE FROM THE DATA MODEL

The data model comprises the *conceptual schema*, or the description of the structure of the database. This is one of three schemas, or designs that database developers refer to. The other schemas include the *external schema*, which is the database as conceived by the end-users, and the *internal schema*, which is the set of actual file structures on disk used by the database management system (SQL Server, Oracle, etc.).

With the conceptual schema created, the next task is to convert the data model into tables, relationships, and data integrity rules. An entity type is represented as a table, where each row in the table represents an instance of that entity type. In relational database terminology, a table is called a "relation." Note that a *relation* is a *table*, not a *relationship*. Later we will also create means to represent relationships. A relation consists of rows, each of which represents an instance of the entity type, and of columns, each of which represents one of the attributes of the entity type.

Each row of a relation is called a *tuple*. Practitioners use the word row more often than tuple, but a tuple is a row of a table, an instance of a relation, an instance of an entity type. Each tuple consists of the values of the attributes for that instance of the entity type.

Another word for attribute is *field*. So, in discussions of relational databases, you must keep in mind these synonyms: relation and table, tuple and row, attribute and field.

The first step is to create a relation for each strong entity in the data model. Each of the attributes of the entity type in the data model will become a column name in the relation. At this time one must choose an attribute, or set of attributes, called a *primary key*, which will uniquely identify each row of the relation.

The ideal key is short, numeric, and never-changing. The ideal is not always possible to achieve, but it can be helpful to keep the ideal in mind when choosing a key. For instance, if the "Student" table includes the attributes of name, address, and *social security number* (SSN), in addition to other attributes, one could probably choose the combination name–address, or the single attribute SSN, to uniquely identify students. Choosing SSN would be wiser, because SSN will be more efficient to process, due to its numeric type, and it will change even less frequently than a name or an address.

Sometimes there is no obviously good key attribute among the attributes of the table. One choice is to concatenate the values of several fields to achieve an identifier that will be unique for each row. If this approach leads to long, alphanumeric keys, it can be better to use a *surrogate key*. A surrogate key is simply a number, generated by the DBMS, which is assigned to each tuple. In the case of the "Student" table, if SSN were not one of the attributes to be stored for each student, one might decide to generate a surrogate key for the Student table and call it "StudentID".

The second step is to create a relation for each weak and ID-dependent entity type. As with strong entities, each attribute of the entity type in the data model becomes a column in the new relation. In addition, one must add a column to the weak or ID-dependent relation that will hold the *foreign key* of the strong entity tuple to which it is related.

A foreign key is a column in a relation, which establishes a relationship with data in another relation. For instance, suppose our data model includes entity type "StudentComputer", and that "StudentComputer" is a weak entity associated with "Student". That is, the database will track the information about each student's computer only as long as the student is part of the database.

In addition to attributes of the student's computer such as make and serial number, the StudentComputer relation will have a column identifying the student who owns the computer. If SSN is the key of the Student relation, the foreign key in the StudentComputer relation will contain values of student social security numbers. It is not necessary for the column names in the two relations to be the same. Thus, even though the key column of the Student relation is named "SSN", the foreign key column in StudentComputer might be called "StudentSSN".

The new relation created for the weak entity must also have a primary key of its own. Choosing the primary key for the weak entity relation involves the same considerations as choosing the primary key for a strong entity relation. If the weak entity is ID-dependent on the strong entity, then make the key of the ID-dependent relation a combination of the foreign key field, and one or more other attributes of the ID-dependent relation.

Another application of ID-dependent entities is in modeling multivalued attributes. For instance, one may want to provide for multiple addresses for each student; many will have one address during the academic year, and another during the summer, for instance. In such a case, model an ID-dependent entity called "Address", and create a relation with attributes such as "Street", "City", "State", etc., as well as a foreign key attribute that will hold values of the primary key for the Student relation.

With relations created for all entities in the data model, it is time to provide for the relationships in the data model. For each 1:1 relationship, choose one relation to be the "parent" and the other to be the "child." To implement the relationship, create a foreign key column in the child relation that will be used to associate each tuple in the child relation with the appropriate tuple in the parent.

If the minimum cardinality on both sides of the 1:1 relationship is 1, it does not matter which relation is chosen as the parent. However, if the minimum cardinality on one side is 0, then make the other relation the parent. For instance, if there were a 1:1 relationship between "Room" and "Projector", but not all rooms had projectors, you would make the Room relation the parent, and put a foreign key column in the Projector relation. This will be more space-efficient, since you will have a foreign key field only when there is a Projector tuple to associate with a Room tuple.

For 1:N relationships, the relation on the 1 side will be the "parent," and the relation on the N side will be the "child." All one must do is add a foreign key column to the child relation so that the "many" children can be related to the "one" parent entity. For instance, to implement the advisor/advisee relationship, simply add a foreign key column to the Student relation, name the foreign key column "FacultyAdvisor", and prepare to populate the column with values of the primary key of the Faculty relation.

Many-to-many relationships are more complex. To implement an N:M relationship, one must create a new table, a new relation. Such a relation is sometimes called an *intersection table* or a *relationship relation*. The intersection table includes foreign key columns for both entities in the relationship. Each tuple in the intersection table will include values of primary keys from both relations. For each association between an instance of one entity type and an instance of the other, there will be a row in the intersection table making the connection.

For instance, to create the M:N relationship between the Student and Course tables, one would create the "StudentCourseIntersection" relation. StudentCourseIntersection would have foreign key columns for Student (perhaps called StudentSSN) and for Course (perhaps called CourseNumber). Each row in StudentCourseIntersection will record the fact that a particular student took a particular course. Any particular student may take many courses, and many students may take any particular course.

The primary key of an intersection table usually is the composite of the two foreign key values. Since the foreign key values must be unique among tuples in their respective relations, the combination of the two keys must be unique among the tuples in the intersection table. This rule would only change in special circumstances. For instance, if one were to decide to record multiple attempts by a student to take a particular course, the primary key of the intersection table would have to be expanded to include another attribute that would allow one to distinguish different attempts by the same student to take the same course.

Recursive relationships sound difficult to create, but they are not. Suppose some students are student advisors. The relationship is 1:N. One can create this recursive relationship by adding a column to the Student relation named "StudentAdvisor". The StudentAdvisor column is essentially a foreign key column that contains values of the primary key from the same relation. Creating a 1:N recursive relationship is just like creating a standard 1:N relationship, except that the "parent" foreign key links to the same table that contains the "child" entity. A 1:1 recursive relationship is handled similarly.

An M:N recursive relationship requires creating an intersection table, just as for standard M:N relationships. In this case, however, the foreign key columns will both contain primary key values from the same relation. Imagine the recursive roommates relationship. Each row in the intersection table will associate one student with a roommate, another student.

NORMALIZATION

Some models are better than others. In particular, poor decisions regarding entity definitions can increase data redundancy and lead to *update anomalies*. Update anomalies include behavior such as requiring information about a second entity (e.g., a dorm) when inserting information about a first entity (e.g., a student), or losing information about a second entity (e.g., a dorm) when an entity of a different type is deleted (e.g., the last student in the dorm). Normalization is the process of subjecting relations to tests. Passing the tests will insure that the relation will show desirable properties.

The goal of normalization is to insure that each relation represents a single theme. For instance, a relation should have information about students, and a relation should have information about dorms, but a relation that has information about both students and dorms will lead to trouble.

There are various normal "forms" which have been identified for relational databases. Higher levels of normalization lead to designs that reduce data redundancy and avoid the update anomalies mentioned above. Any higher normal form also conforms to all lower normal forms. Thus, a relation in *third normal form* (3NF) is also in *second normal form* (2NF), and *first normal form* (1NF).

Discussions of normal forms rely upon the concept of *functional dependency*. When the value of one attribute, or set of attributes, determines the value of another attribute, a functional dependency exists, and the first attribute, or set of attributes, is called the *determinant*.

Suppose that we created a relation with the attributes shown in Figure 8.3.

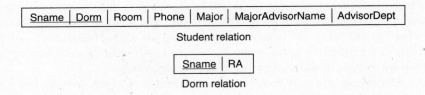

Figure 8-3   Student relation.

The key of the Student relation is the composite of Sname and Dorm (assuming that no students with the same name will live in the same dorm).

This horizontal box representation is a common way to represent a relation—vertical lines separate the attribute names, and the attributes that comprise the key are underlined. The key attributes do not need to be adjacent to one another, and they do not need to be on the left side, but often people choose to show them this way.

The key of any relation is always a determinant; by definition, the key identifies the entire tuple. Given values for Sname and Dorm in the Student relation, the values for all the other attributes are determined.

Not all determinants are keys, however. In the Student relation, there is a functional dependency between MajorAdvisorName and AdvisorDept. Given a value for the advisor name, the department value is determined.

First normal form is simply the definition of a relation. Each attribute must be an atomic, single-valued attribute. For example, if an attribute in the Student relation is TelephoneNumber, any one tuple in the relation can have only one value for TelephoneNumber. If one wants to store multiple telephone numbers for a student, then one must create a separate relation for that purpose. Then each tuple in the new PhoneNumber relation can have a single telephone number, and multiple tuples in the PhoneNumber relation can be associated via a 1:N relationship with a particular student.

Second normal form requires that every nonkey attribute be functionally dependent on the entire key. Said another way, each nonkey attribute value must provide a fact about the entity as a whole, not a fact about a part of the key. If the key of a relation is a single attribute value, for example a surrogate key, any relation is automatically in 2NF. All the nonkey attributes are dependent on (i.e., determined by) the key.

Without thinking too much about it, anyone might think that the Student relation is a reasonable design for a database that will track students. On closer reflection, however, note that the relation includes information about resident advisors (RAs), and faculty advisors, as well as about students.

Is every non-key attribute in the Student relation dependent upon (determined by) values of the entire key? In this case, the answer is "No." Assuming that there is one RA per Dorm, then the value of RA depends upon Dorm, but not upon Sname. To bring the design into 2NF, make a new relation called Dorm, and remove the RA attribute from the Student relation (Fig. 8.4).

Sname	Dorm	Room	Phone	RA	Major	MajorAdvisorName	AdvisorDept

Figure 8-4   2NF.

This is progress, but it's still true that the Student relation tracks information about something other than students. In particular, the relation is tracking information about advisors; it's tracking not just who the advisor for each student is, but also what department the advisor belongs to. If a relation is to focus on a single theme, this doesn't seem right.

Third normal form requires that a relation has no *transitive dependencies*. Said another way, each non-key attribute must provide a fact about the entity as a whole, not about another nonkey attribute. That is what is still wrong with the Student relation. MajorAdvisorName and AdvisorDept are both dependent upon the key of the Student relation, but AdvisorDept is also transitively dependent upon MajorAdvisorName. Once we know who the student is, we can determine the student's advisor, and once we know the advisor, we can determine the advisor's department. This is a transitive dependency: A determines B, and B determines C. To make the design conform to 3NF, one must remove the transitive dependency from the Student relation. Fig. 8.5 shows the design in 3NF.

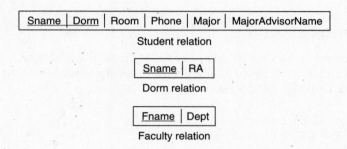

Figure 8-5   3NF.

Now the original Student relation has been broken into three relations, each with a single theme— one records information about students, one records information about dorms, and one records information about faculty members who act as advisors.

In a more complete implementation, one would choose better key values for the Student and Faculty relations. Perhaps one would choose some sort of ID number instead of relying on a name and hoping one never has to deal with the possibility of including two John Smiths in the database. A Faculty relation likely would also have additional attributes, such as office address, salary, etc.

Boyce–Codd normal form (BCNF) is a refinement of 3NF. A relation is in BCNF if every determinant in the relation is a *candidate key*. A candidate key is a valid choice for the key of the relation.

Suppose in our example that room numbers in different dorms were different, such that the value of the room number itself determined which dorm the student was in (room numbers less than 100 were in Arthur Dorm, for instance, and room numbers between 100 and 199 were in Brooks Dorm). Room would then be a determinant, but it obviously would not be a candidate key, so the Student relation would not be in BCNF. To put the Student relation in BCNF, we would have to create a new Room relation in which dorm room number was the key and Dorm was a nonkey attribute.

Normal forms exist at even higher levels. In ascending order, the forms are fourth normal form, fifth normal form, and domain key normal form. In day-to-day work with databases, one is less likely to focus on these higher forms, so this chapter will end its discussion of normalization with BCNF. The important guide to remember is that *each relation should embrace a single theme*, a single topic.

SQL—STRUCTURED QUERY LANGUAGE

IBM first brought SQL to database processing. It is a high-level language for creating databases, manipulating data, and retrieving sets of data. SQL is a nonprocedural language—that is, SQL statements describe the data and operations of interest, but do not specify in detail how the underlying database system is to satisfy the request.

ANSI standards for SQL were published in 1986, 1989, 1992, 1999, and 2003. In practice, different database vendors offer SQL with small differences in syntax and semantics. For any particular vendor, most SQL statements will conform to the standard, and there will also be numerous small differences. As a result, one must always supplement knowledge of standard SQL with information specific to the database vendor one is using. The desktop reference *SQL in a Nutshell* by Kevin Kline (2004) finds it necessary, for example, to include separate sections for ANSI Standard, DB2 (IBM), MySQL (open source), Oracle, and SQL Server (Microsoft) varieties of the standard.

SQL statements are often distinguished as being part of the *data definition language* (DDL) or the *data manipulation language* (DML). DDL statements create database structures like tables, views, triggers, and procedures. DML statements insert data, update data, retrieve data, or delete data in the database.

SQL is not case sensitive. Commands and names may be entered in uppercase or lowercase. However, some people have a style preference for using uppercase and lowercase letters to segregate SQL key words from database names.

DDL—DATA DEFINITION LANGUAGE

The first DDL statement to learn is CREATE. The CREATE TABLE command is the means by which to create a relation. In SQL, a relation is called a table, a tuple is called a row, and an attribute is called a column. Here is the syntax for the CREATE TABLE statement:

```
CREATE TABLE <table_name>
( <column_name> <dataType> <attributes>
  [,<column_name> <dataType> <attributes>]
 [CONSTRAINT [<constraintName>] <constraintType>
  [,CONSTRAINT [<constraintName>] <constraintType>]]
);
```

This syntax specification says that the statement must begin with CREATE TABLE followed by your choice of table name (shown between the less-than and greater-than brackets). Following the table name, you must type an open parenthesis, followed by one or more sets of specifications for the name of each column, the data type of each column, and attributes of each column (such as allowing nulls or not). After the list of column names, you may optionally provide one or more table constraints by typing CONSTRAINT, an optional constraint name, and a constraint type (such as PRIMARY KEY or UNIQUE values). Finally, you must type a close parenthesis and a semicolon.

The database designer is free to specify any name for a table, column, or constraint. The SQL standard specifies rules for names, but each database vendor has its own rules that vary somewhat from the standard. For instance, the SQL2003 standard says that names may be up to 128 characters long, but MySQL limits the designer to 64 characters, and Oracle limits the designer to 30 characters.

The data types for SQL also vary with the vendor of the database management system. In general, these types are available:

- Integer
- Number/Numeric (decimal floating point)
- Varchar (variable length character strings)
- Date/DateTime
- Char (character string of fixed length)

You must consult the documentation for your DBMS to determine correct choices for data types.

The most common attributes one specifies for columns are NOT NULL, DEFAULT, and CONSTRAINT. The NOT NULL attribute requires a value for that column for every row that one adds to the table. By default, a column may contain a null value.

The DEFAULT attribute allows one to provide an expression that will create a value for a column, if a value is not otherwise provided when one inserts a new row. For instance, the following column declaration specifies the default value for the state column to be "NY":

```
State Char(2) DEFAULT 'NY',
```

There are four constraints that can be specified: PRIMARY KEY, FOREIGN KEY, UNIQUE and CHECK. The primary key constraint identifies the column or columns that comprise the primary key.

A foreign key constraint identifies a column that contains values of a primary key in a different table. Foreign keys are the mechanism for creating relationships among rows (entities) in different tables.

A unique constraint requires all rows in the table to have unique values for the column or set of columns specified in the constraint. A unique constraint is sometimes called a *candidate key*, because the unique column(s) could be used as a primary key for the table, in place of the chosen primary key.

Here are examples of several CREATE TABLE commands:

```
CREATE TABLE Student
  (  Sname            VarChar(25)   Not Null,
     Dorm             VarChar(20)   Not Null,
        Room             Integer,
        Phone           Char(12),
        Major           VarChar(20),
     MajorAdvisorName   VarChar(25),
       CONSTRAINT StudentPK         PRIMARY KEY( Sname, Dorm ),
CONSTRAINT StudentDormFK   FOREIGN KEY( DORM )
                       REFERENCES Dorm( Dorm ),
CONSTRAINT StudentFacultyFK FOREIGN KEY( MajorAdvisorName )
                REFERENCES Faculty( Fname )
  );

CREATE TABLE Dorm
(  Dorm             VarChar(20)  Not Null,
   RA               VarChar(25),
     CONSTRAINT DormPK PRIMARY KEY( Dorm )
 );

CREATE TABLE Faculty
(  Fname            VarChar(25)  Not Null,
   Dept             VarChar(20),
     CONSTRAINT FacultyPK PRIMARY KEY( Fname )
 );
```

Another kind of constraint is the CHECK constraint. A CHECK constraint allows one to specify valid conditions for a column. For instance:

```
CONSTRAINT FoundedCheck CHECK ( FoundedDate > 1900),
CONSTRAINT ZipCheck     CHECK ( zip LIKE '[0-9][0-9][0-9][0-9][0-9]' ),
```

The first constraint will insure that the column FoundedDate has a value more recent than 1900, and the second will insure that the column zip will consist of five numeric characters. In the case of the second CHECK constraint, the syntax says that zip must be "like" five characters, each of which is a numeric character between 0 and 9. This syntax, too, varies by database vendor, so you must consult the documentation of your DBMS for implementation specifics.

Having created tables in the database, one sometimes must dispose of them. One might guess that the keyword would be "delete" or "dispose" or "destroy". While "delete" is a key word in SQL, it is used for removing data from the database, not for getting rid of structures like a table. The way to remove a database object like a table is to use the DROP command. Here is the syntax:

```
DROP < object_type > < object_name >;
```

The key word DROP must be followed by the type of database structure and the name of the database structure. Object types include TABLE, VIEW, PROCEDURE (stored procedure), TRIGGER and some others.

To dispose of the Student table, one can use this command:

```
DROP TABLE Student;
```

When one must modify a database object like a table, the command to use is ALTER. For instance, to add a birthdate column to the student table, one could use this command to add a column named Birthdate of data type Date:

```
ALTER TABLE Student ADD COLUMN Birthdate Date;
```

In addition to adding columns, one can use the ALTER TABLE command to drop columns, add or drop constraints, and set or drop defaults.

DML—DATA MANIPULATION LANGUAGE

The first DML statement to learn is SELECT. The SELECT statement provides the means of retrieving information from the database. It is a very flexible command with numberless variations and much to know about using it.

In the simplest case, use SELECT to retrieve values for certain columns in a table, such as the Sname and Major values in the Student table we created in the previous section:

```
SELECT Sname, Major FROM Student;
```

This statement will retrieve one row for each student and display the student's name and major.
One can also be selective about which rows one displays by adding a WHERE clause:

```
SELECT Sname
FROM Student
WHERE Major = 'Computer Science';
```

This statement, or *query*, will return the names of all Computer Science majors, and no others.
If one wants to retrieve all columns for each qualifying row, one can use the asterisk to specify that all columns be displayed:

```
SELECT *
FROM Student
WHERE Major = 'Computer Science';
```

The WHERE clause itself is very flexible. In addition to the equal sign, one can use the comparison and logical operators given in Table 8-1.

Suppose one wants to find all the students named Jones who are not math or computer science majors, and who live in either Williams or Schoelkopf dormitory. One possible query is the following:

```
SELECT *
FROM Student
WHERE Sname LIKE '%Jones'
AND Major NOT IN ( 'Math', 'Computer Science' )
AND ( Dorm = 'Williams' OR Dorm = 'Schoelkopf' );
```

The results of a query can be sorted, too. All one need do is add the ORDER BY clause. For instance:

```
SELECT Sname
FROM Student
WHERE Major = 'Computer Science'
ORDER BY Sname;
```

Table 8-1

Operator	Meaning
=	equal to
>	greater than
<	less than
>=	greater than or equal to
<=	less than or equal to
!=	not equal to
!<	not less than
!>	not greater than
AND	True if both boolean comparisons are true
OR	True if either boolean expression are true
NOT	Reverses the truth value of another boolean operator
IN	True if the operand is one of the listed values, or one of the values returned by a subquery
LIKE	True if the operand matches a pattern % matches anything _ (underscore) matches any one character Other characters match themselves
BETWEEN	True if the operand is within the range specified
EXISTS	True if a subquery returns any rows
ALL	True if all of a set of comparisons are true
ANY	True if any one of a set of comparisons is true
SOME	True if some of a set of comparisons is ture

This will report the CS majors in alphabetical order by name. To sort in reverse alphabetical order, add the word DESC (descending) at the end of the query.

What would this query report?

```
SELECT Major FROM Student;
```

It would return one line for each student, and each line would contain a major field of study. If 300 students major in computer science, there will be 300 lines containing the words "Computer Science". Such a report is probably not what one had in mind. Probably one is interested in a list of the different major fields of study of the students. One can get such a report by adding the word DISTINCT to the SELECT query:

```
SELECT DISTINCT Major FROM Student;
```

What if the information in which one is interested is spread among several tables? Such a query requires a JOIN of the tables. There is more than one way to specify a JOIN, and there are different types of JOINs for different situations. Suppose one is interested in a list of student names and the names of the Resident Advisors in their dormitories. Here is one way to JOIN the Student and Dorm tables to combine the information:

```
SELECT Sname, RA
FROM Student, Dorm
WHERE Student.Dorm = Dorm.Dorm;
```

Conceptually, a JOIN works by concatenating the rows in the two relations where the specified test is true. In this case, each row in the Student table is concatenated with the row in the Dorm table where the value of the Dorm column in the Dorm table is the same as the value of the Dorm column in the Student table (Student.Dorm is how the Dorm column in the Student table is specified. Likewise Dorm.Dorm specifies the Dorm column in the Dorm table.). Then the selection of columns Sname and RA occurs from the concatenated row.

Another way to write the same JOIN query would be to use this syntax:

```
SELECT Sname, RA
FROM Student JOIN Dorm
ON Student.Dorm = Dorm.Dorm;
```

Either syntax is acceptable. In both cases, the column named Dorm, which exists in both tables, must be "disambiguated" by qualifying each use of Dorm with the name of the table to which it applies.

One might add two more tables to the University database to track clubs and student participation in them. Many students can join any club, and each student can belong to many clubs, so the relationship will be M:N. One must create a table to track the clubs, and an intersection table to track club membership:

```
CREATE TABLE Club
(   Cname        VarChar(20)    Not Null,
    Dues         Integer,
    Building     VarChar(20),
    Room         Integer
   CONSTRAINT ClubPK PRIMARY KEY (Cname)
);

CREATE TABLE ClubMembership
(   Cname  VarChar(20)  Not Null,
    MemberName  VarChar(20)  Not Null
    CONSTRAINT ClubMembershipPK PRIMARY KEY (Cname,
MemberName),
   CONSTRAINT ClubMembership_Club_FK
       FOREIGN KEY (Cname) REFERENCES Club( Cname );
CONSTRAINT Member_FK
       FOREIGN KEY (MemberName) REFERENCES Student( Sname );
);
```

To retrieve a list of students, their majors, and the clubs to which they belong, one could use this query that joins the Student and ClubMembership tables:

```
SELECT Sname, Major, Cname
FROM Student JOIN ClubMembership
ON Student.Sname = ClubMembership.MemberName;
```

The "dot notation" in the last line says that we are interested in joining rows where the Sname column in the Student table matches the MemberName column in the ClubMembership table. The results of this query will include a row for each student who participates in a club, and if a student participates in more than one club, there will be multiple rows for that student. What if one also wanted to know which students did not participate in any clubs? A solution would be to use an "outer join."

A standard, or "inner," join assembles information from a pair of tables by making a new row combining the attributes of both tables whenever there is a match between tables on the join condition. In the previous example, whenever there is a match between Sname in the Student table and MemberName in the ClubMembership table, the join creates a new row that includes all the attributes of both tables. The SELECT then reports the values of Sname, Major, and Cname from the combined row.

An outer join includes each row in one or both tables, regardless of whether the row matches on the join condition. For instance, to show all students, regardless of club membership, the query above can be modified with the word LEFT:

```
SELECT Sname, Major, Cname
FROM Student LEFT JOIN ClubMembership
ON Student.Sname = ClubMembership.MemberName;
```

The word LEFT says that the table on the left, Student, not ClubMembership, is the one for which all rows will be reported. Now the query will return one row for every student (more than one for students who belong to more than one club), and if a student is not a member of any club, the Cname column will be NULL.

The word RIGHT can be used to affect the rows reported from the table on the right. Rearranging the order of tables in the join, and switching to the word RIGHT, gives a new query that reports the same result:

```
SELECT Sname, Major, Cname
FROM ClubMembership RIGHT JOIN Student
ON Student.Sname = ClubMembership.MemberName
```

If one wants to include all rows from both tables, regardless of whether the join condition is satisfied, use the word FULL instead of LEFT or RIGHT.

To report only those students who are not members of any club, simply add a WHERE clause:

```
SELECT Sname, Major, Cname
FROM Student LEFT JOIN ClubMembership
ON Student.Sname = ClubMembership.MemberName
WHERE Cname IS NULL;
```

Notice that one uses the word IS, instead of the equal sign, to test for the presence of a NULL value. A NULL value literally has no value. Since the value does not exist, one cannot test for equality of the value to any other, even to NULL. When testing for NULL values, always use IS NULL or IS NOT NULL.

Suppose one wanted to know how many students participated in each club? SQL has built-in functions for simple and frequently needed math functions. The standard five functions are COUNT, SUM, AVG, MIN, and MAX, and many DBMS vendors provide additional nonstandard functions as well. One could report the count of students in each club this way:

```
SELECT Cname, COUNT(*) AS Membership
FROM ClubMembership
GROUP BY Cname
ORDER BY Cname;
```

COUNT(*) says count the occurrences of rows. The AS Membership phrase sets the column heading for the counts in the report to Membership. The GROUP BY phrase tells SQL how to break down the calculations when using the built-in function; that is, count rows (members) for each club.

If there were clubs that no students had joined, and one wanted to include that information in the report, one could use an outer join along with the built-in count function to achieve the desired report:

```
SELECT Club.Cname, COUNT(ClubMembership.Cname) AS Membership
FROM Club LEFT JOIN ClubMembership
ON Club.Cname = ClubMembership.Cname
GROUP BY Club.Cname
ORDER BY Club.Cname;
```

Here a left join on Club and ClubMembership insures that all clubs are included in the report, even if the clubs have no members (no entries in ClubMembership). Also, since Cname is a column heading in both tables, each reference to Cname must also specify which table is being referenced. This query says to execute an outer join on Club and ClubMembership so that all clubs are included, and then count the occurrences of records for each club by grouping on club names.

If one wanted to report the revenues for each of the clubs, this query using the SUM function would work:

```
SELECT CM.Cname, SUM( C.Dues ) AS Revenue
FROM ClubMembership CM JOIN Club C
ON CM.Cname = C.Cname
GROUP BY CM.Cname;
```

This statement introduces the use of aliases for table names. In the FROM clause one may follow the name of the table with an abbreviation. In that case, the abbreviation may be used wherever the table name would otherwise be required, even in the beginning of the SELECT clause before the FROM clause is encountered! Most experienced SQL people make extensive use of table aliases to reduce the size of SQL statements and make the statements easier to read.

SQL queries can also be nested, one within another. Suppose one were interested in finding all those students whose major advisor was not in the Math Department. One way to learn that is to nest one query regarding faculty and departments inside another regarding students:

```
SELECT Sname, Dorm
FROM Student
WHERE MajorAdvisorName
IN (
    SELECT Fname
    FROM Faculty
    WHERE Dept != 'Math'
    );
```

This is called a nested query, or subquery. Usually it is possible to use a join instead of a nested query, but not always. Later we will discuss correlated subqueries, which cannot be translated into join expressions. In this case, however, here is the same query example executed as a join:

```
SELECT Sname, Dorm
FROM Student JOIN Faculty
ON MajorAdvisorName = Fname
WHERE Dept != 'Math';
```

In this case, since there is no ambiguity about which table is being referenced, the column names do not need to be qualified with a table reference.

When using a subquery, the result columns must all come from the table named in the FROM clause of the first SELECT clause. Since that is the case in this example, one has the choice of using a join or a subquery.

We will return to the SELECT statement later to touch on some additional topics, but now we will turn our attention to the other SQL DML statements. Having created the tables for a database, the next step will be to enter data. The SQL statement for adding rows to a table is INSERT. Here is the syntax for INSERT:

```
INSERT INTO <table_name> ( <columnX>, <columnY>..., <columnZ>)
                   VALUES( <valueX>, <valueY>..., <valueZ>);
```

This says that the key words INSERT INTO must be followed by the name of a table. Then you must provide an open parenthesis, a list of one or more column names, and a close parenthesis. Then the key word VALUES must appear, followed by an open parenthesis, a list of column values corresponding to the column names, a closed parenthesis and a semicolon.

And here is an example:

```
INSERT INTO Student( Sname, Dorm, Room, Phone )
VALUES ('Mary Poppins', 'Higgins', 142, '585 223 2112');
```

In this example, notice that some columns are not specified. This student has not yet declared a major. The values for the unspecified columns (`Major`, `MajorAdvisorName`) will be null.

The order of column names need not be the same as the order of the columns in the table, but the order of the values in the `VALUES` clause must correspond to the order of columns in the `INSERT` statement.

In the common case that every column will receive a value, it is not necessary to include the list of column names in the `INSERT` statement. In that case, the order of values must be the order of columns in the table. Here is another example:

```
INSERT INTO Student VALUES ('Mark Hopkins', 'Williams', 399,
               '585 223 2533', 'Math', 'William Deal');
```

With data in the database, changing the information requires one to use the `UPDATE` statement. Here is the syntax for `UPDATE`:

```
UPDATE <table_name>
SET <columnX> = <valueX>, <columnY> = <valueY>...,
<columnZ> = <valueZ>
WHERE <condition>;
```

And here is an example:

```
UPDATE Student
SET Major = 'English', MajorAdvisorName = 'Ann Carroway'
WHERE Sname = 'Mary Poppins';
```

Mary has discovered her major field, and this statement will add that information to the row for Mary in the `Student` table.

The `WHERE` clause in the `UPDATE` statement is the same as, and has all the power and flexibility of, the `WHERE` clause in the `SELECT` statement. One can even use subqueries within the `WHERE` clause. The `WHERE` clause identifies the rows for which column values will be changed. In this example, only one row qualified, but in other cases the `UPDATE` statement can change whole groups of rows.

For instance, suppose the Computer Science department changes its name to Information Technology department. The following `UPDATE` statement will change all `Faculty` rows that currently show `Computer Science` as the department, so that they will now show `Information Technology`:

```
UPDATE Faculty
SET Dept = 'Information Technology'
WHERE Dept = 'Computer Science';
```

This one statement corrects all appropriate rows.

Deleting rows of information from the database is very straightforward with the `DELETE` statement. Here is the syntax:

```
DELETE FROM <table_name>
WHERE <condition>;
```

Again, the `WHERE` clause provides the same flexible and powerful mechanisms for identifying those rows to be deleted.

To remove Mary Poppins from the database, this `DELETE` statement will work:

```
DELETE FROM Student WHERE Sname = 'Mary Poppins';
```

To remove all rows from a table, one simply omits the `WHERE` clause—be careful not to do so by accident! Remember also that to remove the table itself from the database, one must use the `DROP` statement.

Having discussed the DML statements, we will return to the SELECT statement to discuss correlated subqueries. When the evaluation of a subquery references some attribute in the outer query, the nested or subquery is described as a *correlated subquery*.

To imagine the workings of a correlated subquery, imagine that the subquery is executed for each row in the outer query. The outer query must work through all the rows of a table, and the inner query must have information from the row being referenced in order to complete its work.

For example, suppose one wants to know if there are any dormitories in the database that have no students assigned to them. A way to answer this question is to go through the Dorm table, one row at a time, and see if there are, or are not, any students who list that dormitory as their own. Here is such a query:

```
SELECT Dorm
FROM Dorm
WHERE NOT EXISTS (
                  SELECT *
                  FROM Student
                  WHERE Student.Dorm = Dorm.Dorm
                  );
```

The outer query works through the rows of the Dorm table inspecting the Dorm column (Dorm.Dorm). For each value of Dorm.Dorm, the inner query selects all the students who have that dormitory name in the Dorm column of the Student table (Student.Dorm).

This query introduces the NOT EXISTS function (and, of course, there is also an EXISTS function). EXISTS and NOT EXISTS are used with correlated subqueries to test for the presence or absence of qualifying results in the subquery. In this case, whenever no qualifying student is found (the result NOT EXISTS), then that row of the Dorm table qualifies. The result is a list of dormitories to which no students are assigned.

Likewise, one could create a list of all dorms to which students have been assigned by changing the NOT EXISTS to EXISTS.

A famous and mind-bending use of NOT EXISTS can find rows where all rows in the subquery satisfy some condition. For instance, suppose one wants to know if there is any club to which all math majors belong. One can use NOT EXISTS to find clubs to which no one belongs, and then use NOT EXISTS again to find clubs to which everyone belongs. Here is the example:

```
SELECT Cname
FROM Club
WHERE NOT EXISTS (
  SELECT *
  FROM Student
  WHERE Student.Major = 'Math' AND NOT EXISTS (
    SELECT *
    FROM ClubMembership
    WHERE Student.Sname = ClubMembership.MemberName
      AND Club.Cname = ClubMembership.Cname));
```

This query works through each row in the Club table. For each row in the Club table it works through each row in the Student table. Then for each Club row/Student row combination, it works through each row in the ClubMembership table.

The innermost query finds clubs in which at least some math majors *do not* participate. However, if ALL math majors participate in a particular club, the innermost query will return a NULL. If the innermost query is NULL, then the innermost NOT EXISTS will be true (it's NULL; it does not exist; so NOT EXISTS is true). If the innermost NOT EXISTS is true, then that club qualifies, and that club is reported as being one to which all math majors belong.

It can take a while to digest this idea!

STORED PROCEDURES

Most database management systems allow users to create *stored procedures*. Stored procedures are programs that are precompiled and stored in the database itself. Users can access the stored procedures to inquire of, and make changes to, the database, and they can do this interactively using commands, or by using programs that call stored procedures and receive the results.

Stored procedures are written in a language that extends standard SQL to include more programming constructs, like conditional branching, looping, I/O, and error handling. Each vendor's language is different in details, so one must learn the language of the particular database management system to which one is committed.

There are several advantages of stored procedures as a way to access a database. First, a procedure may be complex in its work, and yet be easy for a casual user to invoke. The skilled database programmer can create stored procedures that will make day-to-day use of the database more convenient. For instance, the user may simply want to record a sale to a customer, and the user may not be aware that the database will require updates to both the Customer and Product tables. A stored procedure can accept the facts (customer name, price, quantity, product, etc.) and then accomplish all the updates behind the scenes.

Second, stored procedures usually improve performance. Without stored procedures, SQL commands must be presented to the DBMS, and the DBMS must check them for errors, compile the statements, develop execution plans, and then execute the plans and return the results. On the other hand, if the procedure is precompiled and stored, less error checking is necessary, and the execution plan is already in place. For database applications that are concerned with performance, using stored procedures is a standard strategy for success.

Third, using stored procedures is a way to achieve reuse of code. To the extent that different users and programs can take advantage of the same stored procedures, programming time can be saved, and consistency among applications can be assured.

Fourth, stored procedures are secured with the same mechanisms that secure the data itself. Sometimes the procedures encapsulate important business rules or proprietary data processing, so keeping them secure is important. Stored procedures are stored in the database itself, and access to them is secured just as access to the data is. This can be an advantage compared to separately securing source code.

The only disadvantage of using stored procedures is that using them introduces a requirement for another programming expertise. For example, a programmer may know Java, and may also know SQL, but may not have any experience with Oracle's language PL/SQL. The highest performance approach might be to use stored procedures, but in order to shorten development time, and reduce training and support requirements, a group might decide to simply put SQL statements into Java code instead of writing stored procedures.

The SQL CREATE command is used to create stored procedures. To give the flavor of a stored procedure, here is an example of a stored procedure from an Oracle database. This procedure was written by the authors to support an example database from David Kroenke's book *Database Processing*, 9th Ed., 2004. We will not explain this syntax here, as an entire book could be written on the topic of PL/SQL. We present this code simply to illustrate our discussion with a realistic example.

```
Create or Replace Procedure Record_sale
  (
  v_CustomerName IN Customer.Name%TYPE,
  v_Artist       IN Artist.Name%TYPE,
  v_Title        IN Work.Title%TYPE,
  v_Copy         IN Work.Copy%TYPE,
  v_Price        IN NUMBER,
  v_Return       OUT varChar2          --Return message to caller
  )

AS
    recCount            int;
    v_TransactionFound  Boolean;
    v_CustomerID        Art_Customer.CustomerID%TYPE;
```

```
    v_WorkID               Work.WorkID%TYPE;
    v_ArtistID             Artist.ArtistID%TYPE;
    v_SalesPrice           Transaction.SalesPrice%TYPE;
    v_testSalesPrice       Transaction.SalesPrice%TYPE;

    CURSOR TransactionCursor IS
         SELECT SalesPrice
         FROM Transaction
         WHERE WorkID = v_WorkID
         FOR UPDATE OF SalesPrice, CustomerID, PurchaseDate;

BEGIN
/*
  Selecting and then looking for NULL does not work
  because finding no qualifying records results in
  Oracle throwing a NO_DATA_FOUND exception.
  So, be ready to catch the exception by creating
  an 'anonymous block' with its own EXCEPTION clause.
*/
    BEGIN
      SELECT CustomerID INTO v_CustomerID
        FROM Art_Customer
        WHERE Art_Customer.Name = v_CustomerName;
      EXCEPTION
        WHEN NO_DATA_FOUND THEN
        SELECT CustomerSeq.nextval into v_CustomerID from Dual;
        INSERT INTO Art_Customer (CustomerID, Name)
        VALUES ( v_CustomerID, v_CustomerName );
    END;

    SELECT ArtistID into v_ArtistID
        FROM Artist
        WHERE Artist.Name = v_Artist;

    SELECT WorkID INTO v_WorkID
        FROM Work
        WHERE Work.Title   = v_Title
        AND   Work.Copy    = v_Copy
        AND   Work.ArtistID = v_ArtistID;

    --We need to use a cursor here, because a work can re-enter the
    -- gallery, resulting in multiple records for a given WorkID.
    --Look for a Transaction record with a null for SalesPrice:
    v_TransactionFound:= FALSE;
    FOR Trans_record in TransactionCursor LOOP
        IF( Trans_Record.SalesPrice is null) THEN
            v_TransactionFound:= TRUE;
            UPDATE Transaction SET
                SalesPrice   = v_Price,
                CustomerID   = v_CustomerID,
                PurchaseDate = SYSDATE
                WHERE CURRENT OF TransactionCursor;
        END IF;
```

```
                EXIT WHEN v_TransactionFound;
        END LOOP;

        IF( v_TransactionFound = FALSE ) THEN
                v_Return:= 'No valid Transaction record exists.';
                ROLLBACK;
                RETURN;
        END IF;

        COMMIT;
        v_Return:= 'success';

    EXCEPTION
        WHEN NO_DATA_FOUND THEN
          v_Return:= 'Exception: No data found';
          ROLLBACK;
        WHEN TOO_MANY_ROWS THEN
          v_Return:= 'Exception: Too many rows found';
          ROLLBACK;
        WHEN OTHERS THEN
          v_Return:= ( 'Exception: ' || SQLERRM );
          ROLLBACK;
    END;
```

You probably recognize some SQL statements in this procedure, and you also see statements that are nothing like the SQL discussed in this chapter. PL/SQL is a much more complex language than SQL. Other vendors have their own equivalent procedural language extensions to SQL, too. In the case of Microsoft, for example, the language is called Transact-SQL. We will show an example of Transact-SQL in the next section about triggers.

TRIGGERS

A *trigger* is a special type of stored procedure that gets executed when some data condition changes in the database. Triggers are used to enforce rules in the database. For instance, suppose that room numbers for different dormitories have different *domains*. That is, the room numbers for one dorm use two digits, for another dorm use three, and for another use four. Validating all room numbers automatically would be impossible with standard CHECK constraints, because CHECK constraints do not support such complex logic. However, a trigger could be written to provide for any level of complexity.

Unlike stored procedures that are executed when called by a user or a program, triggers are executed when an INSERT, UPDATE, or DELETE statement makes a change to a table. Triggers can be written to fire BEFORE, AFTER, or INSTEAD OF the INSERT, UPDATE, or DELETE.

Here is an example AFTER trigger written in Microsoft Transact-SQL. Whenever a row is inserted in the Student table, and whenever a row in the Student table is updated, then this code executes after the change has been made to the Student table. The data change *triggers* the code. Again, we provide this code as a realistic example only, and we will not explain the syntax in any detail.

```
CREATE TRIGGER RoomCheck ON Student
FOR INSERT, UPDATE
AS
   declare @Dorm varchar(20)
   declare @Room int

IF UPDATE (Room)
```

```
Select @Dorm = Dorm from inserted
Select @Room = Room from inserted
IF @Dorm = 'Williams' and (@Room > 999 or @Room < 100)
  BEGIN
    PRINT 'Williams dorm has 3 digit room numbers.'
    ROLLBACK TRAN
    RETURN
  END
IF @Dorm = 'Appleby' and (@Room > 9999 or @Room < 1000)
  BEGIN
    PRINT 'Appleby dorm has 4 digit room numbers.'
    ROLLBACK TRAN
    RETURN
  END
IF @Dorm = 'Arpers' and (@Room > 99 or @Room < 10)
  BEGIN
    PRINT 'Arpers dorm has 2 digit room numbers.'
    ROLLBACK TRAN
    RETURN
  END
```

Once again, you see some phrases that look like standard SQL, and you also see many constructs that are not SQL-like at all. One must learn another programming language to take advantage of stored procedures and triggers. Nevertheless, most production databases make use of triggers to enforce data and business rules automatically and efficiently.

DATA INTEGRITY

Database systems provide tools for helping to maintain the integrity of the data. An important set of base rules for insuring good and consistent data in the database is called *referential integrity constraints*.

The built-in rules for enforcing referential integrity are these:

1 Inserting a new row into a parent table is always allowed.
2 Inserting a new row into a child table is allowed only if the foreign key value exists in the parent table.
3 Deleting a row from a parent table is permitted only if there are no child rows.
4 Deleting a row from a child table is always allowed.
5 Updating the primary key in the parent table is permitted only if there are no child rows.
6 Updating the foreign key in a child row is allowed only if the new value also exists in the parent table.

As a database designer, one can count on the DBMS to enforce these basic constraints that are essential if relationships between entities are to be maintained satisfactorily. Many times additional constraints must be maintained in order to satisfy the business rules that must be enforced by the database.

For instance, it is sometimes true that business rules require at least one child row when a parent row is first inserted. Suppose that one is running a database for a sailing regatta. Each boat has a skipper and crew, and the relationship between boat and crew is 1:N (1 boat:many crew). The boat is the parent row to the crew child rows. A data rule could be that a boat may not be added to the database unless at least one sailor immediately is registered as crew (after all, there's no need to store information about boats that aren't racing). Such a constraint would not be naturally enforced by any of the default referential integrity constraints, but one could create a trigger that would automatically prompt for and add a sailor's name when a new boat is inserted. This would be an additional and custom referential integrity constraint.

Another key facility offered by a DBMS to support data integrity is the *transaction*. A transaction is a mechanism for grouping related changes to the database for those occasions when it's important that either all changes occur, or that nothing at all changes.

As we described earlier in this chapter, the familiar example is the act of moving money from a savings account to a checking account. The customer thinks of the act as a single action, but the database must take two actions. The database must reduce the balance in the savings account, and increase the balance in the checking account. If the first action should succeed, and the second fail (perhaps the computer fails at that instant), the customer will be very unhappy, for their savings account will contain less and their checking account will contain what it did. The customer would prefer that both actions be successful, but if the second action fails, the customer wants to be sure that everything will be put back as it was initially. Either every change must be successful, or no change must occur.

Database management systems allow the user (or programmer) to specify transaction boundaries. Every change to the database that occurs within the transaction boundaries must be successful, or the transaction will be *rolled back*. When a transaction is rolled back, the values of all columns in all rows will be restored to the values they had when the transaction began.

Transactions are implemented using write-ahead logging. Changes to the database, along with the previous values, are written to the log, not to the database, as the transaction proceeds. When the transaction is completely successful, it is *committed*. At that point the changes previously written to the log are actually written to the database, and the changes become visible to other users. On the other hand, if any part of the transaction fails, for any reason, the changes are rolled back, i.e., none of the changes written to the log are actually made to the database.

Write-ahead logging is also useful in recovering a database from a system failure. The log contains all the changes to the database, including information about whether each transaction was committed or rolled back. To recover a database, the administrator can restore a previous backup of the database, and then process the transaction log, "redoing" committed transactions. This is called *roll forward recovery*.

Some database systems use a write-ahead log, but also make changes to the database before the transaction is formally committed. In such a system, recovery from failure can be accomplished by restarting the DBMS and "undoing" transactions in the log that were not committed. This approach is called *rollback recovery*.

TRANSACTION ISOLATION LEVELS

When multiple users access a database simultaneously, there is a chance that one person's changes to the database will interfere with another person's work. For instance, suppose two people using an on-line flight reservation system both see that the window seat in row 18 is available, and both reserve it, nearly simultaneously. Without proper controls, both may believe they have successfully reserved the seat but, in fact, one will be disappointed. This is an example of one sort of concurrency problem, and it is called the *lost update* problem.

The database literature describes desirable characteristics of transactions using the acronym ACID—transactions should be atomic (all or nothing), consistent (all rows affected by the transaction are protected from other changes while the transaction is occurring), isolated (free from the effects of other activity in the database at the same time), and durable (permanent). The ideas of consistency and isolation are closely related.

Besides the lost update problem, there are several other potential problems. For instance, *dirty reads* occur when one transaction reads uncommitted data provided by a second simultaneous transaction, which later rolls back the changes it made.

Another problem is the *nonrepeatable read*, which occurs when a transaction has occasion to read the same data twice while accomplishing its work, only to find the data changed when it reads the data a second time. This can happen if another transaction makes a change to the data while the first is executing.

A similar issue is the *phantom read*. If one transaction reads a set of records twice in the course of its work, it may find new records when it reads the database a second time. That could happen if a second transaction inserted a new record in the database in the meantime.

The solutions to all these problems involve locking mechanisms to insure consistency and isolation of users and transactions. In the old days, programmers managed their own locks to provide the necessary protection, but today one usually relies on the DBMS to manage the locks. To prevent the lost update problem, the DBMS will manage read and write locks to insure lost updates do not occur. To address the other possible problems, one simply specifies the level of isolation required, using one of four levels standardized by the 1992 SQL standard. The reason the standard provides different levels of protection is that greater protection usually comes at the cost of reduced performance (less concurrency, and therefore fewer transactions per unit time).

The four transaction isolation levels are, in order from weakest to strongest, read uncommitted, read committed, repeatable read, and serializable. *Read uncommitted* provides no protection against the concurrency issues we have been discussing, but it does provide maximum performance.

Read committed insures against dirty reads by never allowing a transaction to read data that have not been committed to the database. *Repeatable read* also insures against the problem of nonrepeatable reads. *Serializable* provides complete separation of concurrent transactions by locking all the rows necessary during the entire transaction. Such safety comes at the cost of a significant impact on performance for multiuser applications.

Usually the default transaction isolation level is *read committed*.

ACCESSING THE DATABASE PROGRAMMATICALLY

Creating a database and accessing it interactively using SQL can be pretty marvelous in itself, but in almost all cases production databases are accessed and updated via programs. The programs present a familiar face to the user, and they conceal all the details of the SQL language. If a user wants to know, for example, who is the RA for Martin Jones, the user shouldn't have to worry about specifying the JOIN statement, or even about what columns appear in what tables.

There are many paradigms for programmatic access. The Microsoft approach with the .NET languages is one. The JDBC approach is another. PHP has another. In this chapter we will review JDBC as a "neutral" approach that is characteristic of the way databases can be accessed from software.

In general, a program will create a connection with a database using a user name and password, just as a person would. Then the program will send SQL code to the DBMS. The SQL code is the same as would be issued interactively, but the SQL is stored in character strings inside the program, and then sent to the DBMS for execution.

In the case of JDBC, there is also a very first step required, which is to load the driver code for connecting to the database. There are several mechanisms, or types of drivers for JDBC. Some will connect by translating the calls into another standard called open database connection (ODBC); some will convert the JDBC calls into the native application programming interface (API) of the DBMS; some will convert the calls into an independent or vendor-specific network DBMS protocol. One should check with the DBMS administrator for advice about which driver to load for the particular DBMS in use. One can find information about JDBC drivers at: **http://industry.java.sun.com/products/jdbc/drivers**.

A typical snippet of Java code loading a JDBC driver is the following:

```
// Dynamically loads a class called OracleDriver which is in
//    the file classes12.zip
// The environment variable CLASSPATH must be set to include
//    the directory in which the file classes12.zip exists.
Class.forName("oracle.jdbc.driver.OracleDriver");
```

Once the driver is loaded, the program can establish a connection to the database. The Connection class is available by importing the java.sql.* package. To create a Connection, the program needs a user name and a password, just as a person would. Here is a typical snippet of code to create a Connection object for the database:

```
import java.sql.*;
        ...

        // The url means: JDBC driver: Oracle's version:
        //  "thin" driver type, located on cpu reddwarf,
        //   in domain cs.rit.edu, default port number 1521,
        //   database sid "odb"
String url="jdbc:oracle:thin:@reddwarf.cs.rit.edu:1521:odb";
        // Create a connection object
```

```
            //  Note that, by default, a connection opens in
            //    auto-commit mode
            //  (every statement is committed individually).
Connection con = DriverManager.getConnection(url, dbUser, dbPassword);
```

Once the `Connection` is established, the program can read from and write to the database by creating a `Statement` object and supplying the `Statement` with the SQL code to be executed. For instance:

```
Statement stmt = con.createStatement();
            // RETRIEVE STUDENT DATA
String query = "SELECT Sname, Dorm, Room, Phone FROM Student";
```

The `Statement` object has two methods, one for reading from the database, and one for updating the database.

```
    // 1) executeUpdate—statements that modify the database
   // 2) executeQuery—SELECT statements (reads)
      // For a SELECT SQL statement, use the executeQuery method—
   // The query returns a ResultSet object
ResultSet rs = stmt.executeQuery(query);
```

Instead of returning a single value, queries return a set of rows. In JDBC, the set of rows is called a `ResultSet`. To inspect the values in the rows of the `ResultSet`, use the `next()` method of the `ResultSet` to move among the rows, and use the appropriate "getter" method to retrieve the values.

```
            // The ResultSet object is returned
            //  with a cursor pointing above row 1.
            // The next() method of the ResultSet
            //  moves the cursor to the next row.
            // The next() method will return FALSE
            //  when the cursor moves beyond the last row.
while (rs.next()) {

            // Note that you must know the datatype of the column
            //  and use the appropriate method to read it:
            //  rs.getString( <"columnName" or indexStartingAtOne> )
            //  rs.getInt   ( <"columnName" or indexStartingAtOne> )
            //  rs.getFloat ( <"columnName" or indexStartingAtOne> )
            //  others include getDate, getBoolean, getByte, getLong,
            //                  getCharacterStream, getBlob, etc.
            // These work with lots of lattitude. e.g., you can
            //  read a varchar2 column with getInt, if you know
            //  the characters comprise a number.
            // getObject will read ANYTHING
            // getString will read anything and covert it to a String
String studentName  = rs.getString("Sname");
String studentDorm  = rs.getString("Dorm");
int    studentRoom  = rs.getInt("Room");
String studentPhone = rs.getString("Phone");

System.out.println(studentName + ", " + studentDorm + ", " +
                studentRoom + ", " + studentPhone);
}
```

Updating the contents of the database is done similarly, but one uses the executeUpdate() method of the Statement object:

```
stmt.executeUpdate("INSERT INTO Student
                    VALUES('Maggie Simpson', 'Williams', 144,
                           '585-223-1234', 'Biology', 'Ivan Heally')");
```

When the program finishes reading from and writing to the database, the Statement and Connection objects should be closed:

```
// DATABASE CLOSE/CLEANUP
stmt.close();
con.close();
```

There are two other interfaces that inherit from the Statement interface and provide additional functionality. A PreparedStatement object creates a precompiled SQL command that can be executed repeatedly with new values for the column variables. Precompilation leads to efficiency of execution.

PreparedStatements are used for repetitive tasks such as loading a table with data. For instance, the program might repetitively (1) read a record of data to be stored, (2) set each field of the PreparedStatement to the proper value, and (3) executeUpdate().

Here is an example of using a PreparedStatement to insert one of several new students into the database:

```
    // A prepared statement is precompiled, and can be
    // used repeatedly with new values for its parameters.
    // Use question marks for parameter place-holders.
PreparedStatement prepStmt = con.prepareStatement(
        "INSERT INTO Student (Sname, Dorm, Room, Phone)"
                + "VALUES ( ?,   ?,   ?,   ? )" );

    // Now supply values for the parameters using "setter" methods
    // This assignment and execution would usually be within
    //  a loop, so that the same work could be done repeatedly for
    //  different values of the column variables.
    // Parameters are referenced in order starting with 1.
prepStmt.setString( 1, "Jack Horner" );
prepStmt.setString( 2, "Arpers" );
prepStmt.setInt    ( 3, 31 );
prepStmt.setNull   ( 4, Types.VARCHAR );
    // The PreparedStatement object methods:
    // 1) executeUpdate — statements that modify the database
    // 2) executeQuery — SELECT statements (reads)
prepStmt.executeUpdate();
```

Note that the PreparedStatement has different "setter" methods for different data types. Note, too, that if a null value is required, the type of the null must be specified using one of the constants in the Java Types class. The Types class has the Java database types, which may be different from the types used by the DBMS. For instance, Oracle uses a type called VARCHAR2, but the corresponding Java type is VARCHAR.

The last interface we will discuss is the CallableStatement, which extends the PreparedStatement interface. A CallableStatement object provides a single mechanism for a Java program to call a stored procedure in any DBMS. A programmer sets up a CallableStatement object much like a programmer does for a PreparedStatement object, but the syntax uses curly braces, and the stored procedure can return one or more ResultSets as well as other parameters. We will not discuss all the possible configurations of the CallableStatement, but here is an example of a CallableStatement that invokes a stored procedure.

In this case, the stored procedure is named `Add_Student`, and besides adding the new student, it finds and assigns an advisor for the new student, based on the new student's major. All the program needs to do is set the parameters and then execute the stored procedure. The procedure will do all the complex processing, and then return an indication of success in the sixth parameter.

```
        // CallableStatement object to access the stored procedure.
        // Inside the curley braces, you call the procedure, and use
        // question marks for parameter place-holders.
        //  Five are for "IN" variables to be set,
        //  One is for an "OUT" varible to be returned to the program
CallableStatement callStmt = con.prepareCall(
                    "{call Add_Student( ?, ?, ?, ?, ?, ?)}" );

        // Now supply values for the parameters
        // Parameters are referenced in order starting with 1.
callStmt.setString(1, "Billy Bob" );
callStmt.setString(2, "Appleby" );
callStmt.setInt   (3, 1004 );
callStmt.setString(4, "585 223 4599" );
callStmt.setString(5, "Math" );

        // And register the OUT variable
        // This variable returns information to this program
        //  from the stored procedure..
callStmt.registerOutParameter( 6, java.sql.Types.VARCHAR );
        // The CallableStatement object has an additional method*
        //  for use when the stored procedure uses multiple SQL
        //  statements.
        //  1) executeUpdate — statements that modify the database
        //  2) executeQuery — SELECT statements (reads)
        // *3) execute — procedures with multiple SQL
        //                         statements
callStmt.execute();
```

Everything that one might do interactively using SQL commands can be done programmatically from a Java program using JDBC.

SUMMARY

Although several types of database exist, almost all database systems in wide use today conform to the relational database model first described by Codd in 1970. Data are stored in tables where each row is unique, and each column holds the value of a particular item of data. Rows in each table are identified by a unique key value, which can be the value of a particular key column, or a combination of values from more than one column.

Database systems offer advantages by storing data with a minimum amount of redundancy, speeding access to data, providing security and backup of data, and controlling multiuser access. Databases also offer transaction management to insure that related modifications to the database either all succeed, or that no change at all is made. By storing metadata as well as data, databases also allow programs and users to access the information without concern for the details of physical storage.

One creates a database by first modeling the data domain using an *entity-relationship* (E-R) diagram. The E-R diagram identifies the entities, the attributes of the entities, and the relationships between entities the database will track. One then converts the E-R diagram directly to tables and relationships in a database system, using a set of rules for translation.

The *structured query language* (SQL) is the industry-standard language for creating database structures and manipulating data in a database. SQL can be used interactively, or it can be embedded in programs that access the database.

Built-in controls help to insure that the data remain consistent and valid. These controls are called referential integrity constraints. In addition to, or instead of, the standard constraints, a database designer can implement different controls using triggers. Triggers are stored programs that become active when some data element of the database changes.

Transactions group related database commands together in order to insure database consistency. If all the actions in the transaction are successful, the transaction will be committed and the changes made permanent, but if any action fails, the transaction will be rolled back, and the database restored to the state it was in at the beginning of the transaction.

Database management systems also support stored procedures in order to simplify and streamline access to the data. Stored procedures are programs written in an extended version of SQL. They can be invoked passing parameters, and they can return data to users or programs. Stored procedures have the advantage of being precompiled for extra speed and fewer errors. A database programmer can put substantial application logic into stored procedures, which can then be shared among users and application programs.

One can write programs to access databases in a very wide variety of languages. We discussed using JDBC to access databases from the Java language. Other languages use similar techniques to connect to a database, pass commands in SQL, and retrieve sets of data.

REVIEW QUESTIONS

8.1 Consider designing a database for an antique store. What entities would you include? What would their attributes be?

8.2 Create a full ER diagram for the antique store mentioned in question 1. The store handles household furnishings, jewelry, toys, and tools. The owner of the store owns most of what they have for sale, but they handle some items on consignment (i.e., they sell the item for the owner, thus earning a commission on the sale). Some customers require delivery, so the owner maintains relationships with several local movers. The owner wants to keep track of customers in order to do a better job of marketing. In particular, they know that some customers are particularly interested in certain types of antiques, and they'd like to be able to find, for example, all those customers interested in cameo jewelry.

For business auditing and tax purposes, it's very important that the database tracks expenditures and revenues. The owner wants to track what they spent for each item, and what they earned in selling it. These requirements also mean that they have to track store expenses like rent and heat, and their employee expenses (they employ two part-time people to help run the store).

8.3 An inexperienced database designer suggested the following schema for one of the tables in the antique store database:
Sales

Item_ID	Description	Price	Date	Customer_Name	Addr	City	St	ZIP	Phone

Is this schema in 1NF?
Is this schema in 2NF?
Is this schema in 3NF?
If the answer to any of these questions is, "No," redesign the table so that the result is in 3NF.

8.4 Two of the tables in the antique store database will be a table of `Deliveries`, and a table of `Delivery_Services`. Here are the schemas for the two tables:

`Deliveries`

Date	Time	Customer	Delivery_Service	Cost	Invoice_No	Driver

`Delivery_Services`

Name	Phone	Addr	City	St	ZIP	Contact

Write the SQL code to create these tables. Specify which columns may not be NULL, and specify primary and foreign key constraints. Note that the `Delivery_Service` column in the `Deliveries` table is meant to have the same meaning as the `Name` column in the `Delivery_Services` table.

8.5 Here are the schemas for a few more of the tables in one implementation of the antique-store database:
`Item`

Item_ID	Type	Description	Cost	Consignment_Seller_ID	Price_Sold

`Sale`

Invoice_No	Customer_ID	Date

`Line Item`

Invoice_No	Item_ID	Unit_Price	Quantity	Line_Item_Price

`Consignment_Seller`

Seller_ID	Name	Addr	City	State	ZIP	Fee_Percent

Write SQL queries to report the following information:
   a Report all of the consignment sellers located in NY, and list them in order by their consignment fee percentages.
   b Find all of the items in the store that are on consignment from "Parker Smith". Report only the items for sale (`Price_Sold` is NULL).
   c Report the total of all sales during last March.
   d Find all the items on consignment from "Parker Smith" that sold this month.
   e Report the amount due to "Parker Smith" for all sales of his items this month.
   f Report all sales of items not on consignment (`Consignment_Seller_ID` is NULL) this month.
   g Report the profit on all non-consignment items this month.

8.6 When a customer buys an item (or several) from the store, several changes to database tables will occur. Explain what those might be.

8.7 The owner of the antique store doesn't want to train his people in SQL, or to teach them about all the tables in the database. He asks you to write a program that will take sales information, and then make all the changes automatically, including whatever error checking may be necessary. The clerk will enter a customer phone number (assume this is used as the `Customer_ID` primary key in the `Customer` table), an item ID (from a tag on the item), and the sale price.

In pseudocode, outline how your program would record a sale. Show how you would use a transaction to insure the integrity of the database updates. Also, explain the error checking (such as verifying that the customer is already in the database) you would perform in your program, and how your program would recover from problems such as:

- The customer is not in the database.
- The item number is not in the database.
- The item is already sold.

8.8 When an item is sold, should the item row be removed from the Items table? Why or why not?

8.9 What transaction isolation level should apply to this application? Why do you make this choice?

Social Issues

CHAPTER 9

ETHICS THEORIES

Ethics is the rational study of different moral beliefs. A very good book on the subject of ethics with respect to information technology is Michael Quinn's *Ethics for the Information Age*, 2nd Ed., 2006. Quinn discusses a number of ethical theories. An ethical theory is a means by which to reflect on moral questions, come to some conclusion, and defend the conclusion against objections.

Quinn lists six or seven ethical theories, depending upon whether one groups the two forms of utilitarianism together:

1 Subjective relativism
2 Cultural relativism
3 Divine command
4 Kantianism
5 Act utilitarianism
6 Rule utilitarianism
7 Social contract theory

Quinn discards the first three as being inappropriate to reasoned debate of moral questions. The relativism theories provide no objective basis for recommending one action over another, and the divine command theory provides no basis for argument when people of different faiths consider the same moral dilemma.

On the other hand, Kantianism demands that we make our choices only according to rules that we would be comfortable making universal moral rules. As a trivial example, if a Kantian considered the question, "Is it alright to waste printer paper?" the Kantian would consider whether they would endorse a universal moral rule saying, "It is OK to waste printer paper." Since the philosopher probably would not accept that rule as a universal moral rule, the Kantian would conclude that one should not waste printer paper.

The utilitarian positions are consequentialist positions, because they evaluate the consequences of a decision to decide whether it is good or bad. An act or a rule is good if it generates more total good for all concerned. In considering the question of wasting printer paper, the utilitarian would ask what the cost of the paper is, and what the benefits of wasting the paper might be. A complete analysis would include the environmental impact of the waste as well as the values of such things as time saved, clear separation of print jobs, etc.

Finally, social contract theory says that rules are moral when rational people will agree to accept them, on the condition that others do likewise. With respect to the question of wasting paper, the people concerned must discuss the issue. If all agree to be bound by the rule not to waste paper, then wasting paper will be bad and not wasting paper will be good.

Different ethical theories can lead to different decisions with respect to what is right or wrong. For instance, a Kantian might conclude that copying a copyrighted CD is wrong, while a utilitarian might reach a different conclusion, at least in some circumstances (and notwithstanding that breaking the law is itself a problem!).

The study of ethics is very interesting, and certainly one needs some ethical framework in order to consider the social issues and dilemmas that information technology has created or now influences. For our discussion of social issues we will refer to the *Code of Ethics and Professional Conduct* adopted by the Association for Computing Machinery (ACM) in 1992. You can find a complete statement of the code of ethics at http://www.acm.org/constitution/code.html.

The first section of the code of ethics declares its support of general moral imperatives. We list here only the paragraph titles, without the underlying detail, which you can find in the complete statement:

1.1 Contribute to society and human well-being.
1.2 Avoid harm to others.
1.3 Be honest and trustworthy.
1.4 Be fair and take action not to discriminate.
1.5 Honor property rights including copyrights and patents.
1.6 Give proper credit for intellectual property.
1.7 Respect the privacy of others.
1.8 Honor confidentiality.

The code goes on to declare more specific professional responsibilities:

2.1 Strive to achieve the highest quality, effectiveness and dignity in both the process and products of professional work.
2.2 Acquire and maintain professional competence.
2.3 Know and respect existing laws pertaining to professional work.
2.4 Accept and provide appropriate professional review.
2.5 Give comprehensive and thorough evaluations of computer systems and their impacts, including analysis of possible risks.
2.6 Honor contracts, agreements, and assigned responsibilities.
2.7 Improve public understanding of computing and its consequences.
2.8 Access computing and communication resources only when authorized to do so.

The code also recognizes these organizational leadership imperatives:

3.1 Articulate social responsibilities of members of an organizational unit and encourage full acceptance of those responsibilities.
3.2 Manage personnel and resources to design and build information systems that enhance the quality of working life.
3.3 Acknowledge and support proper and authorized uses of an organization's computing and communication resources.
3.4 Ensure that users and those who will be affected by a system have their needs clearly articulated during the assessment and design of requirements; later the system must be validated to meet requirements.
3.5 Articulate and support policies that protect the dignity of users and others affected by a computing system.
3.6 Create opportunities for members of the organization to learn the principles and limitations of computer systems.

As we consider different social issues related to computing, we will discuss them in light of the ACM Code of Ethics.

INTELLECTUAL PROPERTY

Modern societies recognize physical property rights as a necessary foundation of economic activity. Without the incentive to profit from the act of creation, fewer people would invest the time, energy, and resources to create new property. For example, if a farmer builds a new plow, and anyone can come to their farm, take the plow away, and appropriate the plow for the use of someone else, the farmer will not likely build another. The effect of abandoning property rights would be a decline in economic activity, which would impoverish the greater society.

The same thinking has been applied to intellectual property. If authors, scientists and artists cannot profit from their efforts, such activity may decline, leading again to a general impoverishment of society.

Yet, there are differences between physical and intellectual property. For one thing, intellectual property can be copied, while physical property cannot be. One can copy the design of a plow (the intellectual property), but if one wants a second plow (the physical property), one must build a second plow, and that takes material, energy, and time. Making a copy of intellectual property also leaves the original owner in possession of what the original owner had. Copying intellectual property is, therefore, not exactly the same as stealing physical property.

Another difference between intellectual and physical property is that only one person can own a particular intellectual property, but any number of people can own physical property. Only one person can own the design of the plow, but any number of people can build and own physical plows made to the design. Even when more than one inventor independently creates the same intellectual property, the intellectual property must still be assigned, and belong, to only one inventor. In contrast, any number of people can own instances of the physical property. This makes it easier to spread the benefits of physical property ownership among multiple people.

The interest of society as a whole is to maximize the good for the largest possible number of its members. While most think rewarding inventors for their ideas is for the good, most also feel that disseminating better ideas widely, so they can be used by many, is also for the good. There is a tension between the desire to make creativity rewarding to inventors, so they will continue to invent, and the desire to let many in society benefit from new inventions.

With physical property, property rights are almost absolute. Only in special cases such as eminent domain, where a community can appropriate, after compensating the owner, private property for public use, is there a limit on one's right to what one owns. With intellectual property, the tension between promoting the good of the inventor and promoting the good of the larger group has resulted in more limitations on the rights of property owners. Intellectual property is not perfectly analogous to physical property, as we discussed above, so the rules relating to intellectual property are different.

There are four recognized ways in which people protect their intellectual property, and each has its limitations. The four are trademarks, trade secrets, patents, and copyrights.

Trademarks and Service Marks

Trademarks are the symbols, names, and pictures that companies use to identify their companies and products. Service marks are essentially the same thing, but they identify a service, such as insurance, rather than a tangible product. The Kodak logo, for instance, is a trademark. So is the Kleenex brand name. The name "Novell Online Training Provider" is a service mark of the Novell Corporation.

Trademarks are granted by the government, and they can have a very long life. A trademark granted by the US Patent and Trademark Office has a term of 10 years, and it can be renewed indefinitely for 10 year terms. The application is relatively inexpensive, and can cost as little as a few hundred dollars. Renewals also carry a fee, and with each renewal the owner must submit an affidavit of use, attesting to the owner's ongoing use of the trademark.

A company can lose its exclusive right to use a trademark if the term used becomes part of the language. This is called trademark *genericide*. In Britain, the word "hoover" has come to be the common word for vacuum cleaner, so Hoover is no longer a registered trademark in Britain (however, Hoover remains a trademark in the US). Today the trademarks Xerox and Band Aid are in danger of genericide, and you will perhaps see advertisements for "Xerox *copies*" and "Band Aid brand *strips*," which are attempts by the companies to preserve their trademarks.

Trade Secrets

Of more importance to software creators are the other three approaches to protecting intellectual property. First, a trade secret is just that, a secret kept by a company because the secret provides the company an advantage in the marketplace. A famous trade secret is the formula for Coca-Cola. By the way, the name Coca-Cola is trademarked, and some say it is the most widely recognized brand in the world. The formula for Coca-Cola is a trade secret, and has been since Coca-Cola was invented in 1886 by John Pemberton, a pharmacist in Atlanta, GA. We know the formula has changed over the years, because originally it included some cocaine, which today's formula does not! In any case, the formula has always been a closely and successfully guarded secret, and resides in a bank vault in Georgia.

Writers of software can protect their work by keeping the code secret. In the early days of computing, customers often received source code to the software they ran. However, as software has become appreciated as valuable intellectual property itself, software publishers have begun to regard their source code as a trade secret. What gets shipped to the customer today is almost always the object code, in machine language, which is not easily readable by humans. And what the customer buys today is not ownership of the software, but a license to use the software; the software supplier remains the owner of the intellectual property.

Intellectual property can be protected as a trade secret provided the owner of the secret takes care to protect the information. The owner must restrict access to the information, so that only those with authorization can get to it. The source code could be kept in a secure archive, for instance. The owner must also limit access to the information. Even though the code is in a secure archive, the owner also must be vigilant in providing access only to authorized individuals. The owner must also require those who have access to the information to sign an agreement not to disclose to others anything about the code. Such an agreement is called a nondisclosure agreement, and it may be required of employees as well as any outsiders who might have a need to see the source. To protect their trade secret rights, the owner must also mark any material related to the secret as proprietary. The source code itself, training manuals, and other documentation should include a statement that the software is proprietary.

A trade secret can last indefinitely, and it costs nothing except being serious about protecting the secret. The courts will enforce the owner's rights to the trade secret, as long as the owner remains diligent in efforts to protect the secret. However, if the owner becomes sloppy about security surrounding the secret, the owner can lose the trade secret rights. Suppose, for instance, that (perhaps mistakenly) the owner posts the source code on a web page for a while. Such disclosure of the secret to the public could invalidate any future claim of the owner to legal protection of the secret.

Patents

A patent protects an inventor's intellectual property for a limited period of time. After 20 years, the patented idea becomes public property, and anyone can use it. During the lifetime of the patent, the patent gives the owner the right to prevent others from making or using the invention, unless the owner grants permission. The purpose of seeking a patent, which often costs many thousands of dollars in legal and filing fees, is to gain protection from competition, so the inventor can bring the invention to market and profit from it. A patent is a short-term monopoly right granted to reward the genius of the inventor.

To be patentable, an invention must be novel, nonobvious, and useful. Many suitcases today have wheels on them, so they can be rolled about as well as carried. If someone tried to patent a three-wheeled suitcase, arguing that only two- and four-wheeled suitcases existed prior to the patent application, the patent would probably be denied as being obvious. A three-wheeled suitcase might be novel, and it might be useful, but once someone comes up with the idea of a wheeled suitcase, the number of wheels seems to be a minor detail—something obvious to someone in the business of designing suitcases.

Since 1981, software has been patentable in the United States, if the software is part of a patentable device. In general, software is not patentable because "scientific truths" and the "mathematical expressions" of scientific truths are not patentable. The 1981 case involved a patent for a rubber curing device which incorporated a computer for control. Since software was part of a patentable rubber molding device, the software was patentable.

Mathematical algorithms remain unpatentable, so a new sorting algorithm could not be protected by a patent (It could be protected as a trade secret, of course.). Since 1981, software has been patentable if the software is part of an invention of a new machine or process. A key to making the distinction has been whether the software manipulates measurements obtained from real-world sensors. A program controlling a toaster, or a robotic warehouse, for example, would likely be patentable.

Patents granted to software have not been as protective as patents granted to more traditional inventions. When deciding whether an invention is novel, patent examiners usually rely on inspection of earlier patents. Since software has only recently become patentable, the "prior art" of the field is difficult for examiners from outside the field to learn. As a result, many "bad patents" have been issued for software, with the result that software patents are more subject to challenge than other types of patents, and the individual holding a software patent is more responsible for defending the patent against charges that prior art invalidates it. These considerations add to the cost of a software patent, and limit the protection the patent affords.

Copyright

Copyrights apply to written and artistic works, and a copyright gives the author of the work exclusive rights to copy, distribute, perform, and display the work, and it gives the author exclusive rights to any derivative work (e.g., *The Return of...*). The author can be an individual, a group of individuals, or a company. Copyright to work created by employees in the course of their employment belongs to the company for which they work.

To consider all the industries that rely on copyrighted works, one must include book, journal and newspaper publishing, the recording industry, the film industry, the software industry, advertising, theater, and radio and TV broadcasting. In addition, a substantial set of related industries print, copy, or distribute copyrighted materials, and so are dependent upon the copyright industries. In the United States, in 2001, the copyright industries accounted for over $535 billion, or 5.24 percent of the total GDP of the United States. If one also includes the dependent industries, the total jumps to $791 billion and 7.75 percent of GDP. The copyright industries have been growing at a rate of 5.8 percent per year (Stephen Siwek, "Copyright Industries in the U.S. Economy: The 2002 Report," Economists Incorporated, 2002, http://www.iipa.com/). Clearly, copyrights and the copyright industries are very important to the economy.

One copyrights one's particular expression of an idea, not the idea itself. Your poem about the beauty of the sunset can be copyrighted, but others may also write about the beauty of sunsets, in their own words, of course.

Obtaining a copyright to one's work product is free and automatic. As soon as one creates the work, one owns the copyright to the work. The law does not require that the work be published, and does not require even that notice of copyright be made on the product. Nevertheless, it is good practice to put a notice of copyright on one's work, using the copyright symbol © or the word "copyright," followed by the year of creation and the author's name. Such notification often will put the author in a stronger position in court when prosecuting an infringer.

While not necessary to secure copyright protection, an author can also register a copyright with the government. One completes an application, and submits two copies of the work along with a filing fee of $45. Registration creates a public record of the copyright, and strengthens further one's position in court should someone later infringe on the copyright. For one thing, successful prosecution of an infringer will result in the infringer having to pay court and legal costs of the prosecution, as well as any damages the court awards (http://www.copyright.gov/).

Copyright protection continues from the date of creation of the work until 70 years after the author's death. If the copyright is held by a company, the protection extends 120 years from the date of creation, or 95 years from the date of publication, whichever is shorter.

Copyrights are free or inexpensive, easy to obtain, long-lasting, and economically important. These characteristics make copyright an attractive protection for the intellectual property in software. However, a copyright protects only the expression of an idea, not the idea itself. If an author creates an excellent accounting program and protects it with only a copyright, someone else could look at the program, rewrite it in a different language, and sell the new version without violating the copyright of the original creator.

Software companies usually protect their intellectual property by distributing only the object code, the machine language program, and protecting the object code with copyright. Companies protect the source code as a trade secret by keeping it confidential. What the user buys is not the software itself, but a license to use the software. Usually the license agreement grants the user the right to make a copy of the software for backup purposes, but it may not even permit that. The license agreement may also prohibit the user from disassembling the object code in an attempt to recover a version of source code. Note that the user may not copy the software and distribute it to anyone else, for pay *or for free*, without violating the copyright.

There are those who argue that society's interests are better served when software source code is distributed freely. When no one owns the intellectual property in software, they argue, many people can contribute to the product, and this benefits all. Further, users of the software need not fear the failure of their vendor, and need not wait for their vendor to implement changes the users desire. Those who take this position have created the open source movement. Apache is an open-source web server that runs more than half of all internet servers,

Linux is a popular open-source operating system, and there have been many other very successful examples of open-source products as well.

Whether you side with the vendors of proprietary software or with the open-source advocates, you must know and respect the copyright and patent laws. Sections 1.5, 1.6, and 2.3 of the ACM Code of Ethics clearly require the computer professional to recognize and respect copyright and patent protections.

PRIVACY

There is no question that information technology poses risks to our traditional beliefs about privacy. Governments and companies can and do collect vast amounts of personal information about all of us. Usually the information is collected and used for appropriate purposes, but the existence of the information does pose risks.

When you enter a toll road using an electronic tag to pay the toll, your travel will be tracked from the on-ramp to your exit. When you use a grocery store card to get a discount on your shopping, the store will be collecting your personal shopping history. When you complete your taxes, your personal financial details get stored in a vast database of the tax-paying citizenry. When you use a charge card, your purchases and payment history are recorded for purposes of rating your credit.

There have been occasions when such databases have been used in ways that some would say infringed on rights of privacy. For instance, supposedly confidential census records were used by the US government during WWII to locate Japanese Americans and confine them to internment camps.

Data mining has also permitted governments and organizations to associate personal information from a variety of sources in order to learn more about individuals. Many companies, and even governments, make available for use or for sale various databases. Such *secondary use* of data has a commercial value, because companies can refine their profiles of individuals and tailor marketing to them. The government can use data mining to identify people who probably have underreported their taxes, or who apparently have links to terrorist organizations.

It's also true that information technology has been used to collect information from sources we usually consider private. Governments have listened in to telephone conversations, both by wiretapping and by monitoring the radio transmissions of cell phones, for example, and also intercepted e-mail messages. These actions have usually been justified as necessary for national security, or required as part of an ongoing investigation.

In the United States, a citizen's right to privacy is inferred from the Fourth Amendment which insures, "the right of the people to be secure in their persons, houses, papers, and effects, against unreasonable searches and seizures ..." That's all there is. Privacy is not a right on the same plane as the rights to life, liberty, and property.

In fact, there is a tension between the individual's right to privacy and the needs of others to know about the individual. After all, a person needs to know certain things about another before deciding whether or not to trust the other in a business or personal relationship. For instance, have you ever "Googled" a person with whom you were considering a first date? Governments enforce privacy rights in a balance between the individual's desire for privacy and the needs of others to know.

We usually think of our e-mail and instant messaging conversations as personal correspondence, but think again, if you communicate in such ways at work. The American Management Association reported in 2003 that over half of all US employers now monitor e-mail (quoted in Nord, G.D., McCubbins, T.F., & Nord, J.H., E-"Monitoring in the Workplace," *Communications of the ACM*, 49:8, August 2006, pp. 73-76.). Such monitoring varies from storage of messages for later review, to active software surveillance.

There is very little legal constraint on the monitoring of employee communications when the communications are carried on at work, on company time, using company facilities. Employers monitor such behavior because they have an interest in employee productivity, because they want to protect trade secrets and company data, and because they want to avoid liability for bad behavior by their employees (Nord et al. [2006] report that over 10 percent of US companies have been subpoenaed as a result of employee e-mail!). The courts in most cases support the employer's right to monitor, based on the employer's legitimate need to know.

As a software professional, the ACM Code of Ethics provides excellent guidelines for people collecting, managing and reporting private information. They are summarized in section 1.7. Information professionals should:

- Protect the privacy of data.
- Collect only data that is required.

- Insure the accuracy of data.
- Provide a means for individuals to review data about themselves for accuracy.
- Provide a means for correction of inaccurate data.
- Protect against "secondary use" of data.

ENCRYPTION

Related to the question of privacy is encryption. In an effort to keep communications secure from eavesdropping, people encrypt their communications. Before 1976, if one wanted to encrypt communications, one probably used a single key, or symmetrical encryption, mechanism. Each user knew the key, and each user encrypted their messages with the key, and decrypted incoming messages using the same key. The problem with this method is that all users had to share in advance the secret of the key. Passing the single key around to all users created risks of discovery for all.

In 1976 Diffie and Hellman published an asymmetric key cryptosystem. It and several related mechanisms became known as public key encryption. In this system, each user has a pair of keys, one of which the user publishes and is therefore public, and one of which the user keeps secret only to themselves. If Joe wants to send Mary a secret message, Joe encrypts the message using Mary's public key. In this system, the only way to decrypt such a coded message is to use Mary's private key. Joe cannot even decrypt the message using the public key he used to encrypt the message!

Because of the mathematical relationship between the public and private keys, it is theoretically possible to deduce the private key value from the public key. However, the problem of guessing the private key becomes much greater as the size of the key becomes larger. Large keys, such as 128-bit keys, are thought to provide good security. It should take something like 1000 years using a powerful computer to directly break (as contrasted with a lucky guess) such a public key encryption code.

In the last quarter of the 20th century, the US government prohibited the export of encryption technology in an effort to prevent the spread of public key encryption systems that offered strong security. The reason for this was that the government had an interest in monitoring certain communications for reasons of national security and the prosecution of criminals. After the technology spread outside the US anyway, some people felt the government's actions seemed to punish or hold back US companies, while the rest of the world went ahead using strong encryption anyway.

Starting in 1999, the government's efforts to restrict export of strong encryption technology suffered reversals in the courts. In 1999, for example, the US 9th Circuit Court of Appeals ruled 2–1 in the Bernstein case that the restriction on exporting source code for encryption products was an infringement of free speech, since source code is "expressive." The court said the government did not have the right to impose a "prior restraint" on such speech.

While the ruling could have been appealed further, the US State Department decided to discontinue its efforts to control encryption technology. Such public key systems can now be used and exported to support private communications between computer users.

VIRUSES, WORMS, AND TROJAN HORSES

Viruses are programs that are concealed within another program. When the user executes the "host" program, the virus gets control and may perform actions unrelated to the host program's apparent function. While it has control, the virus program also replicates itself by attaching itself to another executable on the user's computer. The self-replication property of a virus permits it to spread rapidly among networked computers.

A Trojan horse is similar, in that a Trojan Horse is a program with a second, unadvertised function in addition to its apparent function. A Trojan horse does not self-replicate, however, so the spread of a Trojan horse depends upon tricking users into downloading its code. Sometimes this is accomplished using "social engineering" to trick naive users into clicking on an internet link which then downloads an executable file with the hidden functionality.

Trojan horses are often spread with pornography, for example. The file download may promise, and perhaps deliver, erotica, but it also delivers a Trojan horse which could make the user's computer accessible to the attacker remotely. Such a variety of Trojan horse is called a *remote access Trojan* (RAT).

KaZaA is a file-sharing community used to exchange music files, video and movie files, and games. The company has a checkered record of conflicts over its facilitation of copying of copyrighted materials (http://en.wikipedia.org/wiki/Kazaa). A study in 2003, and reported in *Wired* magazine (Zetter, K., "Kazaa Delivers More Than Tunes," *Wired*, January 11, 2004), found that 45 percent of the 4778 executable files the researchers downloaded from KaZaA during one month contained viruses or Trojan horses!

A worm is a program that travels through the network by exploiting weaknesses in the security systems of computers on the network. Often the weakness has to do with an array of data where there is no checking being done on the boundaries of the array. Programs written in the C programming language, perhaps the most popular system programming language, can be vulnerable, because C does not provide built-in boundary checking on arrays. A worm program can change data beyond the boundary of an array, thus altering, perhaps, the return address on the call stack so as to cause the method to transfer control to the worm.

Why do people write and release viruses, Trojan horses, and worms? Sometimes it is for clearly criminal intent. The perpetrator wants to gain access to private information, perhaps with the intention of stealing money or credit. Sometimes it is for a quasi-commercial purpose, such as gaining access to another's computer to employ it to send spam e-mail to others. Sometimes it is simply to prove one's technical ability, and perhaps also to gain recognition among one's peer group or reference group.

Sometimes the perpetrators claim to be doing the victims a favor by exposing a weakness in the victims' security! That argument can be addressed by analogy. What would a homeowner think if some stranger came to the front door, the back door, the basement door, the windows, etc. looking for a way to get in? Most would think they were under assault, and would call the police! Most people feel they have a right to what is theirs, and to their peace of mind, regardless of the quality of their locks.

Software professionals should never condone the spreading of viruses, Trojan horses, or worms. The ACM Code of Ethics provides clear guidance:

1.2 Avoid harm to others.
1.3 Be honest and trustworthy.
1.7 Respect the privacy of others.
2.8 Access computing... resources only when authorized to do so.

HACKERS

Hackers are people who believe themselves to be, and who often are, astute technically. One page on the web defines hackers this way (http://tlc.discovery.com/convergence/hackers/glossary/glossary.html):

hacker n. 1. A person who enjoys exploring the details of programmable systems and how to stretch their capabilities. 2. One who programs enthusiastically. 3. A person who is good at programming quickly. 4. An expert at a particular program, as in "a Unix hacker." 5. [deprecated] A malicious meddler who tries to discover sensitive information by poking around. The correct term for this sense is 'cracker.'

The current sense of the word is generally positive. That is, a hacker knows a lot and uses that knowledge to improve systems and expand capabilities. Hackers do not create viruses or worms. They might, on the other hand, create a new operating system (Dennis Ritchie and Ken Thompson—Unix), found the Free Software Foundation (Richard Stallman), or design a new computer (Steve Wozniak—Apple I).

In the past, the word hacker also meant a technically sophisticated person who used their skills in sometimes illegal ways. Robert Morris unleashed a computer worm in 1988 from Cornell University. Kevin Poulsen got control of the telephone lines going to a Los Angeles radio station in 1990 in order to insure himself of a win of a Porsche in a contest to be the 102nd caller. Vladimir Levin managed to trick Citibank computers out of $10M in 1995 (Hackers Hall of Fame, http://tlc.discovery.com/convergence/hackers/bio/).

Even though today "hacking" may be seen as a positive and creative attitude combined with exceptional skills, it may also be true that a certain technical arrogance among hackers may lead to inappropriate behavior. There may be a tendency among hackers to feel that the rules governing ordinary users should not apply to them, and that authority need not be respected in the technical domain of hackers. Hackers may also see bypassing the rules, without being caught, as a kind of on-line game. A hacker may enjoy finding a way to learn credit card numbers, for example, even though they may have no intention of committing fraud with the information.

In any case, the US law provides serious penalities for both "harmless" hacking and computer fraud. The Computer Fraud and Abuse Act was first passed in 1986, and it was amended in 1994, 1996, and 2001. Accessing a government computer without authorization, and communicating any information with respect to national defense or foreign relations to anyone not otherwise authorized, carries a penalty of a large fine and imprisonment for up to 20 years.

Accessing the computer of any financial institution when one is not authorized to do so can be punished with up to 10 years in prison, and a large fine. Simply obtaining the information is a crime, whether one does anything with that information or not. Trafficking in password information can also draw a 10-year prison term.

Simply damaging a computer, for instance by releasing a computer virus, can be punished with 5 years in prison. Even *causing damage by accident* while improperly accessing another computer can be punished with a year in prison!

Many sections of the ACM Code of Ethics appropriately warn against unauthorized access of another's computer. These include sections 1.2, 1.3, 1.7, and 2.8, as well as:

1.8 Honor confidentiality.

2.3 Know and respect existing laws pertaining to professional work.

3.3 Acknowledge and support proper and authorized uses of computing resources.

CAN COMPUTERS KILL?

In particular, can software kill? Can software maim? Can software inflict damaging financial loss? As software and computers have become ever more integrated into all the appliances, tools, medical devices and weapons of the modern world, the question of software quality has become a question of more urgency.

Most of the time, developers experience the failure of a program as an unfortunate but correctable defeat. From time to time, however, software failures can be very serious. Some are merely expensive, though dramatically so. In 1999 the Mars Climate Orbiter, launched in 1998, crashed when the NASA spacecraft team used different units of measure for distance than the navigation team. One team used English units, and the other used metric units (http://mars.jpl.nasa.gov/msp98/news/mco990930.html).

Three months later, the companion project, Mars Polar Lander, crashed when the jolt from the deployment of its parachute made the software respond as if the probe had touched the surface of the planet, and the software turned off the retro rockets. Without the braking rockets, the craft fell from about 130 feet and was destroyed. These two mission failures were due to problems with software, and wasted about $180 million (http://news.bbc.co.uk/2/hi/science/nature/4522291.stm).

One can argue that the problems were not with the software but with the humans who created the software. That way of looking at the problem focuses attention on the responsibility of the engineers. That is why these failures are properly reviewed in a chapter on the ethics and the social issues of computing.

With software controlling pacemakers, automobile engine controls, antilock brake systems, missile targeting, medical equipment, driverless transports, elevators, robotic equipment, and industrial processes, when software fails, the results can be fatal. One example is the overexposure to radiation suffered by cancer patients in Panama during 2000.

During November of 2000, 28 people being treated for cancer at the National Cancer Institute in Panama were accidentally exposed to much more radiation than prescribed. At least five died of the experience, and many of the others risked "serious radiation-related complications" from excessive exposure to radiation, according the the US FDA (http://www.fda.gov/cdrh/ocd/panamaradexp.html, July 6, 2001). When investigated, the cause turned out to be an erroneous software algorithm in the Multidata software controlling the Theratronics Cobalt-60 machine.

The Multidata software provided a way for operators to digitize representations of metal shields called blocks, which are used to protect healthy, delicate tissue from exposure to x-rays. The doctors prescribed the use of various blocks for individual patients. The machine operators entered descriptions of the blocks into the software, and the Multidata software then calculated the amount of radiation to deliver.

When investigating the cause of the radiation overexposures, investigators found that operators could enter data about the blocks in such a way that the software would "misunderstand" the digitized representation, mistaking holes in the pattern of blocks for the block itself. Multidata later recognized the problem as the "self-intersecting shape outline" problem. In that circumstance, the software calculated radiation doses that were too high by margins of 20 percent to 100 percent.

Because the problem only manifested itself with certain combinations of blocks, and with certain data input practices of individual operators, the cause of the few overexposures (the hospital treated about 100 people per day) was difficult to determine. You can read a more complete account of the accidents and the investigation in an eWEEK article from March 2004 at http://www.findarticles.com/p/articles/mi_zdewk/is_200403/ai_ziff121063.

In 1991 during the first Gulf War, a software anomaly caused a Patriot missile battery protecting a barracks of the US Army in Dhahran, Saudi Arabia to fail to fire at an incoming Iraqi Scud missile, even though the system detected the missile en route. Twenty-eight soldiers died. The cause of the Patriot missile's battery failure turned out to be an obscure software bug related to truncation of a variable used to keep time. The Information Management and Technology Division of the US General Accounting Office provided a complete report (http://www.fas.org/spp/starwars/gao/im92026.htm).

Originally the Patriot missile was designed to operate against aircraft and cruise missiles. It is a mobile system designed to be set up in a location and operated for a few hours at a time before moving again. The system was adapted to attack faster short-range ballistic missiles. To avoid firing the Patriot battery at false alarms, the software controlling the battery would confirm the presence of an incoming missile by predicting the incoming missile's future position based on the battery's early detection of the missile target.

To compute the predicted position of the enemy missile, the Patriot battery relied on highly accurate time-keeping to focus the attention of its radar on a "range gate." If the incoming missile were again detected in the range gate at the predicted time, the Patriot battery concluded that the incoming missile was real, and automatically launched its attack.

The problem discovered in the tragic Dhahran incident was that the time-keeping variable used in the Patriot software lacked sufficient precision, and this resulted in truncation of the time measurement. That truncation slowly accumulated a difference between actual and computed time. In Dhahran, the missile battery had been in place for over 100 hours, and the time difference had accumulated to 0.34 seconds. Since the Scud was moving fast, the Patriot battery miscalculated the predicted position of the Scud by about a half mile. As a result, the battery did not detect the incoming missile in its range gate, and so concluded that no attack was in progress. The battery sat silent as the Iraqi missile killed the US soldiers.

Such subtle problems in software illustrate the tremendous challenge, and the tremendous responsibility, developers have to create and test their programs and systems. As someone observed, in most states you need a license to cut hair, but not to write software, even for medical and military systems! Computing professionals must shoulder their ethical burden and use every means at their disposal to insure their systems are correctly specified and implemented.

Testing is important, but it is not enough. Any system of reasonable complexity will be impossible to test exhaustively. Many authorities have made this point. For example, Jeffrey Voas of the Defense Advanced Research Projects Agency (1998, http://www.stsc.hill.af.mil/crosstalk/1998/11/voas.asp) cites, "the many practical and theoretical deficiencies of software testing." In addition to testing, developers need to use best practices throughout specification and creation of their systems, and to perform their work with the utmost conscientiousness.

The ACM Code of Ethics again provides guidance:

1.2 Avoid harm to others... computing professionals must minimize malfunctions by following generally accepted standards for system design and testing...
2.1 Strive to achieve the highest quality, effectiveness... in both the process and products of professional work.
2.2 Acquire and maintain professional competence.
2.5 Give comprehensive and thorough evaluations of computer systems and their impacts, including analysis of possible risks... Computer professionals are in a position of special trust, and therefore have a special responsibility to provide objective, credible evaluations to employers, clients, users, and the public... Any signs of danger from systems must be reported to those who have opportunity and/or responsibility to resolve them...

SUMMARY

Ethics is the rational study of different moral systems. We described very briefly some of the different ethical theories, and then introduced the ACM Code of Ethics, developed to guide the behavior of people in the computing industry.

The development of the software industry has brought new emphasis to the topic of intellectual property rights. Software is now considered valuable intellectual property, and companies and individuals protect their rights with a variety of tools. We discussed trademarks, trade secrets, patents, and copyrights. The most common ways of protecting software rights are to maintain source code as a trade secret and protect object code with copyright.

Individual privacy can be endangered in this age of large databases and marketing of data resources to commercial interests. In addition, actions many consider by their nature to be private, such as e-mail communications, may in fact not enjoy the protection of the laws, if the communications occur at the workplace. For people working with data resources, the ACM Code of Ethics prescribes a set of rules to fairly protect individual privacy.

Encryption can be viewed as a matter of privacy rights. But privacy rights are not absolute, since there is a tension between the individual's right to privacy, and others' need to know with whom they are interacting. In the past, the US Government resisted the export of strong encryption technology, because the government monitors certain communications for the purposes of insuring national security and prosecuting criminals. Since 1999, however, the government has withdrawn its export controls on encryption technology.

Viruses, worms and Trojan horses are misleading or malicious programs that can damage or subvert a victim's computer. Whether the purpose of such a program is simply mischievous, or destructive, or criminal, the law provides severe penalties of up to 20 years in prison for offenders. The ACM Code of Ethics clearly rejects such behavior.

Hacker is a word meaning someone with great computer skills whose work contributes in an unusual way to the industry. Today the word is generally positive, but in the past the word hacker also included those who created cleaver but destructive or criminal applications of computer technology. Today the word used for the "bad guys" is cracker. In any case, hackers must be careful to avoid a feeling of superiority that might tempt them to think that rules which apply to others do not apply to them.

Finally, as computers become ever more highly integrated into many critical applications, more and more responsibility falls on developers to take every precaution in creating reliable applications. Computer-controlled weapons, medical equipment, transportation systems, food processing, chemical manufacturing, and other applications make quality computing systems a matter of life and death. Thorough testing must be part of the activities of developers, but since testing cannot be exhaustive for most systems, because of their complexity, developers must use a combination of best practices and relentless conscientiousness to create safe and effective systems.

REVIEW QUESTIONS

9.1 Should software be copyrightable or patentable? Ignoring the law for the moment, argue the question from the Kantian, Utilitarian, and Social Contract Theory perspectives.

9.2 Why does a copyright provide better protection for object code than for source code?

9.3 How can you apply the ACM Code of Ethics to the practice of sending "spam" e-mail (unsolicited messages to strangers). What sections of the ACM Code apply, and does the ACM Code permit the practice?

9.4 Inspection of a computer program controlling a weapons system shows 54 "if" statements (23 with "else" clauses), 4 "switch" statements (with 5, 7, 4, and 8 "cases"), and 17 "for" or "while" loops with parameterized looping boundaries. How would you exhaustively test such a program to prove its safety?

9.5 Assume you have just created a program to schedule taxicabs in real time. You're sure that your approach is entirely new and much better than anything else available. Every taxi company in the world is going to want your software. Explain how you would best protect your work—patent? copyright? secret?

APPENDIX

Answers to Review Questions

INTRODUCTION TO COMPUTER SCIENCE

1.1 Write an algorithm for your morning routine, from the time the alarm clock rings until you leave the house for work or school.

> Awake to alarm clock.
> Get out of bed.
> Go downstairs to the kitchen.
> Fix and eat breakfast.
> Go to my room.
> Check the temperature and listen to the weather forecast.
> Get dressed.
> etc.

1.2 Find or invent an algorithm to calculate the square root of any number. Apply the algorithm to the number 2046, finding its square root to 2 decimal places. Do not use a computer or calculator!

> First take a guess: in this case 40.
> Divide the number by the guess: 51.15
> Find average of guess and quotient: (51.15 + 40) / 2 = 45.575
> Repeat with the new guess (45.575 after the first round).
> Second round result: 45.23
> Third round result: 45.232
> (from: http://www.homeschoolmath.net/teaching/square-root-algorithm.php)

1.3 Perl is a computer language that is often used for quick, one-off programming jobs, like converting text in a document from one format to another. ADA is a language used for Department of Defense applications where human life may be at stake. What differences would you imagine to find when you compare Perl with ADA?

> Perl: little type checking of variables
>   lots of default assumptions and short-cuts

180

    informal code style
    emphasis on speed of coding

  ADA: rigorous type checking
    no default assumptions — full declarations required
    documentation/comments required
    emphasis on correct and verifiable process

1.4 Why might a computer scientist with a primary interest in databases also need to know about networking?

   Today many databases are accessed over a network, and some are even distributed over multiple networked computers. Understanding networking will be essential to understanding issues of database security and performance.

1.5 The acronym API stands for Application Programming Interface. What do you suppose API means with respect to an operating system?

   The API of an operating system documents the manner in which programs can request operating system services, like accessing peripheral devices, writing files, starting other processes, and accessing the network.

1.6 If you were offered a job with Microsoft and permitted to choose between working on operating systems, database products, or applications products like Word or Excel, which would you choose, and why?

   This is a matter of opinion. The question is designed to stimulate thinking about the different programming demands and rewards in different arenas.

1.7 Whom do you believe should be credited as "the inventor of the modern computer?"

   This, too, is a matter of opinion. Some will argue John Atanasoff, some will argue Howard Aiken, some will argue Konard Zuse, and some will argue Mauchly and Eckert.

1.8 What applications of computing seem to you to be unethical? What are some principles you can declare with respect to the ethical and unethical use of computers and software?

   Unethical uses of computers include using computers to defraud others, using computers to improperly obtain personal information, using computers to cause damage to others, and using computers to steal intellectual property.

   Computing should be used in ways that protect individual rights and property.
   Computing should be used in ways that conform to the law.
   Computing should be used to benefit society.
   Computing should cause no harm.

1.9 List some important ways in which computing has contributed to the welfare of man. What people, if any, have suffered from the advance of computing technology?

   Molecular modeling of drugs has speeded development of medical cures.
   Election results are reported much faster and more accurately than before.
   Manufacturing and service industries have streamlined their processes, resulting in less expensive and higher quality goods and services.
   People of limited education have found fewer low-level jobs available as a result of automation.
   Professional people have found themselves competing with people around the world, as the Internet has advanced globalization.

ALGORITHMS

2.1 Write pseudo code for an algorithm for finding the square root of a number.

```
guess <-- number / (1 + count of digits in the
number)
while(absoluteValue((guess * guess) - number) > .01
){
 guess = (guess + number/guess) / 2
}
return guess
```
(from: http://www.homeschoolmath.net/teaching/square-root-algorithm.php)

2.2 Write pseudo code for finding the mean of a set of numbers.

```
mean( list_of_numbers )
length <-- length of list_of_numbers
index  <-- 1
sum    <-- 0

while index <= length {
 sum <-- sum + list_of_numbers[index]
 index <-- index + 1
}
return sum / length
```

2.3 Count the primitive operations in your algorithm to find the mean. What is the order of growth of your mean algorithm?

```
setup 4
loop 5 * length (length = n, the count of numbers to be averaged)
return 2
```
$$\Theta(n)$$

2.4 Write pseudo code for finding the median of a set of numbers.

```
median( list_of_numbers )
    length <-- length of list_of_numbers

    merge_sort( list_of_numbers )

if length is odd
    // return middle number
    return list_of_numbers[(length + 1) / 2]
else
    // find subscripts of 2 middle values
    m1 <-- length / 2
    m2 <-- m1 + 1
    // and return the average of the middle two
    return (list_of_numbers[m1]+list_of_numbers[m2]) /
2
end
```

2.5 What is the order of growth of your algorithm to find the median?

```
Θ( n( lg n ) ), based on merge_sort
```

2.6 Suppose that your algorithm to find the mean is $\Theta(n)$, and that your algorithm to find the median is $\Theta(n \lg n)$, what will be the execution speed ratio between your algorithm for the mean and your algorithm for the median when the number of values is 1,000,000?

```
mean : median ::   1,000,000 : 1,000,000 * lg 1,000,000
mean : median ::   1 : lg 1,000,000
mean : median ::   1 : 20
It will be 20 times faster to find the mean than the median.
```

2.7 A sort routine which is easy to program is the bubble-sort. The program simply scans all of the elements to be sorted repeatedly. On each pass, the program compares each element with the one next to it, and reorders the two, if they are in inverse order. For instance, to sort the following list:

   6 7 3 1 4

Bubble-sort starts by comparing 6 and 7. They are in the correct order, so it then compares 7 and 3. They are in inverse order, so bubble-sort exchanges 7 and 3, and then compares 7 and 1. The numbers 7 & 1 are in reverse order, so bubble-sort swaps them, and then compares 7 & 4. Once again, the order is incorrect, so it swaps 7 & 4. End of scan 1:

   6 3 1 4 7

Scanning left to right again results in:

   3 1 4 6 7

Scanning left to right again results in a correct ordering:

   1 3 4 6 7

Write pseudo code for the bubble-sort.

```
bubbleSort( list )
    length          <-- length of list

    // look through the whole list to find
    //   mis-ordered pairs, and continue until
    //   we get through the whole list without
    //   swapping any pairs
    do {
        // start at the left end of the list: index = 1
        swapped_pair <-- false
        index        <-- 1
        while index <= length - 1 {
            // if this pair is mis-ordered, swap them
            if list[index] > list[index + 1] {
                swap( list[index], list[index + 1] )
                swapped_pair = true
                // increment the index to look at the
                //   next pair up
                index <-- index + 1
            }
        }
    // quit only when we have gone through the whole
    //   list and found it unnecessary to swap any pair
    } while( swapped = true )
end
```

2.8 What is the bubble-sort Θ?

   $\Theta(n^2)$

2.9 How will the bubble sort compare for speed with the merge sort when the task is to sort 1,000,000 social security numbers which initially are in random order?

```
bubble-sort:merge-sort::(1,000,000)2:1,000,000*lg 1,000,000
bubble-sort : merge-sort  ::  1,000,000 : lg 1,000,000
bubble-sort : merge-sort  ::  1,000,000 : 20
bubble-sort : merge-sort  ::  50,000 : 1
```
The merge-sort will run 50,000 times faster than the bubble-sort!
If the merge-sort takes 10 seconds, the bubble-sort will take
almost 6 days!

COMPUTER ORGANIZATION

3.1 Write the number 229 in base-2.

    11100101

3.2 What is the base-10 value of 11100101?

    229

3.3 What are the units (values) of the first 3 columns in a base-8 (octal) number?

    64s 8s units

    8^2 8^1 8^0

3.4 What is the base-2 value of the base-8 (octal) number 377?

    11111111

3.5 Convert the following base-10 numbers to base-2:

    37
    470
    1220
    17
    99
         100101
      111010110
   10011000100
        10001
     1100011

3.6 Convert the following base-2 numbers to base-10:

    00000111
              7
    10101010
           170
    00111001
          57
    01010101
          85
    00110011
          51

3.7 Assume a 16-bit signed integer data representation where the sign bit is the msb.

    a What is the largest positive number that can be represented?
    b Write the number 17,440.
    c Write the number −20.
    d What is the largest negative number that can be represented?

    a 32,767
    b 0100010000100000
    c 1111111111101100
    d −32,768

3.8 Using ASCII encoding, write the bytes to encode your initials in capital letters.

```
CHR
C    67    1000011
H    72    1001000
R    82    1010010
```

3.9 Referring to the list of Intel x86 instructions in this chapter, arrange a set of instructions to add the values stored in memory locations 50 and 51, and then to store the result in memory location 101. You need not show the bit pattern for each instruction; just use the mnemonics listed, followed in each case by the appropriate operand(s).

```
MOV 50, EDX   // copy what's in 50 to the register
ADD 51, EDX   // add what's in 51 to the register
MOV EDX, 101  // store the result in 101
```

3.10 What Intel x86 instructions would you use to accomplish subtraction using 2's complement addition? This instruction set has a SUB instruction, but don't use that; write your own 2's complement routine instead.

```
MOV 51, EDX   // copy what's in 51 to the register
NEG EDX       // take 2s complement of register
ADD EDX, 50   // subtract contents of 51 from 52
MOV EDX, 101  // store the result in 101
```

3.11 What are the advantages of a larger computer word size? Are there disadvantages? If so, what are the disadvantages?

Advantages:
Easy to represent large numbers.
Easy to address large memory space.

Disadvantages:
Memory use is likely to be less "bit-efficient" when numbers are small.
Processors and supporting hardware are more expensive.

3.12 Assume that cache memory has an access time of 10 nanoseconds, while main memory has an access time of 100 nanoseconds. If the "hit rate" of the cache is .70 (i.e., 70% of the time, the value needed is already in the cache), what is the average access time to memory?

```
.70 * ( 10ns ) + .30 * ( 100ns ) = 37ns average access time
```

3.13 Assume our 1GHz computer, which averages 3 cycles per instruction, is connected to the Internet via a 10 Mbit connection (i.e., the line speed allows 10 million bits to pass every second). From the time the computer receives the first bit, how many instructions can the computer execute while waiting for a single 8-bit character to arrive?

8 bits * 1 sec./10,000,000 bits = .0000008 sec./character
1Billion cycles/sec. * 1 instruction/3 cycles * .0000008
sec./character = 267 instr/char

3.14 What complexity does DMA present to the management of cache memory?

DMA directly updates main memory, or directly reads from main memory. If the CPU takes advantage of cache memory to accelerate reads and writes, a "cache coherency" can develop. The CPU may be reading memory location x via a cached copy that has been changed in main memory via a DMA transfer. The cached value is, therefore, "stale." Likewise, if DMA is being used to write values from main memory to a device, and values the CPU has written to cache memory have not yet been "flushed" to main memory, stale or incorrect values may be written.

3.15 Discuss the concept of a "memory hierarchy" whereby memory closer to the CPU is faster, more expensive, and smaller than memory at the next level. Arrange the different types of memory we have discussed in such a hierarchy.

The smallest, fastest, most expensive memory locations are the registers on the CPU. Adjacent to the CPU are cache memories that are smaller, faster and more expensive than main memory, but larger, slower, and less expensive than the set of registers. The next level in the memory hierarchy is main memory, which modern machines have in some abundance, often measured in gigabytes. After main memory, the next level in the memory hierarchy is mass storage, today almost always on magnetic disk drives. Such memory is more expansive, less expensive per byte, and slower than main memory. Beyond magnetic disks, optical disk memory today represents the next step in the memory hierarchy, with lower costs, higher densities, and slower speeds.

SOFTWARE

4.1. Why was it important to the history of programming languages that, even at its introduction, FORTRAN generated efficient programs?

There was a widespread belief that a higher-level language could never approach the efficiency of hand-coded assembly language. If FORTRAN had been less efficient, it would have been much more difficult to persuade the assembly-language-oriented programmers of the 1950s to try higher-level languages. Such resistance would have slowed the development of language theory, higher-level languages, and the productivity of the software industry.

4.2 Given what you know of computer languages, what language would be a good choice for

a Processing a file of text, such as a system error log, looking for particular types of events?

Perl, awk, sed, PHP, Ruby, and Python

b Developing an artificial intelligence application to diagnose disease, given a list of symptoms?

Lisp
Prolog

c Writing driver software for a new computer printer?

C, C#, C++

4.3 Here is a C function that computes the sum of a range of integers. You can assume that `begin` will always be less than or equal to `end` (begin <= end):

```c
int summation( int begin, int end ) {
    int result = begin;
    begin = begin + 1;

    while( begin <= end ) {
        result = result + begin;
        begin = begin + 1;
    }
    return result;
}
```

Rewrite this function so that it uses recursion instead of iteration.

```c
int summation( int begin, int end ) {
    if( begin == end ) return begin;
    return begin + summation( (begin + 1), end );
}
```

4.4 Assume that a language describes a *statement-sequence* as a sequence of one or more *statements* separated by semicolons (assume statements are defined elsewhere), but with no punctuation at the end of the statement-sequence. Write the EBNF production.

```
statement-sequence → statement { ; statement }
```

4.5 Given the following grammar:

```
expr    → term + expr | term
term    → factor * term | factor
factor  → ( expr ) | number
number  → number digit | digit
digit   → 0|1|2|3|4|5|6|7|8|9
```

Draw the full parse tree for the expression:

```
        2 * (3 + 5) + (6 + 8)

         term              +        expr
        2*(3+5)                     6+8

  factor  *   term           term  +  expr
  number      factor         factor   term
  digit       (expr)         number   factor
   2          (3+5)          digit    number
                             6        digit
                                      8
          term + expr
          factor term
          number factor
          digit  number
           3     digit
                  5
```

Abstract parse tree on next page . . .

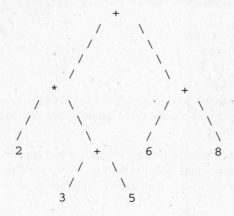

```
              +
             / \
            /   \
           /     \
          /       \
         *         +
        / \       / \
       /   \     /   \
      /     \   /     \
     2       + 6       8
            / \
           /   \
          3     5
```

4.6 Describe the form in which a program is passed from

    a the scanner to the parser.

       stream of tokens

    b the parser to the semantic analyzer.

       parse tree

4.7 Here is a context-free grammar in BNF form:

```
expr   --> expr + term  | expr - term  | term
term   --> term * factor | term / factor | factor
factor --> ex ** factor  | ex
ex     --> ( expr ) | id
```

Rewrite this grammar in EBNF form.

```
expr   --> term   { ( + | - )  term  }
term   --> factor { ( * | / ) factor }
factor --> ex     { ** ex }
ex     --> ( expr )  | id
```

4.8 What does this Scheme function do?

```scheme
(define whatsThis
  (lambda (n)
    ( cond((null? n) 0)
          ((null? (cdr n)) (car n))
          ((> (car n) (whatsThis (cdr n))) (car n))
          ( else (whatsThis (cdr n)))
      )))
```

The function whatsThis returns the largest element in a list:

```scheme
> (whatsThis (list 1 2 4 5 3))
5
>
```

4.9 Give an example of an irregularity in a language with which you are familiar.

In Java, one can test for the equality of two variables of a primitive type, such as int x and int y, using the double equal sign (==) operator, but objects must be compared using the equals() method. The Java switch statement takes only "integral" data types (e.g., int, char, short, byte) for case values, and many times it would be convenient to use Strings or other objects as case labels.

Return values in Visual BASIC look like assignments.

In C, a function cannot return an array.

Etc.

4.10. Would it ever make sense to write a program in one language, planning from the beginning to rewrite the program later in a different language? Give an example of a situation in which such a plan might make sense, and not simply result in wasted time and effort.

This strategy is often used. A prototype for a system will be built using a language that is particularly suited to rapid development, thus leading quickly to working code for testing. When the concept has been proved, the algorithms can be rewritten in a language particularly suited for high performance and scalability.

PROGRAMMING IN JAVA

5.1 Write a Java program that divides the number 74.3 by 12.6 and reports the result of the division. Store the dividend and divisor in variables named dividend and divisor before performing the division. What will be the type of these variables? What will be the type of the result? What is the quotient?

```
public class Divide {
//A Java program that divides the number 74.3
//  by 12.6 and reports the result

public static void main( String[] args ) {
    double dividend = 74.3;
    double divisor  = 12.6;
    double result   = dividend / divisor;
    System.out.println( "Result: 74.3 / 12.6 = " + result);
  }
}

Result: 74.3 / 12.6 = 5.896825396825397
```

5.2 Write a Java program to compute the area of a circle whose radius is 5. For the value of PI, use 3.14. Now rewrite your program so that it uses the very precise value of PI available as a static constant in the Math class that comes with Java. Here is how you use the Math class constant:

```
double pi = Math.PI;
```

How much does your result change?

```
public class CircleArea {
//A Java program to compute the area of a circle
//  whose radius is 5

  public static void main( String[] args ) {
      double r = 5.;
      System.out.print  ( "Using pi = 3.14: " );
      System.out.println( "Area when r = 5: " + 3.14*r*r );
      System.out.print  ( "Using Math.PI:    " );
      System.out.println( "Area when r = 5: " + Math.PI*r*r );
  }
}

Using pi = 3.14: Area when r = 5: 78.5
Using Math.PI:   Area when r = 5: 78.53981633974483
```

5.3 Write a Java program that prompts the user for a number, and then tells the user whether the number is an even multiple of 5. Use Scanner to read the number from the user, and use the modulo operator (%) to decide whether the number is a multiple of 5.

```
import java.util.Scanner;
public class Mod5 {
//A Java program to detect a multiple of 5
public static void main( String[] args ) {
    Scanner sc = new Scanner(System.in);
    System.out.print( "Enter an integer: " );
    int number = sc.nextInt();
```

```
    if( number % 5 == 0 ) {
      System.out.println( number + " is a multiple of 5." );
    }
    else {
      System.out.println( number + " is not a multiple of 5.");
    }
  }
}
```

```
Enter an integer: 115
115 is a multiple of 5.
```

5.4 Write a Java program that asks a user to enter five Strings, one at a time. Have it save the Strings in an array of strings. Then have the program display the words in reverse order. Use a for, or a while, or a do while loop to read in the Strings, and another for, while, or do while loop to print them out.

```
import java.util.Scanner;
public class FiveStrings {
//A Java program to read and display 5 Strings

        public static void main( String[] args ) {
                Scanner  sc           = new Scanner(System.in);
                String[] stringList  = new String[5];

                for( int i=0; i< 5; i++ ) {
                        System.out.print( "Enter a String: " );
                        stringList[i] = sc.nextLine();
                }
                System.out.println( "In reverse order:" );
                int n = 4;
                while( n >= 0 ) {
                        System.out.println( stringList[n] );
                        n--;
                }
        }
}
```

5.5 Write a Java program that can categorize vehicles based on the number of wheels the vehicle has. Your program should prompt the user for the number of wheels on the vehicle, and then read the number into an int variable. If the user says the vehicle has 2 or 3 wheels, the program will report that it is a motorcycle, if it has 4 wheels the vehicle will be labeled a "car or light truck," if it has 6, 8, 10, 12, 14, 16, or 18 wheels, it will be categorized as a truck. Any other number of wheels will be reported as an error. Use a switch statement to compute the decision.

```
import java.util.Scanner;
public class Wheels {
//A Java program to categorize a vehicle

        public static void main( String[] args ) {
            Scanner sc = new Scanner(System.in);
            System.out.print( "How many wheels? " );
            int number = sc.nextInt();

            switch (number) {
                case 2: case 3:
```

```
                    System.out.println( "motorcycle" );
                    break;
          case 4:
                    System.out.println( "car" );
                    break;
          case  6: case  8: case 10: case 12:
          case 14: case 16: case 18:
                    System.out.println( "truck" );
                    break;
          default:
                    System.out.println( "Error: "
                                     + number + " wheels?" );
        }
      }
    }
```

5.6 Write a Java class called `Vehicle`. The `Vehicle` class will have instance attributes for color, make, model, speed, number of occupants, and maximum number of occupants. The `Vehicle` class will also have a static variable called `vehicleCount` that can be used to track the number of vehicles in the application.

The constructor for `Vehicle` should expect values for make, model, maximum number of occupants, and color, and it should set the vehicle speed to zero, the number of occupants to 1, and increment the count of vehicles each time the constructor is called. Each of the instance and static variables should have an accessor (`get`) method that will return the appropriate value, and all except the `vehicleCount` variable should also have a mutator (`set`) method so that the value can be modified.

You should also give the `Vehicle` class an instance method called `changeSpeed`. The `changeSpeed` method should expect a floating-point value for the new speed, and it should return a floating-point value representing the difference between the new speed and the previous speed of the vehicle.

Include a `public static void main( String[] args)` method that creates a few vehicles, sets some speeds, and reads some variable values, so that you can test your code by launching the class from the command line.

```
    // The Vehicle class
    public class Vehicle {
          private String color;
          private String make;
          private String model;
          private double speed;
          private int     maxOccupants;

          private static int vehicleCount = 0;

          public Vehicle( String mk, String mdl, int maxOcc, String clr )
            {

                  make         = mk;
                  model        = mdl;
                  maxOccupants = maxOcc;
                  color        = clr;
                  speed        = 0.;
                  vehicleCount++;
            }

          public String getColor()          { return color; }
```

```java
        public String getMake()        { return make; }
        public String getModel()       { return model; }
        public double getSpeed()       { return speed; }
        public int    getMaxOccupants() { return maxOccupants; }

        public void setColor( String clr ) { color = clr; }
        public void setMake ( String mk )  { make  = mk; }
        public void setModel( String mdl ) { model = mdl; }
        public void setSpeed( double spd ) { speed = spd; }

        public double changeSpeed( double newSpeed ) {
                double accel = newSpeed - speed;
                speed = newSpeed;
                return accel;
        }

        public static void main( String[] args ) {
            Vehicle v1, v2, v3;

            v1 = new Vehicle( "Ford", "Mustang", 2, "red" );
            v2 = new Vehicle( "BMW",  "328i",    4, "silver" );
            v3 = new Vehicle( "Chrysler", "PT Cruiser", 4, "gold" );

            System.out.println( "There are " + vehicleCount +
                                " vehicles." );
            System.out.println( "Make of v1 (Ford): " + v1.getMake() );
            System.out.println( "Model of v2 (328i): " +
                                v2.getModel() );
            System.out.println( "Color of v3 (gold): " +
                                v3.getColor() );
            System.out.println( "Max occupants of v1 (2): " +
                                v1.getMaxOccupants() );
            double accel = v1.changeSpeed( 70. );
            System.out.println( v1.getModel() + " accelerated by " +
                                accel + "mph to " +
                                v1.getSpeed() + "mph." );
            v1.setMake( "Chevrolet" );
            v1.setModel( "Malibu" );
            v1.setColor( "white" );
            v1.setSpeed( 60. );
            System.out.println( "v1 is now a " + v1.getColor() + " "
                                + v1.getMake() + " " + v1.getModel() +
                                " going " + v1.getSpeed() + "mph." );
        }
}
```

5.7 Write a `Skateboard` class that inherits from `Vehicle`. Override the `changeSpeed` method for the `Skateboard` class, so that instances of the `Skateboard` class can never exceed 10mph. If a larger value is supplied, the method will simply set the speed of the `Skateboard` to 10.

```java
    class Skateboard extends Vehicle {

        public Skateboard( String mk, String mdl, String clr ) {
            super( mk, mdl, 1, clr );
        }
```

```
        public double changeSpeed( double newSpeed ) {
                if( newSpeed > 10. ) { newSpeed = 10.; }
                double accel = newSpeed - speed;
                speed = newSpeed;
                return accel;
        }
    }
```

5.8 Write a `Bus` class that inherits from `Vehicle`. An instance of the `Bus` class must always have a named driver. In the constructor for a `Bus`, make sure that your code expects and stores the name of the driver. Also, the `Bus` class should have accessor and mutator methods for returning and changing the name of the driver.

```
    class Bus extends Vehicle {
        private String driver;
        public Bus( String driver ) {
                // A "convenience constructor" that defaults all the
                //   parameters except for driver name.  The "this"
                //   says create a bus passing the 4 default parameter
                //   values, plus the driver name, to the other
                //   constructor for the Bus class.
                this( "GM", "Metro", 42, "Silver", driver);
        }
        public Bus( String mk,  String mdl, int maxOcc,
                    String clr, String driver  ) {
                // super says create a vehicle instance for this bus
                //   super invokes the vehicle (superclass) constructor
                super( mk, mdl, maxOcc, clr );
                // We also need to store the name of the bus driver.
                // this.driver refers to the private instance variable
                //    that has the same name as the constructor
parameter
                this.driver = driver;
        }

        public String getDriver() { return driver; }

        public void    setDriver( String driver ) {
                this.driver = driver;
        }

        public static void main( String[] args ) {
                // A main method for testing use only
                Bus firstBus  = new Bus( "Joe" );
                Bus secondBus = new Bus( "Mercedes", "B302", 60,
                                          "Black",     "Mary" );
                System.out.println( "First bus: "  + firstBus.getMake() +
                            " driven by " + firstBus.getDriver() );
                System.out.println( "Second bus: " + secondBus.getMake() +
                            " driven by " + secondBus.getDriver() );
                secondBus.setDriver( "David" );
                System.out.println( "Second bus: " + secondBus.getMake() +
                            " driven by " + secondBus.getDriver() );
        }
    }
```

5.9 To the class `Vehicle`, add a `refuel` method that expects two parameters, `fuelQuantity` and `milesSince LastFueling`. Also add instance variables to the `Vehicle` class for `totalMileage` and `totalFuelConsumed`. Further, add an accessor method called `fuelEconomy` that will return the total miles per gallon of the vehicle.

```
private double totalFuel  = 0.;
private double totalMiles = 0.;
      .
      .
public void reFuel( double fuelQuantity,
                    double milesSinceLastFueling ){
     totalMiles += milesSinceLastFueling;
     totalFuel  += fuelQuantity;
}

public double fuelEconomy() {
     return totalMiles / totalFuel;
}
```

What will you do to make the `refuel` method work properly when invoked on an instance of Skateboard?

```
class Skateboard extends Vehicle {

     public Skateboard( String mk, String mdl, String clr ) {
          super( mk, mdl, 1, clr );
     }

     public double changeSpeed( double newSpeed ) {
          if( newSpeed > 10. ) { newSpeed = 10.;  }
          double accel = newSpeed - this.getSpeed();
          this.setSpeed( newSpeed );
          return accel;
     }

     public double fuelEconomy()
                     throws UnsupportedOperationException {
          throw new UnsupportedOperationException(
               "Skateboard uses no fuel" );
     }

     public void reFuel(double gallons, double miles)
                     throws UnsupportedOperationException {
          throw new UnsupportedOperationException(
               "Skateboard uses no fuel" );
     }
}
```

Write a test class called `ManyVehicles` that creates a variety of different `Vehicles`, exercises all the methods you have created, and checks for proper execution. Try to set the speed of a `Skateboard` to 60, for example, or to refuel a `Skateboard`. Check that the fuel economy calculations are being performed correctly.

```
public class ManyVehicles {
     // main method: tests the Vehicle class
     public static void main( String[] args ) {
          Vehicle v1, v2, v3, v4;
```

```
        v1 = new Vehicle( "Ford", "Mustang", 2, "red" );
        v2 = new Vehicle( "BMW",  "328i",    4, "silver" );
        v3 = new Vehicle( "Chrysler", "PT Cruiser", 4, "gold" );

        System.out.println( "There are " + Vehicle.vehicleCount
                            + " vehicles." );
        System.out.println( "Make of v1 (Ford): " + v1.getMake() );
        System.out.println( "Model of v2 (328i):" +
                            v2.getModel());
        System.out.println( "Color of v3 (gold: " +
                            v3.getColor());
        System.out.println( "Max occupants of v1 (2):
                            " + v1.getMaxOccupants() );

        double accel = v1.changeSpeed( 70. );
        System.out.println( v1.getModel() + " accelerated by "
                            + accel + "mph to " + v1.getSpeed()
                            + "mph." );
        v1.setMake( "Chevrolet" );
        v1.setModel( "Malibu" );
        v1.setColor( "white" );
        v1.setSpeed( 60. );
        System.out.println( "v1 is now a " + v1.getColor() + " "
                            + v1.getMake() + " " + v1.getModel()
                            + " going " + v1.getSpeed() + "mph."
    );

        v4 = new Skateboard( "Mako", "Shark", "red" );
        accel = v4.changeSpeed( 5. );
        System.out.println( "v4 is a " + v4.getMake() + " "
                            + v4.getModel() + " " + v4.getColor()
                            + " Skateboard going "
                            + v4.getSpeed() + "mph.");
        accel = v4.changeSpeed( 22. );
        System.out.println( "The Skateboard is now going "
                            + v4.getSpeed() + "mph." );

        v2.reFuel( 11.3, 295.); //should be 26.1 mpg
        System.out.println( "The " + v2.getMake() + " mileage: "
                            + v2.fuelEconomy() );
        try{
            System.out.println( "Refueling skateboard" );
            v4.reFuel( 0., 5.);
        }
        catch( Exception e ) {
            System.out.println( e.getMessage() );
        }
    }
}
```

5.10 Write a class that extends Exception and is called TooManyOccupantsException. Have the Vehicle class mutator for number of occupants throw such an exception if the numberOfOccupants would exceed the maximum number of occupants for the vehicle. What will you need to change in your ManyVehicles test class?

```
public class TooManyOccupantsException extends Exception {
   TooManyOccupantsException( int occupantCount ) {
      super( "Vehicle cannot accommodate " + occupantCount );
   }
}
```

In `ManyVehicles` test class:

```
try{
      System.out.println( "adding people to Ford" );
      v1.setOccupants( 6 );
}
catch( Exception e ) {
      System.out.println( e.getMessage() );
}
```

5.11 Change your `ManyVehicles` class so that it reads from a text file called `Vehicles.txt` the specifications for the `Vehicles` to create. Use a `BufferedReader` or a `Scanner` to read the file. Using a `Scanner` is probably easier in this case. Here is a sample `Vehicles.txt` file. The first word in a line is the class, the second word in a line is color, the third word in a line is the make, the fourth word is the model, and the fifth word is the maximum number of occupants. In the case of a bus, there is a sixth word in the line giving the driver's name:

```
Vehicle     red     Ford              F-150       3
Vehicle silver BMW      328i     4
Bus         blue    GM                bus         32 Jones
Vehicle     gold    Chrysler          PTCruiser   4
Skateboard  orange  WorldIndustries ProBoard      1
```

If there is a file name on the command line, read from the file; otherwise simply create some hard-coded examples in the `ManyVehicles` main method. This is the code snippet that decides how to create the `Vehicles` and then creates them:

```
if( args.length == 0 ) {
      //There is no file name on the command line, so
      //  make up some vehicles with hard coding

      vehicles[0] = new Vehicle( "Ford", "Mustang",
                                 2, "red" );
      vehicles[1] = new Vehicle( "BMW",  "328i",
                                 4, "silver" );
      vehicles[2] = new Vehicle( "Chrysler", "PT Cruiser",
                                 4, "gold" );
      System.out.println( "There are "
                          + Vehicle.vehicleCount + " vehicles." );
      System.out.println( "Make of vehicles[0]:    "
                          + vehicles[0].getMake() );
      System.out.println( "Model of vehicles[1] (328i):   "
                          + vehicles[1].getModel() );
      System.out.println( "Color of vehicles[2] (gold):   "
                          + vehicles[2].getColor() );
      System.out.println( "Max occupants of vehicles[0]: "
                          + vehicles[0].getMaxOccupants() );
}
```

```
    else {//There is a file name on the command line, so
         //  read from a file using Scanner.
         Scanner sc = null;
         try {
              sc = new Scanner(
                             new File(args[0]) );
         }
         catch(Exception e) {
              System.out.println( e.getMessage() );
         }
         int    index = 0;

    while( sc.hasNext() ) { //read line in file
              vehicle     = sc.next();
              color       = sc.next();
              make        = sc.next();
              model       = sc.next();
              maxOccupants = sc.nextInt();

              if( vehicle.equals( "Vehicle" ) ){
                vehicles[index] = new Vehicle(
                      make, model, maxOccupants, color );
              }
              else if(vehicle.equals( "Bus" ) ) {
                vehicles[index] = new Bus( make, model,
                   maxOccupants, color, sc.next() );
              }
              else if(vehicle.equals("Skateboard") ) {

                vehicles[index] = new Vehicle(
                   make, model, maxOccupants, color );
              }
              else {
                System.out.println(
                   "Unrecognized vehicle type: "
                   + vehicle );
                   System.exit(1);
              }
              System.out.println( "Created "
                      + vehicles[index].getModel() );
              index++;
    }//while
    }//else
```

Note that you must also add these import statements at the very beginning of your source code file, above even the declaration of public class ManyVehicles {...

```
import java.util.Scanner; //for access to the Scanner class
import java.io.*;         //for access to file I/O
```

5.12 Write a Java program that iterates through the integers from 1 to 20, computing the square of each number and writing the information to a file called squares.txt. Use a PrintWriter to write the file of the first 20 integers and their squares. Arrange for 2 columns with a line of column headings at the top. You will find this easy to do using the println() method of the PrintWriter.

```java
import java.io.*;
public class Squares {
      public static void main( String[] args ){
            PrintWriter output = null;

            try {
                  output = new PrintWriter( new File(
                                                "Squares.txt" ) );
            }
            catch( Exception e ) {
                  System.out.println( e.getMessage() );
                  System.exit(1);
            }

            output.println( "number\tsquare\n_____\t_____" );

            for( int i = 1; i <= 20; i++ ) {
                  output.println( i + "\t" + i*i );
            }

            output.close();
      }
}
```

OPERATING SYSTEMS

6.1 What is the advantage of managing I/O with interrupts? If an active typist is typing 30 words per minute into a word processor, and the computer operates at one million machine instructions per second, how many machine instructions can be executed in the time it takes a character to be typed on the keyboard?

> While the I/O device is performing the transfer, independent of the CPU, the CPU can be doing other useful work, instead of simply waiting for the I/O device to complete its work.

> 30 words-per-minute * 5 characters-per-word = 150 characters-per-minute
> (1 min / 150 chars) * (60 sec / min) = 60/150 = .4 seconds-per-character.

> .4 seconds * 1,000,000 instructions / sec = 400,000 instructions executed per character typed.

6.2 Explain why a DMA channel would or would not be useful in a computer without an interrupt-based I/O system.

> A DMA channel would be much less useful in a computer without an interrupt-based I/O system. The benefit of a DMA channel is that it proceeds with an I/O task independently of, and in parallel with, the CPU. For full efficiency, the CPU should not have to stop and poll the DMA channel periodically for its state; the CPU should be allowed to continue its other work until the DMA channel accomplishes the entire transfer and signals the CPU with an interrupt.

6.3 What scheduling concept was critical to the development of timesharing computers, and has remained an important part of scheduling for interactive computer systems?

> The round robin scheduler was the basis of the first timesharing computers. Each user in turn received his "time slice." The effect was to make each user feel he was the sole user of the machine. Variations on round robin scheduling continue to be important mechanisms for providing interactive computing on multiuser computers.

6.4 Categorize the following programs as system software or application software, and explain your categorization:

> Java Virtual Machine
>> system software—facilitates program development and execution

> Excel
>> application software—used specifically for spreadsheet applications

> Powerpoint
>> application software—used specifically for creating presentations

> C compiler
>> system software—facilitates program development and execution

> C library
>> system software—facilitates program development and execution

> Oracle database management system
>> difficult to say, but I would choose system software. A general database management package is a tool for application development

> Employee payroll system
>> application software—very specific to the payroll function of a company

> Web browser
>> difficult to say, but I lean toward calling a browser system software, because of the generality of a browser's application. A browser supports a multitude of user intentions, and it includes features that facilitate web-based applications of many types

Media player
> application software—specific to presenting audio and video material

Control panel
> system software—the control panel makes configuration and management of the system easier, and system administration supports all applications

Email client
> application software—specific to the email application

6.5 Why is it that threads are faster to create than processes?

> When the operating system creates a process, it must allocate memory for the process and create a process control block. To create a thread, the operating system need only create a much smaller thread control block. Because threads within a process share memory and other resources (e.g., open files) available to the process, the operating system has much less set-up to do when creating a new thread.

6.6 What advantage do kernel threads provide over user threads? Give an example of a user thread package.

> A major advantage of kernel threads is that when a kernel thread blocks for I/O, other threads continue to execute. This is because a kernel thread is visible to the operating system, and each thread can separately scheduled. User threads, on the other hand, are not visible to the OS. With a user thread package, the process is the only entity of which the operating system is aware. POSIX is a user thread package, although some operating systems (e.g., Solaris) implement the POSIX interface using calls to the kernel threads offered by the operating system.

6.7 When a process is multithreaded, which of these resources are shared among the threads, and which are private to each thread?

Memory
> shared between threads

Program counter
> private to each thread

Global variables
> shared among all threads

Open files
> shared among all threads

Register contents
> private to each thread

Stack/local/automatic variables
> private to each thread

6.8 List four events that transfer control to the operating system in privileged mode.

> I/O interrupt
> System clock interrupt
> Process makes a system call (e.g., read, write, file open, etc.)
> A process page-faults
> A process causes a memory protection error

6.9 How can a semaphore be used to insure that Process First will complete before Process Second executes?

> The semaphore must be shared between processes First and Second. The semaphore must be set to 0 initially. At the beginning of Second, Second must execute a P() operation (also called test,

wait, acquire, etc.) on the semaphore. The P() operation will block Second. When First completes, the last thing First must do is execute a V() operation (also called increment, release, signal, etc.) on the semaphore. The V() operation will release the waiting process Second, thus guaranteeing that First will complete before Second.

6.10 Describe how transaction logging might apply to a file system, and give an example of a file system that employs transaction logging.

Microsoft's NTFS is one file system that uses transaction logging to protect the file system from corruption due to system failure. When a change must be made to the file system, such as adding a new file, the file system first writes the changes to a write-ahead log. When the system has recorded all the changes in the write-ahead log, the system marks the transaction as committed. When the system finds it convenient to do so, the system writes the committed changes to the file system itself. When all the changes have been transferred to the file system, the system can delete the record of the transaction in the write-ahead log.

If the system should fail some time during this process, the system can look in the write-ahead log when the system recovers to see what transactions were committed but not yet written to the file system itself. The system can roll back partially complete transactions.

6.11 If a memory access requires 100 nanoseconds, and the computer uses a page table and virtual memory, how long does it take to read a word of program memory?

It takes 100ns to read the page table entry, plus 100ns to read the memory location itself. The total access time is 200ns.

6.12 If we add a TLB to the computer in the previous question, and 80% of the time the page table entry is in the TLB (i.e., the required memory access results in a "hit" in the TLB 80% of the time), on average, how long does it take to read a word of program memory?

Assuming that TLB access time is negligible:

.8 * (100ns) + .2 * (200ns) = 120ns

6.13 A paging system uses pages with 1024 addresses per page. Given the following page table:

Page	Frame
0	4
1	10
2	6
3	7
4	5

What are the physical addresses corresponding to the following logical addresses?

Logical address	
0	4096
430	4526
2071	6167
4129	5123
5209	memory protection error

6.14 Why do virtual memory systems include a "modified" bit in the page table entry?

If a process has written to a page, it will take more time to reallocate that memory to a new page. If a page has been modified, the system must write the page to disk before the frame of memory can be used for another page mapping. On the other hand, the system does not need to write and unmodified page to disk before remapping the frame for other use, because an unmodified page is always available in its original form on the disk already. Often page replacement algorithms take this difference into account in order to speed execution. Other things being equal, the system will remap an unmodified page before it will remap a page that has been modified.

6.15 Why would fixed-length record files be a good choice for storing data from database tables?

With fixed-length record files, the system can easily calculate the exact address within the file of any record in the file. Databases often use fixed-length record files to speed indexed access to information in its tables.

6.16 How would you expect process scheduling policies to be different on batch computing systems and interactive systems?

Interactive computer systems like Unix and Windows use scheduling policies that share the computer in some "fair" way among the concurrent users. This means some variation of round robin or time-slice scheduling, perhaps mixed with additional policies for background, non-interactive processing.

Batch computer systems will use scheduling policies that in some way maximize the number of jobs accomplished per hour or day. There is no moment-to-moment concern with fairness, but there is still pressure to be as efficient as possible. Perhaps a FCFS or SRJF policy will be used, or a policy that queues waiting jobs by priority.

6.17 How would you measure the success of a batch operating system? Would you measure the success of an interactive system like Unix or Windows the same way? If not, how would you measure the success of an interactive operating system?

Batch operating systems are often measured by the average number of jobs they complete per hour, or by average CPU utilization.

Interactive operating systems are evaluated differently. Often the measure of success for interactive operating systems is response time; when a user enters a command, how much time elapses before the user receives the first response from the system?

NETWORKING

7.1 Explain how an IP packet might become duplicated and arrive twice at its destination.

> Suppose a TCP message is sent from Host A to distant Host Z. Because of network congestion, Host A does not get a confirmation from Host Z within its timeout period for the message confirmation. Therefore, Host A assumes the message was lost, and it sends the message again. Perhaps all of the IP packets will eventually arrive at Host Z, and that will mean that many or all packets are duplicated at Host Z.

> It's also possible that an error in a router's routing table could result in a packet being sent twice by different paths to the distant host.

7.2 Some researchers in networking complain that networking protocols have become "ossified." What do they mean by that, and why might that be so? Who benefits from "ossified" protocols?

> As the Internet and its protocols have become central to many business applications, the consequences of any change to the protocols have become much more serious. When only a hundred academics used the Internet regularly, there was more opportunity to try new protocols and approaches. Now with millions of people, thousands of businesses, and billions of dollars dependent on current protocol definitions, it is almost unthinkable to disturb the protocol infrastructure.

> Our "ossified" protocols support the business, shopping and communications of end users of the Internet.

7.3 Using Google or some other source, find a list of other "well known ports" in networking besides port 80.

> See http://en.wikipedia.org/wiki/List_of_TCP_and_UDP_port_numbers

7.4 Most Internet communications use the TCP protocol, but some do not. Some communications use only the IP protocol. Another name for the IP protocol is *user datagram protocol* (UDP). Why would an application choose to use UDP? Can you think of a category of applications that might prefer UDP?

> UDP is a low-overhead, high-speed protocol. By doing away with checks for out-of-order, duplicated, or lost packets, UDP offers higher performance. Many networks have extremely low error rates anyway, so the cost of reduced reliability may be small, and the gain in speed substantial.

> Audio and video streams may well be communicated via UDP. If the error rate on the network is low, the occasional bad packet will hardly be noticed, except for the infrequent audio or video "glitch."

7.5 IPv6 uses addresses that are 16 bytes long (128 bits). How many addresses is that per person in the world?

> The population of the world in 2007 is about 6.6 billion; 128 bits can represent numbers up to $3.4 * 10^{38}$. With addresses occupying 128 bits, we have approximately $5 * 10^{28}$ addresses per person!

7.6 What classes does Java provide to make network programming easier? Which classes are for TCP communications? Which classes are for UDP communications?

> For TCP: ServerSocket, Socket
> For UDP: DatagramSocket, DatagramPacket

7.7 It's hard to imagine today how hot the competition was between different vendors of proposed networking standards in the 1980s. Today most wired LANs are implemented using 802.3 "Ethernet" protocols. General Motors strongly backed a competitive standard called manufacturing automation protocol (MAP) that became IEEE standard 802.4. Do some research to answer these questions: Why did GM favor 802.4 over 802.3? Why did most of the world end up choosing 802.3?

GM was concerned with the predictability of response on the network. GM anticipated robots and other automated equipment attached to the network, and predictability of response to a problem was very important. MAP was a token-passing protocol that provided relatively uniform access time to each device on the network. In contrast, Ethernet's CSMA/CD protocol could not guarantee any worst case access time to the network, because the frequency of collisions and retries on the network depended on the loading of the network.

GM also liked the broadband, cable TV wiring specification of MAP. With broadband, the wiring could handle many channels at once, allowing for networking, video, and other communications over common cable. The broadband wiring also provided greater immunity to electrical noise, such as that from welders and other equipment in the factory.

Ethernet, or 802.3, was more successful with most customers, partly because it had a head start. Also, the imagined problems of responsiveness with Ethernet generally did not occur in practice. In addition, the wiring was less expensive and less complicated.

7.8 The HTTP protocol is essentially a protocol providing for file transfer between the server and the client. Therefore, the HTTP protocol is said to be "stateless;" i.e., the server receives a request, and the server satisfies the request with a file transfer, regardless of what has happened before with this client. This statelessness has been a challenge to those developing applications to be delivered over the web. For instance, a banking application will need to keep track of the account number of the individual making inquiries, even though the individual makes repeated inquiries and updates using several different screens (web pages). How is application state maintained in such applications?

Web applications often use "cookies" to store information about the current interaction with the user. Cookies are files kept on the client's computer and facilitated by the client's web browser.

A second way of saving information about the current interaction is to use "hidden fields" in the web page sent to the client. The browser does not display these fields to the client, but information saved from the previous transactions with the client can be stored in the hidden fields, so that the server has that context available when the user submits his next page to the server.

A third way to save transaction state is with a user session object on the server. When a user logs in to the server, the server creates a "session" on the server that is identified by a session_ID. The server can then attach the session_ID to each form exchanged with the client.

Some application "frameworks" provide additional tools. For instance, Microsoft's .Net framework provides a ViewState property for each "control" (button, table, etc.) on a web page. The state of the control (whether the button was pushed, whatever data are shown in the table, etc.) is saved invisibly in the ViewState property of the control as the web page is passed back and forth between server and client.

DATABASE

8.1 Consider designing a database for an antique store. What entities would you include? What would their attributes be?

Entities and attributes:

> Item: ID, type, description, cost, sales price, consignment seller
> Customer: ID, Name, Phone, Address
> ConsignmentSeller: SellerID, Name, Address, Phone, Commission%
> Sale: InvoiceNo, Customer, Date
> Sale Item: InvoiceNo, ItemID, ItemPrice, Quantity
> Etc.

8.2 Create a full E-R diagram for the antique store mentioned in question 1. The store handles household furnishings, jewelry, toys, and tools. The owner of the store owns most of what he has for sale, but he handles some items on consignment (i.e., he sells the item for the owner, thus earning a commission on the sale). Some customers require delivery, so the owner maintains relationships with several local movers. The owner wants to keep track of his customers so that he can do a better job of marketing. In particular, he knows that some customers are particularly interested in certain types of antiques, and he'd like to be able to find, for example, all those customers interested in cameo jewelry.

For business auditing and tax purposes, it's very important that the database track expenditures and revenues. The owner wants to track what he spent for each item, and what he earned in selling it. These requirements also mean that he has to track store expenses like rent and heat, and his employee expenses (he employs 2 part-time people to help him run the store).

> There is no single correct answer to such a challenge, but here is a possible E-R diagram for an antique store database:

Antique Store

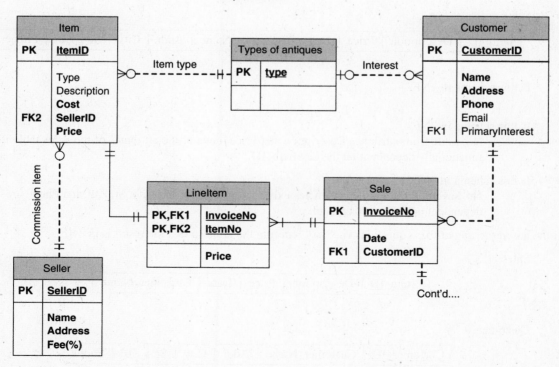

Cont'd....

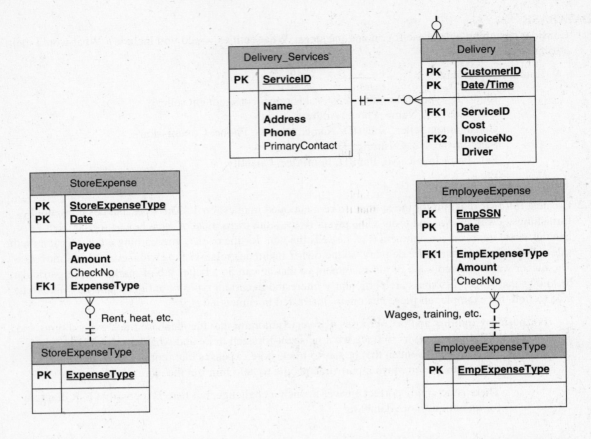

8.3 An inexperienced database designer suggested the following schema for one of the tables in the antique store database:

Sales

| Item_ID | Description | Price | Date | Customer_Name | Addr | City | St | ZIP | Phone |

Is this schema in 1NF?
> yes

Is this schema in 2NF?
> No, aside from attributes Description and Price, none of the attributes of the Sales table is functionally dependent on the key Item_ID.

Is this schema in 3NF?
> No, several transitive dependencies exist; for instance, Addr, City, St, ZIP, and Phone are dependent upon Customer_Name.

If the answer to any of these questions is, "No," redesign the table so that the result is in 3NF.

Sales

| Item_ID | Description | Price | Date | Customer_Name |

Customer

| Customer_ID | Customer_Name | Addr | City | St | ZIP | Phone |

8.4 Two of the tables in the antique store database will be a table of `Deliveries`, and a table of `Delivery_Services`. Here are the schemas for the two tables:

`Deliveries`

Date/Time	Customer_ID	Delivery_Service	Cost	Invoice_No	Driver

`Delivery_Services`

Name	Phone	Addr	City	St	ZIP	Contact

Write the SQL code to create these tables. Specify which columns may not be NULL, and specify primary and foreign key constraints. Note that the `Delivery_Service` column in the `Deliveries` table is meant to have the same meaning as the `Name` column in the `Delivery_Service` table.

```
CREATE TABLE DELIVERIES (
        DATETIME              TIMESTAMP      NOT NULL,
        CUSTOMER_ID           INT            NOT NULL,
        DELIVERY_SERVICE      VARCHAR(20)    NOT NULL,
        COST                  NUMERIC(8,2),  NOT NULL
        INVOICE_NO            CHAR(8)        NOT NULL,
        DRIVER                VARCHAR(20),
PRIMARY KEY(DATETIME, CUSTOMER_ID),
FOREIGN KEY(DELIVERY_SERVICE) REFERENCES
                              DELIVERY_SERVICES(NAME)
);

CREATE TABLE DELIVERY_SERVICES(
        NAME      VARCHAR(20)   NOT NULL,
        PHONE     CHAR(12)      NOT NULL,
        ADDR      VARCHAR(30)   NOT NULL,
        ST        CHAR(2)       NOT NULL,
        ZIP       CHAR(5)       NOT NULL,
        CONTACT   VARCHAR(20),
PRIMARY KEY(NAME)
);
```

8.5 Here are the schemas for a few more of the tables in one implementation of the antique store database:

`Item`

Item_ID	Type	Description	Cost	Consignment_Seller_ID	Price_Sold

`Sale`

Invoice_No	Customer_ID	Date

`Line Item`

Invocie_No	Item_ID	Unit_Price	Quantity	Line_Item_Price

`Consignment_Seller`

Seller_ID	Name	Addr	City	State	ZIP	Free_Precent

Write SQL queries to report the following information:

a   Report all of the consignment sellers located in NY, and list them in order by their consignment fee percentages.

```
SELECT name, fee_percent FROM CONSIGNMENT_SELLER
WHERE state = 'NY'
ORDER BY fee_percent;
```

b   Find all of the items in the store that are on consignment from "Parker Smith". Report only the items for sale (`Price_Sold` is NULL).

```
SELECT item_id, description
FROM ( ITEM JOIN CONSIGNMENT_SELLER ON
                Consignment_Seller_ID = Seller_ID)
WHERE name = 'Parker Smith' AND Price_Sold IS NULL;
```

In all of these examples, the specific syntax may vary by database product. Here is the proper syntax for Microsoft Access:

```
SELECT item_id, description
FROM Item INNER JOIN CONSIGNMENT_SELLER ON
                Item.Consignment_Seller_ID =
                Consignment_Seller.Seller_ID
WHERE name = 'Parker Smith' AND Price_Sold IS NULL;
```

c   Report the total of all sales during last March.

```
SELECT SUM (Line_Item_Price)
FROM (Sale JOIN Line_Item ON Invoice_No)
WHERE Date LIKE '%2007-03%';
```

```
In Access:
SELECT Sum (Line_item.line_item_price)
FROM Sale INNER JOIN Line_item
          ON Sale.Invoice_no =
Line_item.Invoice_No
WHERE Sale.date Like "*3/*2007*";
```

d   Find all the items on consignment from "Parker Smith" that sold this month.

```
SELECT item_id
FROM (Sale JOIN Line_Item ON Invoice_No)
WHERE Date LIKE '%2007-11%'
      AND item_id IN
                (SELECT item_id
              FROM ( Item JOIN Consignment_seller ON
                    Consignment_Seller_ID = Seller_ID)
              WHERE name = 'Parker Smith'
                AND Price_Sold IS NOT NULL);
```

In Access:

```
SELECT item_id
FROM Sale INNER JOIN Line_Item ON
     Sale.Invoice_No = Line_Item.Invoice_No
WHERE Date LIKE '*11*2007'
   AND Line_item.item_id IN
          (SELECT Item.item_id FROM Item INNER JOIN
               Consignment_Seller ON
                    Item.Consignment_Seller_ID =
                    Consignment_Seller.Seller_ID
               WHERE name = 'Parker Smith'
                  AND Price_Sold IS NOT NULL);
```

e   Report the amount due to "Parker Smith" for all sales of his items this month.

```
SELECT SUM (Line_Item_Price * fee_percent) as
Smith_comission
FROM ( ( ( Sale JOIN Line_Item ON Invoice_No  )
               JOIN Item       ON Item_ID )
               JOIN Consignment_Seller ON
                  Consignment_Seller_ID = Seller_ID )
WHERE name = 'Parker Smith' AND Date LIKE '%2007-11%';
```

In Access:

```
SELECT SUM(Line_Item.Line_Item_Price *
     Consignment_Seller.fee_percent) AS Smith_comission
FROM ((Sale INNER JOIN Line_Item ON
               Sale.Invoice_No = Line_item.Invoice_No)
       INNER JOIN Item ON
               Item.Item_ID = Line_Item.Item_Id)
       INNER JOIN Consignment_Seller ON
               Consignment_Seller.Seller_ID =
               Item.Consignment_Seller_ID
WHERE Consignment_Seller.name = 'Parker Smith'
               AND Sale.Date LIKE '*11*2007*';
```

f   Report all sales of items not on consignment (Consignment_Seller_ID is NULL) this month.

```
SELECT Item_ID
FROM ( ( Sale JOIN Line_Item ON Invoice_No  )
               JOIN Item       ON Item_ID )
WHERE Consignment_Seller_ID IS NULL
               AND Price_sold IS NOT NULL
               AND Date LIKE '%2007-11%';
```

In Access:

```
SELECT Line_item.Item_ID
FROM (Sale INNER JOIN Line_Item ON
     Sale.Invoice_No = Line_Item.Invoice_No)
     INNER JOIN Item ON
     Line_Item.Item_Id = Item.Item_ID
WHERE Item.Consignment_Seller_ID Is Null
```

```
AND Item.Price_sold Is Not Null
AND Sale.Date Like '*11*2007*';
```

g   Report the profit on all non-consignment items this month.

```
SELECT SUM(Line_Item_Price) - SUM(Cost) as Profit
FROM ( ( Sale JOIN Line_Item ON Invoice_No  )
             JOIN Item       ON Item_ID )
WHERE Consignment_Seller_ID IS NULL
          AND Price_sold IS NOT NULL
          AND Date LIKE '%2007-11%';
```

In Access:

```
SELECT SUM(Line_Item_Price)-SUM(Cost) AS Profit
FROM (Sale INNER JOIN Line_Item ON
      Sale.Invoice_No = Line_Item.Invoice_No)
      INNER JOIN Item ON
      Line_Item.Item_ID = Item.Item_Id
WHERE Item.Consignment_Seller_ID Is Null
      AND Item.Price_sold Is Not Null
      AND Date Like '*11*2007*';
```

8.6 When a customer buys an item (or several) from the store, several changes to database tables will occur. Explain what those might be.

    a If the customer does not yet exist in the database, a customer record must be added.

    b The row in table Item for the antique the customer purchases must have the column Price_sold updated.

    c The sale must be recorded in tables Sale and Line_Item.

8.7 The owner of the antique store doesn't want to train his people in SQL, or to teach them about all the tables in the database. He asks you to write a program that will take sales information, and then make all the changes automatically, including whatever error checking may be necessary. The clerk will enter a customer phone number (assume this is used as the Customer_ID primary key in the Customer table), an item ID (from a tag on the item), and the sale price.
In pseudo code, outline how your program would record a sale. Show how you would use a transaction to insure the integrity of the database updates. Also, explain the error checking (such as verifying that the customer is already in the database) you would perform in your program, and how your program would recover from problems such as:

- The customer is not in the database.
- The item number is not in the database.
- The item is already sold.

    a Select the customer from the Customer table.
        One row should be returned. If so, continue at b.
        If no row is returned, we must add the customer to the database.
        Insert a new customer row in the Customer table to add this new person to the database.

    b Start the sale transaction.

    c Select the row for the Item_ID from the Item table.

One row should be returned.
Check the `Price_sold` column to be sure it is null
(has not been sold already).
If the `Sale_price` is null, proceed to d,
otherwise report the error and roll back the transaction.
If no row exists for the `Item_ID`, report the error, and
give the clerk the option of entering a corrected Item_ID,
or canceling the transaction.
If the clerk cancels the sale, roll back the transaction.

d Insert new rows in the `Line_item` and `Sale` tables.

e Update the `Price_sold` column in the `Item` table for this `Item_ID`.

f Commit the transaction.

8.8 When an item is sold, should the item row be removed from the `Items` table? Why or why not?

Probably not. The rows in the Items table maintain information about costs and revenues, which allow us to calculate profit. These rows also provide information about consignment sales, and we need that information to pay our consignment sellers correctly.

Very old entries in the `Items` table may be deleted, perhaps on an annual basis, to keep the size of the database smaller. However, we must be sure not to delete any information that may be required for business and tax reporting.

8.9 What transaction isolation level should apply to this application? Why do you make this choice?

This is a rather undemanding database application. Apparently there are only three people, the proprietor and two part-time workers, who will be accessing the database. Probably there will also be only one computer from which to access the database, unless the owner, working from home, also logs in.

In these conditions, one could argue that the default `read_committed` isolation level will be more than adequate. One could also argue that the modest performance requirements of this application mean that we should use the serializeable isolation level. Such precaution will give us the most protection, and no one will notice any performance impairment, since the application is undemanding of high performance.

SOCIAL ISSUES

9.1 Should software be copyrightable or patentable? Ignoring the law for the moment, argue the question from the Kantian, Utilitarian, and Social Contract Theory perspectives.

While there is not a single correct answer to this question for all people, answers to this question should include observations along the following lines:

The Kantian would ask the question, "Am I comfortable with everyone being able to copyright or patent their software?"

The Utilitarian would try to sum the advantages and disadvantages to all concerned. The writers would gain because they could demand payment for use of their software. The users would lose because buying software would be more expensive. On the other hand users might gain because more software may become available to buy.

The Social Contract Theorist would ask, "Are most people willing to agree to allow copyrighting and patenting of software, probably because it achieves a reasonable balance between the needs of the writers and the needs of the users, so that all agree to be bound by such rules, as long as the others are also?"

9.2 Why does a copyright provide better protection for object code than for source code?

Copyrighting protects the expression of the idea, not the idea itself. Since a programmer can read source code, a programmer could readily adopt a good idea expressed in C, and create a similar program in another language, perhaps Java. Because the "expression" of the idea is now different (in a different language), the copyright holder would have no means of protecting his idea from free adoption by others.

Object code, on the other hand, is not generally readable by humans. Therefore, copyrighting the object code, and shipping only object code, is a fairly effective way of protecting both the idea and its expression via copyright.

9.3 How can you apply the ACM Code of Ethics to the practice of sending "spam" e-mail (unsolicited messages to strangers)? What sections of the ACM Code apply, and does the ACM Code permit the practice?

Several sections of the ACM code apply to the practice of spamming email:

1.2 Avoid harm to others: Spam email imposes costs on others, on the ISPs that must store and forward the spam, and on the receiver who must spend time deleting unsolicited messages. Also, often to goal of spam is to trick the receiver into revealing information about the receiver's identity, so that the spammer can then steal the receiver's money or identity.

1.3 Be honest and trustworthy: Spam is nothing if not dishonest. The receiver did not ask for the spam message, and the spammer designs the message to trick the receiver into responding to it.

1.5 Honor property rights: Spammers often create messages using the trademarks of legitimate businesses. This is a violation of property rights, as well as a deliberate attempt to deceive the receiver and make him vulnerable to further attack or theft.

1.7 Respect the privacy of others: Spammers violate this principle directly. The whole point of spam is to gain surreptitious access to private information about the receiver.

2.3 Know and respect existing laws pertaining to professional work: The US Can-Spam Act of 2004 prohibits the practice of spamming. The name of the act stands for Controlling the Assault of Non-Solicited Pornography and Marketing.

2.8 Access computing and communication resources only when authorized: Clearly, spammers are not authorized by the receivers to send their unsolicited messages.

By violating all these principles, spamming is clearly not acceptable to the ACM Code of Ethics.

9.4 Inspection of a computer program controlling a weapons system shows 54 "if" statements (23 with "else" clauses), 4 "switch" statements (with 5, 7, 4, and 8 "cases"), and 17 "for" or "while" loops with parameterized looping boundaries. How would you exhaustively test such a program to prove its safety?

> To exhaustively test all possibilities, you would have to test all paths through the program:

> 31 * 2 (if statements) * 23 * 3 (if else) * 5 * 7 * 4 * 8 (switches) * 17 (loops) * 4 (loop test cases per loop) ~ 325 million test runs

9.5 Assume you have just created a program to schedule taxicabs in real time. You're sure that your approach is entirely new and much better than anything else available. Every taxi company in the world is going to want your software. Explain how you would best protect your work—patent? copyright? secret?

> There is no single correct answer to this question.

> I would probably not use a patent to protect this program. First, such software may not be patentable. If I wanted to patent the program, however, I would argue its patentability on the basis of its connection to a real world taxi scheduler.

> Another risk would be that filing for a patent would force me to reveal the details of my implementation, and such details might well allow another to take advantage of my thinking, while allowing the other to change his implementation sufficiently to avoid violating my patent.

> Probably the best protection for me would be secrecy. I will simply keep my source code secret as a trade secret. I will be obligated to maintain the secret carefully, exposing the source code only to individuals who have a need to know, and I will have such individuals sign a non-disclosure agreement with me first.

> To protect the software that I sell, I will ship only object code, and I will copyright the object code. Such copyright will make it illegal for my customers to copy the object code without my permission.

INDEX

Tables and **figures** in **bold**